T5-AGS-343

Global Ecotourism Policies and Case Studies

Channel View Publications

Dynamic Tourism: Journeying with Change
Priscilla Boniface
Journeys into Otherness: The Representation of Differences and Identity in Tourism
Keith Hollinshead and Chuck Burlo (eds)
Natural Area Tourism: Ecology, Impacts and Management
D. Newsome, S.A. Moore and R. Dowling
Tourism Collaboration and Partnerships
Bill Bramwell and Bernard Lane (eds)
Tourism and Development: Concepts and Issues
Richard Sharpley and David Telfer (eds)
Tourism Employment: Analysis and Planning
Michael Riley, Adele Ladkin, and Edith Szivas
Tourism in Peripheral Areas: Case Studies
Frances Brown and Derek Hall (eds)

Please contact us for the latest book information:
Channel View Publications, Frankfurt Lodge, Clevedon Hall,
Victoria Road, Clevedon, BS21 7HH, England
http://www.multilingual-matters.com

Global Ecotourism Policies and Case Studies

Perspectives and Constraints

Edited by

Michael Lück and Torsten Kirstges

CHANNEL VIEW PUBLICATIONS
Clevedon • Buffalo • Toronto • Sydney

Library of Congress Cataloging in Publication Data
Global Ecotourism Policies and Case Studies: Perspectives and Constraints/Edited by Michael Lück and Torsten Kirstges.
Includes bibliographical references.
1. Ecotourism. 2. Ecotourism–Case studies. I. Lück, Michael II. Kirstges, Torsten.
G156.5.E26 G58 2003
338.4'791–dc21   2002153678

British Library Cataloguing in Publication Data
A catalogue entry for this book is available from the British Library.

ISBN 1-873150-40-7 (hbk)

Channel View Publications
An imprint of Multilingual Matters Ltd

UK: Frankfurt Lodge, Clevedon Hall, Victoria Road, Clevedon BS21 7SJ.
USA: 2250 Military Road, Tonawanda, NY 14150, USA.
Canada: 5201 Dufferin Street, North York, Ontario, Canada M3H 5T8.
Australia: Footprint Books, PO Box 418, Church Point, NSW 2103, Australia.

This book is also available as Vol. 5, Nos 3&4 (2002) of the journal *Current Issues in Tourism.*

Typeset by Archetype-IT Ltd (http://www.archetype-it.com).
Printed and bound in Great Britain by Short Run Press.

Contents

Acknowledgements

We owe great debt of gratitude to friends and colleagues who have contributed chapters to this volume of *Current Issues in Tourism*. A compilation like this covers so many issues and the expertise and experience of the contributing authors help identify crucial issues of ecotourism, both positive and negative. Theory and practice join in this book with the aim to gain a better understanding about the complex chances and constraints of the growing ecotourism market.

The editors also want to thank Brett Derecourt, C. Michael Hall, Alec Holt, Brent Lovelock, Gaby Pfeiffer and Sue Russell for reviewing the chapters. This part takes place 'behind the scenes', but is so important to achieve a quality piece of work.

Hector Ceballos-Lascuráin is one of the 'gurus' of ecotourism. Often cited as the first person that used this term consciously, his definition appears in the majority of works related to ecotourism. We are grateful to him for having written the Preface, which completes this project appropriately.

Finally, we would like to thank Chris Cooper, C. Michael Hall, and Ruth Harwood as well as the team at Multilingual Matters, Clevedon.

Michael Lück
Torsten Kirstges

Correspondence

Any correspondence should be directed to Michael Lück, Department of Recreation and Leisure Studies, Brock University, St. Catharines, Ontario, Canada L2S 3A1 (mlueck@brocku.ca / michael.lueck@brocku.ca).

Preface

Hector Ceballos-Lascuráin
Director General PICE

Much action has taken place over the last two decades in the fascinating and complex field of ecotourism, and even more has been written on these developments.

Over 17 years have elapsed since I coined the term 'ecotourism' and provided its preliminary definition. Since then, many developments have taken place in the fields of tourism, ecotourism, conservation and sustainable development throughout the world.

Over these years, ecotourism has proven to be more than a theory and is already providing many benefits to societies, businesses and natural areas around our planet. Of course, since ecotourism is a human invention, as all human inventions it is imperfect. Many critics of ecotourism point out its imperfections and shortcomings, stating that there is no place in the world where ecotourism is happening in a 'pure' form. I agree. But I believe in ecotourism, not 'eco-purism'. Democracy is another example of a human invention, and I do not know of a perfect example of democracy that has occurred in any country or at any time in history. Nonetheless, many societies around the world strive to attain a high level of democracy, knowing perhaps that the ultimate echelon will forever be unattainable. Conceivably, the situation in ecotourism is analogous, and hopefully many persons and human groups around the world will continue trying hard to achieve a satisfactory level of ecotourism, one that will truly contribute to conserve the natural and cultural heritage of our planet and play a part in achieving a higher plane of sustainable development and human happiness.

I am happy and honoured for having been asked to write the Preface to this issue. *Global Ecotourism Policies and Case Studies: Perspectives and Constraints* undoubtedly provides new insight into ecotourism thought and development. By reading its different papers one attains the knowledge of different 'real world' situations and approaches that show different levels of success and opportunities, but also serious problems of implementation and downright failures.

There are many case studies in this document that should prove to be helpful both to students and to practical doers. After reading the different contributions, perhaps what struck me most is that there still seems to be a general lack of agreement on a single, accepted definition of ecotourism, as well as on standards and sound certification processes in the wide world of ecotourism.

Agreeing upon a definition of the word 'ecotourism' still poses a challenge in most parts of the world. This buzzword remains a vague term in many countries and is used to market anything related to nature or environmental tourism, 'selling everything from community development projects to jet skis', as Ron Mader says in his contribution to this issue.

Speaking of Ron Mader, it is pertinent to mention here that during the very successful Sustainable Ecotourism in North America On-line Conference that he organised in May 2000, hosted by Planeta.com, Ron asked me to be the moderator/facilitator of the Definitions and Applications Group of the Conference. Many of the discussions of our group and the conclusions to which we arrived seem to me to transcend the North American sphere (North America understood here as comprising the whole of the Western Hemisphere between Alaska and Canada in the north to Panama in the south, including also the whole of the Caribbean) and may be applied at a worldwide scale, so I would like briefly to refer here to some of the conclusions of our forum.

The challenge that this discussion group posed was formidable, since it was considered indispensable to implement a single, accepted definition of ecotourism in North America.

It was generally agreed by the participants in the forum that a big obstacle for choosing a single definition is in the intrinsic nature of ecotourism, it being a complex, interdisciplinary and multi-sectoral phenomenon. It is also a new concept, which is still not fully understood. Another serious problem is that, in many cases, the notion of ecotourism is confused with the broader concept of sustainable tourism or with certain types of adventure tourism that have nothing to do with ecotourism. This causes much difficulty in proper communication when discussing these different concepts.

There was wide consensus that the main components and issues that should be considered in defining ecotourism are, broadly speaking: nature, local community, economics, conservation, and culture.

In a more detailed way, it was agreed upon by most participants that ecotourism should be characterised by the following standards:

(1) Tourism activity is carried out in a relatively undisturbed natural setting.
(2) Negative impacts of tourism activity are minimised.
(3) Tourism activity assists in conserving the natural and cultural heritage.
(4) It actively involves local communities in the process, providing benefits to them.
(5) It contributes to sustainable development and is a profitable business.
(6) Education/appreciation/interpretation component (of both natural and cultural heritage) must be present.

A vast majority of the participants in this on-line forum agreed that a single, commonly agreed definition of ecotourism is urgently required, since we need a point of reference, especially for planners, governments and operators, and to keep all of us on track. Several of the participants urged that this agreed definition be of worldwide application, and not only constrained to the North American context, since clear communication in the field of ecotourism is required at the whole international level.

However, it was recognised that the really important thing is, first to reach a certain level of consensus, and then from there move on to more practical and tangible actions – proceed from idea to action.

After much discussion, and recognising that IUCN (The World Conservation Union) is one of the institutions with the widest coverage and influence of all the international conservation organisations, it was suggested by a considerable number of participants that the official IUCN ecotourism definition (adopted during the First World Conservation Congress organised by IUCN in Montreal in October 1996, by means of Resolution CGR 1.67 'Ecotourism and Protected

Area Conservation') be endorsed for application in the North American context. The IUCN definition is:

> Ecotourism is environmentally responsible travel and visitation to relatively undisturbed natural areas, in order to enjoy and appreciate nature (and any accompanying cultural features – both past and present) that promotes conservation, has low negative visitor impact, and provides for beneficially active socio-economic involvement of local populations.. (Ceballos-Lascuráin, 1996)

Another key area of ecotourism that requires more attention and successful results is that of physical planning and architectural design of ecotourism facilities, including ecolodges.

According to The International Ecotourism Society (TIES), 'the term ecolodge is an industry label used to identify a nature-dependent tourist lodge that meets the philosophy of ecotourism' (Hawkins *et al.*, 1995: x).

At a purist level an ecolodge will offer a tourist an educational and participatory experience, be developed and managed in an environmentally sensitive manner and protect its operating environment. An ecolodge is different from mainstream lodges, like fishing and ski lodges and luxury retreats. It is the philosophy of ecological sensitivity that must underlie, and ultimately define, each operation.

It must be stressed that 'the most important thing about an ecolodge is that the ecolodge is not the most important thing' (Ceballos-Lascuráin, 1997: 4), i.e. it is the quality of the surrounding environment that most counts: the nearby natural and cultural attractions – and the way ecotourism circuits are set up, operated and marketed, also the way in which local populations are actively involved in the process. The main reason for a tourist coming to an ecolodge is that it provides the opportunity of being in close contact with nature (in some cases, supplemented by interesting cultural elements). There is already a good number of successful and attractive ecolodges around the world, but more effort has to be channelled into achieving an appropriate, environmentally friendly architectural design, which should always be in harmony with the natural and cultural environment.

One of the more difficult problems is the larger resorts which may have many commendable environmental practices, and even good social practices, but still siphon off their dollars to non-regional (or international) investors. Many large resorts, however 'green', fail to convince that they are in the ecotourism business, even more so when they are owned by outside interests, which do little to benefit the host country and local communities. On the other hand, it is absolutely fair to congratulate any operation which is moving to be more environmentally, socially and economically sensitive, whatever their scale and wherever they are located, and without worrying too much about definitions. We also need to build awareness in each individual concerning the impact of everyday choices about lifestyle and consumer habits.

If ecotourism is to make further progress around the world, we need to have a positive proactive agenda first, and not just a list of rules for everybody to conform to. Something new that adds value to the industry is urgently required. Once we have the world's attention, then things will really start happening in the field of ecotourism.

The generalised lack of standards and sound certification processes in the world of ecotourism is another major problem. This is an area where governments and trade organisations need to concentrate their efforts for achieving appropriate accreditation.

To my knowledge, the country where the ecotourism certification process has advanced the most is Australia. The Ecotourism Association of Australia (EAA), an incorporated non-profit organisation that was created in 1991, launched the National Ecotourism Accreditation Program (NEAP) in 1996. This programme arose out of the fundamental problem of how to distinguish between genuine ecotourism operators and other operators who work in natural areas. EAA recognised early that this is a real dilemma that retailers and marketers such as the state and national government tourism promotion agencies are faced with. The Accreditation Program has been critical in helping ecotourism operators improve the profile of their products, which in turn has led to greater customer recognition and an emerging market edge. NEAP expounds eight principles of ecotourism which should guide every ecotourism operation. Preferential marketing opportunities for NEAP accredited operators are now being provided by regional, state and national tourism marketing bodies.

Perhaps we should recognise that ecotourism has become the tourism industry's leader in sustainability around the world. Nonetheless, we should also acknowledge that ecotourism alone will not lead to a sustainable tourism industry. In that sense, we should all endeavour to assist and orient every conventional tourist operator and hotel manager to become more sustainable through cooperative initiatives.

As Michael Lück asserts in his contribution to this issue:

> ... it is possible for large-scale ventures, such as a large tour operator or a charter airline, to operate according to a code of conduct. Compliance to self-set regulations is strictly enforced and contributes to a better environment not only at the destination. Taking responsibility means investing in the future and in the host communities. It also comprises taking action and active support of vital research for a better understanding of the impacts tourism has on the host communities and the environment in general.

I agree with Pam Wight when, in her contribution to this issue, she states:

> While it is true that we need sustainable tourism at all levels and of all types, to look for one answer (such as sustainable mass tourism) may be a simplistic, if not impossible quest. Any role that ecotourism plays in contributing to sustainable tourism would seem to be beneficial. It seems that ecotourism's influence is having far reaching impacts toward extending principles of sustainability into other forms of tourism.

It is to be hoped that some day all tourism activities around the world – and not only ecotourism – will contribute strongly to conserving the best values our planet possesses and to provide a better livelihood for communities everywhere.

Correspondence

Any correspondence should be directed to Arq. Hector Ceballos-Lascuráin, Director General PICE, Program of International Consultancy on Ecotourism,

Camino Real al Ajusco 551, Col. Xolalpa (Tepepan), Tlalpan 14649, Mexico DF, Mexico (ceballos@laneta.apc.org).

References

Ceballos-Lascuráin, H. (1996) *Tourism, Ecotourism, and Protected Areas*. Gland, Switzerland: IUCN.

Ceballos-Lascuráin, H. (1997) *Uso Público en Areas Protegidas de la Amazonia*. Report for FAO/United Nations. Manu Biosphere Reserve, Peru.

Ecotourism Association of Australia (1998) *National Ecotourism Accreditation Program (NEAP)*. Queensland, Australia: Ecotourism Association of Australia.

Hawkins, D.E., Epler Wood, M. and Bittman, M. (1995) *The Ecolodge Sourcebook for Planners and Developers*. North Bennington, VT: International Ecotourism Society.

Basic Questions of 'Sustainable Tourism': Does Ecological and Socially Acceptable Tourism Have a Chance?

Torsten Kirstges
University of Applied Science, Wilhelmshaven, Germany

This paper examines the tourism market and its effects on the national economy. Ecological and socio-cultural problems cannot be denied. Due to an ever-increasing number of tourists, studies of tourism specific problems are necessary. To suggest and understand steps for the realisation of sustainable tourism, the author demands a glance at the whole tourism system, which he does by giving an overview of the tourism industry with obvious problems in that field. There is an analysis of the development of tourism demand, and the question whether there is something like 'sustainable mass tourism'. The increasing awareness of the environment plays an important role when it comes to tourism and selecting a tourism destination. The paper tries to find answers to promote a more sustainable tourism through tour operators and tourism companies, which can be a niche strategy for small or medium sized businesses. Strategical points (approaches) of a more sustainable tourism are shown. The realisation of sustainable tourism can be an economical opportunity for tourism companies in the long term, but according to the author the immediate risks involved in such a strategy can outweigh the benefits. There are also limits in carrying out more sustainable tourism programmes.

Essential Features of Tourism Criticism

The tourism market is renowned as *the* growing market. For decades the numbers of tourists, the turnover and the profits have been growing in Germany. In addition, German tourism companies have experienced two-figure growth rates, and for a long time it seemed that the tourism market was unlimited. The motto of the expansion of many companies and tourism areas during that time was 'close your eyes and just do it'. However, for a few years now there have been signs of an end of this rather pleasant trend for tourism companies. For many national economies, the absence of tourists would be a disaster. Therefore it is to be expected that the tourism industry in western nations will have politically and economically more influence in the future. Even though the economical opportunities, especially the chances of employment in the field of tourism, cannot be denied, many tourism critics argue that eventually the negative consequences of a 'rough' tourism – often only recognisable in the long term – outweigh the benefits. As such consequences can be defined:

Economical and socio-cultural problems

- It is the norm that the majority of jobs are available for only a certain period of time; natives are offered less qualified jobs; tasks of disposition are done by non-locals.
- Tourism mono-structures are developed which will lead to dangerous dependency due to their one-sided nature.

- Where there is inflation due to tourism, the price level in the centres of tourism increases, therefore those natives, who do not participate in the development of income are unable to afford many goods. Property and real estate prices increase rapidly.
- Support of land-leaving. Young people especially leave agricultural back-up areas to move to centres of tourism.
- The tourism meeting is superficial and therefore results in more prejudices towards developing countries.
- Commercialisation of the culture. Religious ceremonies are taken out of their surroundings and their actual meaning is lost for the sake of photo-seeking tourists.
- Begging, crime, prostitution and alcoholism increase. This is because the behaviour of tourists helps increase the desire to do and have the same standard of living.

Ecological problems

- The landscape is used for the purpose of relaxation. Natural landscape gets transformed into leisure areas.
- The permanent ecological pressure increases directly due to the behaviour of the holiday-makers (rubbish, sewage, exhaust fumes, trampled on and runover of plants and animals, noise, etc.).

People travelling in a 'rough' way are those who are short on time and prefer the fast way of transport. They see the sights just for the sake of taking a picture, do not prepare themselves for their holidays mentally and try to import their way of living to the country they spend their holidays in. Therefore 'rough' tourism does not only damages the natural resources, it also has negative effects on the individual recreational value of the holidays as well as the social environment of the host country. On the other hand, an exact definition of 'Eco tourism' does not exist. The fact that every type of tourism harms the environment will lead to discussions of it as a more sustainable tourism under which certain forms of travelling and measures can be understood which try in an even stronger way to reconcile with the social and natural environment.

With an expected increase in the travelling population, the importance of scientific studies regarding problems in the field of tourism is of high importance. However, at this point the discussion about the expected and long-term consequences of tourism, as well as the role of the tourism companies, destinations and politics cannot be repeated. Any reader interested in that topic should refer to the relevant literature. This paper will illustrate the problems associated with tourism and provide examples. The paper will also provide solutions to overcome such problems successfully.

With the obvious problems in sight, there is a plead for no consumption of tourism services at all. The total abandonment of tourism would be the most dramatic thing to reduce the damage of the environment caused by the consumption. As tourism plays quite an important economic role, every claim for a full abandonment or turning away from tourism (as is sometimes demanded by environmental protection parties) seems to be absolutely unrealistic and even reprehensible because of the effects upon the (world) economy!

Solutions have to be found in the field of tourism that can reconcile the natural and social environment with the economy. It is desirable to refer to a partial abandonment to influence (potential) travellers to be more conscious towards particular methods of travel (for example towards a possible damaging effect) and to consume it with a 'lighter dosage'.

The Problem: General Conditions of the Realisation of Better 'Eco Tourism'

The structure of the tourism system

To suggest and understand steps for the realisation of better 'Eco tourism' it is necessary to look at the entire tourism system. Normally there are single organisations that help to create the final tourism product, like a package holiday. Construction companies and real estate agencies, that build and rent hotels and apartment complexes in respective destinations can already be included in the term of the tourism system. Such real estate agencies have sometimes bought land speculatively years ago. They create complexes and then sell the whole hotel complex to hotel groups or other investment companies. For instance, huge holiday complexes are a popular investment for insurance companies. Alternatively they sell single apartments of an apartment complex to private investors. The holiday properties are mostly used by their owners; others see it as some kind of capital investment. Therefore it seems that in many tourism destinations, building new complexes is not only for providing more capacity of accommodation; the real estate market follows its own regularities –independent from tourism. Accommodation built in such a way is fundamental for tourism potential.

In the context of the actual tourism industry the following classifications can be found:

Service providers: responsible for a single output regarding the tourism industry which is offered to tour operators (e.g. hotels, owners of apartments, airlines, bus companies).

Tour operators: combine the single output of the different companies to marketable offers (package holiday).

Travel agents: sell the marketable offers of the tour operators.

In addition, there are destination agencies in some countries which at times look after apartments, as well as rent them in cases of apartment complexes and single persons owning an apartment. Such destination agencies are often founded by local authorities to market the tourism service of the relevant places in an even better way. The destination agencies that have different apartments on offer get in contact with tour operators who use the service as a part of their holiday package tour.

With regard to the mentioned single functions, different forms of distribution of tourism service are illustrated (Figure 1).

A more sustainable tourism is only possible if all partners of the whole tourism system co-operate. Not only at the same market level can competition be found; it is also very obvious in a vertical direction (for example competition

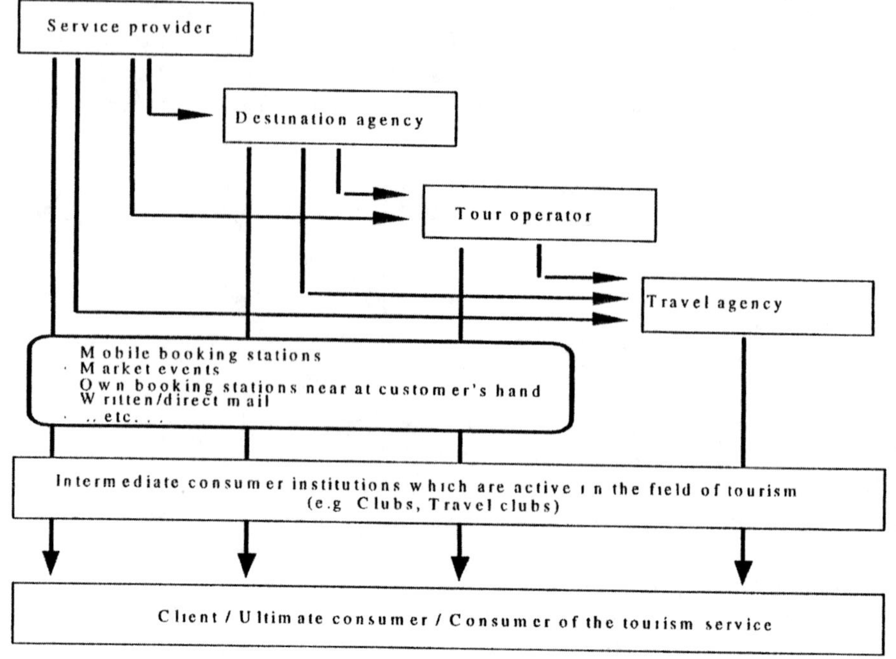

Figure 1 Alternative ways of distribution of tourism service

between hotels as service providers and tour operators that purchase their services with regards to pricing). Therefore a co-ordinated behaviour fails because of the differing aims.

Tour operators initiate tourism production processes whilst making inquiries for accommodation capacity at holiday destination. The larger tour operators are able to use the effects of quantity due to the fact of the regularity of mass production. When a tour operator selects a certain holiday destination as a part of the offered programme, the company should be interested in getting as many tourists in this country as possible to be able to function economically. Therefore an infrastructure able to serve mass tourism in the holiday destination must be found. Through the pressure of inquiries the capacity is calculated almost 100 days of peak season. At the end the tour operators control the destinations and take them in a certain direction through their product policy. Therefore a joint responsibility of the tour operators for production processes in certain holiday destinations and its effects cannot be denied.

Only when it is possible to convince the mass of the (middle class) companies in the respective markets, as well as in the holiday destinations of the necessity, the opportunity of realisation and the economical advantages of a more sustainable tourism, is there hope for more and appropriate forms of tourism.

On the other hand the middle class companies as well as the small tourism destinations seem to be unable to do anything in organisational, personnel and financial respect. So before there are any demands (mainly too high) to an environmental efficiency of those who take part in the field of tourism, every critic has to think of their financial as well as their organisational background conditions.

The opportunities of engagement of smaller companies in the field of a more sustainable tourism are limited because of:

- A relatively small yield. It is not that small organisation units differ in that respect from larger companies; but because of their smaller turnover it is more difficult to deal with dropping profits or unexpected additional costs, including costs for the field of sustainable tourism.
- A relatively small privately owned capital. The low annual profits only allow – if at all – a slow increase of the privately owned capital. Therefore the realisation of financing plans with capital resources is quite difficult. The drop in profit due to turning away from ecologically harmful holiday offers which are on the other hand really marketable, cannot be financed with capital resources for a long time. Additional financial costs for environmental oriented steps are proving difficult to meet, due to a lack of the capital resources required.
- It is quite difficult to have access to the capital market. Due to the lack of security, it is sometimes impossible to get a loan. Such disadvantages in providing capital can affect the chances of the realisation of bigger projects (of a more sustainable tourism).
- The permanent dilemma between overwork and an explosion in personnel costs. The tourism industry has a relatively high demand in staff, therefore an expansion is often only possible with even more staff. This leads to high semivariable costs. Therefore, hiring new staff is avoided until the overtime of the old staff is enough for a new employee. During the cycle in which a company exists, there is never any staff capacity available to realise 'special projects' in the field of sustainable tourism.
- Weaknesses in disposable areas. In many small firms the owner manages the company, marketing, human resources, organisation, and finances alone which often leads to sub-optimal results. It is difficult to find qualified staff for management under the aspect of bearable costs for 'no name' middle class companies. Innovative projects that are quite normal in the field of sustainable tourism can only be realised by the company owner or qualified staff of the management.

The potential of sustainable tourism as well as the target and realisation planning, which is necessary for the realisation of such tourism by middle class companies, can only be started systematically and sufficiently in some cases. Even if there would have been suitable strategies were acquired, their realisation could require finances and / or staff that make the carrying out for the company rather difficult. That speaks well for the thesis that usable instruments of sustainable tourism are reduced with a decrease in the size of a company. Large companies are able to get more usage out of the spectrum of usable instruments through the cost (in its absolute amount, employment of an environmental expert) than small firms. This restriction has to be considered when deriving strategies and operative steps of sustainable tourism – if they are supposed to be relevant for middle class companies.

Development of the tourism demand

'All of the ecologically harmful hotels at the Spanish Mediterranean Sea should be closed.' Such claims made by racial environmentalists often do not take into account that especially those areas with 'bunkers made out of concrete' are the most popular, and have the most visitors. Those who want to state destination oriented claims must measure these with the reality of the travel stream.

For the future – of the German source market – it is possible that as a result of increasing real wages and increasing leisure time, more people are able to afford a second or a third holiday per year although the stated increase of several travels during the 1990s will not continue in the same way. Fewer persons (= market volume in persons) will be going on more holidays (= volume in travels). Even if one takes the possible negative development of the population into account and the intensity of travel stagnating on a high level, the market volume which is counted in travels will be slightly increasing within the next few years. Therefore a 'process of self curing' regarding the ecological and social damages in the destination areas of (German) tourism cannot be expected. On the contrary: the burden of the holiday destinations due to tourism will even be increasing at least in a quantitative way!

As the trend to shorter holiday trips increases, the majority of travellers do not replace a longer holiday but rather supplement one with a shorter excursion. Short holiday trips are especially the extreme of the 'rough' tourism if they are done by car as the way of transport: energy consumption, pollution of the environment, personal 'stress of travelling', etc. are proportionally high in comparison with longer holiday trips. But it is unrealistic to expect a contribution towards the reduction of such a consumer trend from a single tour operator or a holiday destination. The general development of leisure time (shortening of work time, flexible work time, time in lieu) leads to such increasing demand in short-trip holidays. Although some companies have got understandable, selfish thoughts according with the market-economy system they cannot close their mind to such demand.

To blame only the tour operators should be avoided. Here too, it has to be taken into account that only a part of all travels are produced by tour operators. Their influence on the entirety of all travel streams and therefore their influence on better forms of sustainable tourism is less than expected: Fewer than half of all holidays are booked via a tour operator. In other (European) countries the proportion is even less. Therefore it is a wrong perspective if, because of a changed behaviour of tour operators regarding sustainable tourism, one is going to expect 'healed' conditions. Even if all the tour operators were able to 'convert' their clients to environment-conscious and social-conscious behaviour the mass of people individually travelling (so called individual travellers) can still contribute to the damage of the natural and social environment at the destination areas.

The problem increases on one hand due to the fact that the holiday budget influences the decision of holidays very much (sustainable offers are more likely to be more expensive than 'rough' ones because external costs are optionally converted into internal costs). On the other hand, in most companies and destination areas the offers regarding sustainable tourism are still missing. This is not only because the needed capacity of accommodation in expected quality (i.e.

equipment, location, etc.) is not available at the destination regions. In addition the companies and destination regions missed the opportunities to use chances in an innovative way. These opportunities result from a changing leisure time behaviour. However in many areas middle class special interest tour operators as well as incoming agencies, often quite small firms, were able to develop an offer which met consumers' requirements and have been marketed successfully.

The paradox of 'sustainable mass tourism'

'The tourist destroys what he is looking for whilst finding it.' That is such a short formula for the phenomenon, which can be seen to be quite paradoxical. The economical importance of tourism and the enormous size of the stream of travellers have been mentioned before. Let us assume it would be possible to convince all the people who go on holiday of the necessity of a better and rather soft form of travelling. Everyone would be willing to pay more would avoid ecologically harmful hotels, and would be 'gentle' and so on. Everyone would only think of environment-conscious and social-conscious motives when travelling. Let us assume that the necessary 'eco offers' are available (no overcrowding). What would happen?

After the first season, in which all the 'gentle tourists' turn away from the ecologically harmful and badly built Mediterranean Sea destinations and become environmental friendly hikers in the Austrian mountains instead, Austria would already have to close its mountains because of natural damage and danger of congestion. Or let us assume that everyone who goes alpine skiing would avoid the tabooed mechanical help for getting up the mountains (i.e. lifts, chair lifts, etc.) and would instead do cross-country skiing or snow walks. The consequences for the environment would be catastrophic!

So 100% sustainable tourism is not possible considering today's streams of travellers. The only possible way out is that travelling has to be forbidden or there has to be a distribution of authorised tickets to control the quantity and temporal distribution of the travel streams. This, as well as the distribution of 'quality certificates' for travellers, is absolutely impossible in a liberal society. Individual freedom of travelling normally comes with mass movements, but every mass movement goes against the ideals of sustainable tourism. Therefore it is perhaps possible to have an influence in a more sustainable tourism in the main dimensions of tourism.

Often it is said that the 'package tour travellers' are the bad tourists. Individual travels (i.e. travels without support of tour operators) are supposed to be better, gentler. In my opinion this is an error of judgement. Co-ordinated travel streams – let us take coach tours as an example, often smiled at with their 'umbrella carrying tour guide' – are more likely to fulfil the demands of sustainable tourism than so called individual travellers who are touring around Europe by car with only two people in it, with their backpack on the back using Indian hospitality or damaging lonely bays in Greece whilst camping. And even if a single individual traveller pays attention and follows the rules of sustainable tourism what would happen if all holiday-makers follow this apparent ideal?

The Chance: Change of Values Amongst the Population

The characteristics of values are the 'concepts of something desirable'. They can have the character of an aim and used as criterion for judging. Values are a guide to orientation standards, key-rules and guidelines for human behaviour in certain directions. The notice of values and changes of values are important for the estimation of the chances of a more sustainable tourism. The values make it easier to give a long-term prognosis regarding tendencies of behaviour of travelling than attitudes which often depend on the situation. Observed values indicate a potential of behaviour in that respect that can sooner or later lead to the actual behaviour. The change of values can therefore be an indicator of a possible change of behaviour.

The socio-political appreciation of the difficulties of Germans has become stable on a relatively high standard during the last few years. The social values, preservation of the environment and environmental protection, as well as the preservation and creation of places of work are high on the priority list in the social related value system. In an international comparison the people of Germany are very environment-conscious. However, other western nations are slowly attaining the same consciousness. A very distinct environmental consciousness is required to get holiday-makers to accept the need to make sacrifices for an even better environmental protection and give up other needs and behave environmentally correct as well.

In particular the environmental consciousness shows very clearly the noticeable shortage. In addition the ecological damage done by leisure time activities combined with the industrial pollution and pollution from private homes lead to even more shortage of the good 'intact environment'. As a result of this shortage, especially in the field of leisure time, there is a growing sensibility towards the environment and nature. The longing for untouched nature gains a bigger meaning. Nowadays the holiday motive 'being surrounded by nature' is an important requirement for a successful holiday. For a long time the holiday motive 'relaxation and silence' had been dominant amongst Germans. Many things contribute to the thesis that the central motives of a holiday for the majority of the population in the future will be a mixture of

- sun, silence, nature ;
- contact, contrast, comfort;
- fun, freedom, activity.

The majority of people travelling are only or mainly looking for untouched nature. Amongst the trippers the experience of the scenery and the nature is even more tempting to do weekend-trips. In the centre is getting to know the ecological connections and not the 'pure consumption of nature' such as the admiration of fantastic natural spectacles and natural beauty. Within the bounds of the trends towards naturalness and authenticity the 'sand deserts' made out of sand and concrete are especially criticised.

Families with children are particularly sensitive towards the environment. The quality of the environment at potential holiday destinations plays an important role when making decisions where to spend the holidays. Parents and children want to spend their holidays together and are very interested in beautiful surroundings, nature, and a clean environment. They therefore avoid holiday destinations with dirty beaches and a badly built area. This target group gets plenty of information about the environmental situation at the destination regions before making the decision.

The increasing sensitivity towards the environment and the growing meaning of the holiday motive nature in the course of changing of values is already obvious in that travellers are now more aware of environmental problems. Results of travel surveys verify it. In 1985 only 21.9% of holiday-makers were aware of the environmental problems in the destination regions; today the proportion is more than 50%.

It already seems that tourists who became critical do not agree with some important destination regions anymore. The Spanish holiday-destinations, led by the Canary Islands, has had a drop in bookings for some time. The destination areas of mass tourism in which there are obvious damages due to tourism will have to fear an abstinence of holiday-makers considering a more critical attitude towards consumption. In fact, the situation of capacity stops an increase in the streams of tourists moving away to other regions. However, there are the first signs for a start of a reorientation of important inquiry segments.

Firstly the meaning of the awareness of the environment for leisure time and holiday behaviour is characterised by the knowledge of each individual person about the consequences of their own behaviour, as well the ecological damage caused by institutions and companies. Empirical studies show that only about one-third of German people think they do harm the environment because of their holiday and leisure time behaviour. Different to the general social behaviour, the awareness of the environment in the field of leisure time has not yet led to an awareness of their own behaviour. The German citizen is now far more aware of his own competence for realising social aims than he was back in the early 1980s. He mainly sees his responsibilities in the fields of ecological preservation as well as the realisation of aims regarding health. Definite fields of activity form the information about current problems, the discussion with it and their own responsible behaviour. This is reflected in the fact that among two-thirds of the consumers there are signs of a social-conscious as well as an ecological-conscious style of behaviour.

The small willingness for personal sacrifices limit these behaviour tendencies. There is still a big difference between a strong awareness of the environment and an active environmental engagement. This discrepancy between the verbal-ideational level and the behaviour level of ecology orientated values has become noticeably smaller during the 1990s.

These inconsistencies show the following: the conversion of behaviour and to a changing of the awareness formed by social models into a new behaviour of an individual is – especially in the field of leisure time and holiday – a long process. First of all, the increased awareness of the environment, which could still rise because of further shortening of the environment, leads to growing requests of the travellers with regards to the products of the tourism industry. The individual awareness of the behaviour – the knowledge of a share of responsibility and the willingness of changing the personal behaviour are not well developed yet. There is the danger of a pure thought of requirement for tourism companies and holiday regions without an increasing willingness to have personal (for example financial) sacrifices among the tourists. So it is a difficult task to offer products on one hand that guarantee ecologically quality but on the other hand to show people inquiring that an intact environment on holidays is a luxury and everyone has to pay their share.

The tourist in between this area of conflict of social problem awareness and individual action awareness for the marketing of tourism organisations. The willingness of taking over social responsibility as a part of the tourism industry is necessary to avoid the danger of public opinion against tour operators. To fulfil the allocated responsibility is also a necessity. The willingness of the population to make (financial) sacrifices themselves – in their role as consumers while travelling – depends on what the industry does as a part of their share to solve the problems.

Steps for the Promotion of a More Sustainable Tourism Through Tourism Companies

Establishment of the environmental orientation in the entrepreneurial target system

In the following sections there are some chosen strategic attempts of a more sustainable tourism put forward. With the first step, tourism companies should establish environmental protection policies and respectively sustainable tourism in general among the entrepreneurial targets in their target system explicitly (!). This only guarantees

- that the ideals of sustainable tourism will be followed by the companies consequently and convincingly;
- that this is obvious to their own employees and will be effective in their behaviour as a maxim;
- that it is believably demonstrated outside the company.

Finally it is to determine to which entrepreneurial area the ecological orientated target must is aimed. Here it can be quite useful to put a maxim, formulated as an entrepreneurial main target, for the individual areas and hierarchies of the company in concrete terms. In a tour operating company the general effective main target could be 'to avoid pollution of the natural environment'. It could be put in concrete terms for instance for the purchasing departments ('only hotels with a connection to a sewage plant'; 'only aeroplanes with environmentally beneficial power plants'); for creating the catalogue ('only non-chlorine bleached paper') or for distributing the catalogue ('building of a re-distribution system for not distributed catalogues'). It is also possible to formulate targets for the individual production areas.

It would be unrealistic to demand the establishment of the targets of sustainable tourism as the *highest* entrepreneurial target for tourism companies, either in Germany or in the destination areas. Empirical surveys show that the environmental protection in entrepreneurial target systems still have a low priority. On the other hand it is quite satisfactory that environmental protection targets are seen as complementary sub-targets among other targets, especially long-term orientated targets of growth.

Quality leadership through to sustainable tourism

The offers of softer forms of travelling could also secure the position of tourism companies and destination regions with regard to quality leadership internationally. Next to the basic service today, through to the high standards expected by travellers, the environmental protection could be as a new quality dimension of a (package) holiday, an additional opportunity of distinction to get quality regarded competitive advantages. Such a quality leadership seems to be especially relevant as a strategy of individual destination areas and tourism resorts. An intact scenery and untouched nature are – as shown above – for a majority of the population main requirements for qualitative successful holidays.

But indirectly it has also strong effects that relate to the quality of the service offered by tour operators. Their most important components are still the original factors of the destination areas.

Quality leadership allows the supplier to achieve a higher price level at the market compared with the competitors. The quality leader normally is the price leader too, especially when the high quality level comes with a well-known brand. The price leader is able to realise higher prices compared with the competitors. Therefore, in the field of tourism, it is possible to bring the targets of a sustainable tourism in accord with the business management-ecological targets through to a quality orientated strategy of distinction.

However, there are only a few starting-points that allow sustainable tourism to appear meaningful in the way of business management under the aspect of cost leadership. The optional integration of the otherwise normal external costs goes against the efforts to have a low level of costs compared with their competitors. Scale effects – often the requirement for a cost leadership – can hardly be done with actions of sustainable tourism or go against the basic idea of ecological and social tolerated tourism (compare above: The paradox of 'sustainable mass tourism').

Sustainable tourism as a niche strategy and for selected market segments

Especially for smaller or middle class tourism companies sustainable tourism can be a market niche where – protected from rough competition on the 'big' tourism market – a circle of clients can create a distinctive personal image for themselves. Meanwhile the company can withdraw from the widely spread and therefore tough to realise requirements of the different groups of interests of sustainable tourism. On the other hand it then has to pay more attention to the specific requirements of the selected niche target group and take them into account. Various providers for cycling or trekking tours could be named as such niche specialists for the German tourism market. In the field of travel agencies too, there are already companies that stand out due to a programme policy which is orientated to sustainable tourism. Their requirements include ecologically orientated tour operators as well as additional services (for example selling of 'alternative' travel guides).

For tourism companies, that

- want to work on more than one market niche;
- want to put up with certain challenges of sustainable tourism in an innovative way;

- want to avoid a rather strong mark as a 'sustainable provider' in other areas;
- or want to initiate the first steps towards sustainable tourism without the risks of a total 'strategic change of direction';

the establishment of specific 'soft demand potentials' would provide a solution. These demand potentials are useful for specifically dealing with offers that are sufficient for the requirements of an ecologically and socially correct tourism. Also, it is possible to distinguish and work on other segments without a specific mark due to sustainable tourism.

Organisational establishment of sustainable tourism

Sustainable tourism can only become reality if it is organisationally established within the company. There is an implicit solution where the environmental protection is established as a sight task of each employee. Adding to this, there is the opportunity of an explicit solution where own organs for the establishment of targets of sustainable tourism in the enterprise can be created. For such an institutionalisation of the environmental protection task there are some reasons:

- **Reduction of the complexity**
  The 'right' conversion of the ideals of sustainable tourism partly requires specific know-how, not only in the economical and ecological field but in the scientific and technical areas (for example sewage plants, catalogue printing methods). This complexity of individual environmental tasks requires a certain professional way not only to give enough competence towards clients, service providers, and the public in general (press, organisations, environmentalist groups, etc.). Due to the organisational concentration of all the tasks of sustainable tourism, this complexity is reduced. Then professional and competent appearance and decision making are more likely to be possible.
- **Relief of other departments**
  The individual tasks which appear within the framework of realisation of targets set for sustainable tourism can hardly be done 'just next to other tasks' with the necessary care. A single organisational unit can co-ordinate the daily environmental tasks which arise in all entrepreneurial departments better, completely and more effectively as the other departments are relieved.
- **A better controlling**
  An official organisational unit's performance can be supervised, controlled and judged in a far more effective way than a multitude of departments and persons. A professional approach to working and specialisation in certain tasks are also the requirements for offensive and controlling environmental protection policy. Due to an explicit organisation solution it gets easier for external authorities to communicate and supervise.
- **Promotion of innovation**
  An innovative environmental protection management is influenced by the form of establishment of the ideals of sustainable tourism in the entrepreneurial organisation. Here the classical strategy-structure-dilemma is obvious, because to initiate and plan offensive environmental protection strategies there are already organisational requirements necessary.

For the field of tourism in Germany there are no laws regarding the explicit organisational establishment of the environmental protection until now, for instance, having a representative for environmental protection. Nevertheless, since November 1990 TUI employs a representative for environmental protection on an optional basis and is the only German tour operator with such a position. Dr Wolf Michael Iwand has held the position to date. It is his task to tackle environmental questions systematically, orientated on results and experience.

Creating special jobs to convert the environmental protection within or through the own enterprise involves high costs which normally cannot be paid for by small and middle class businesses. Therefore an institutionalisation of sustainable tourism in the form of a project team is possible. A permanent existing central group (environmental committee) that consists of members of the different departments should meet on a regular basis (for example once a month) to secure a continuing consideration of the topic and a lasting conversion of passed measurements. Furthermore project specific and additional or extended meetings and/or work circles (project teams) can be formed to realise bigger plans with regards to planning, decision making or conversion.

As an extra variant there should be – at least partially – external conversion named. So representatives of travel agents, service providers, associations and others can be considered when it comes to entrepreneurial decisions in the form of an integrative committee.

The second area of decision in case of an explicit establishment of sustainable tourism in an enterprise is the question of the hierarchical arrangements of environmental protection. If the hierarchical arrangement of the job of the environmental protection representative is rated high and there is full authority to issue directives, then it will lead to the establishment of higher targets for sustainable tourism that relate to concrete decisions and actions of the individual organisational members. The positive extreme could be that one of the managers of the company declares himself to be responsible for this area. The negative extreme would be that a department with hardly any authority to issue directives is in charge of the environmental protection but just as an alibi function (for example press department). Even with little authority to issue directives – for instance to make it possible to work efficiently in the departments – the representative for environmental protection could be equipped with a veto right. This would allow him to stop decisions and actions made by the departments that are questionable or rather critical considering the (entrepreneurial) targets of sustainable tourism and would lead to abnormal developments. Should the situation arise the final decision has to be made by the highest management, after a veto had been made prior to that by the department of environmental protection. Internal business disputes with regard to the environmental protection would automatically always be a top management matter if there is no agreement between the representative for environmental protection and the department. The conflicts caused by such rules are of a constructive nature and should be supported to produce an awareness discussion of all employees in the company with the consequences of their own behaviour.

Particularly in larger companies it seems to be useful to have a combined solution (explicit and implicit organisational conversion) in accordance with a distribution and a hierarchical specification of the environmental protection meaning.

This is the only way to reach a total penetration of the entire organisation with the targets of sustainable tourism. On each level, environmental tasks can be transferred to certain managers. In this case the representative in the 'head office of environmental protection' would specifically have – as a field promoter within the business – an information and co-ordination function as well as a representation function outside the company. Therefore he/she is also the institutionalisation of the risk management while the chance orientated innovation function gets especially implemented in the form of a decentralised competence, project teams or environmental committees within the company.

Environmental orientated service arrangements

The most important parameter for the arrangements for a more sustainable tourism is the product policy. Due to (among other things) an environmental orientated selection of the offered destination areas as well as method of transport, middle class suppliers can fulfil the mentioned requirements. Questions regarding the selection of accommodation could be:

- Is the type of construction typical for the country/area?
- Has there been any damage to originally protected nature because of construction?
- Is accommodation really tourist (human being) friendly?
- Are locals employed?
- Is sewage and waste management ecologically acceptable? Do sewage plants exist?

Optional self-restriction should be tried in certain destinations if there are signs of strain or over-capacity. Bounds of limitation do exist in the view of

- ecological capacity: maximum of capacity of the eco-system;
- socio-psychological capacity: to what degree do locals accept the stream of tourists and their behaviour;
- economical capacity: at what load factor could be counted on a rapid increasing, over dimensional infrastructure, with price increases abnormal for the country, etc.;
- technical capacity: restrictions due to area requirements and physical conditions;
- relaxation capacity: ability of a destination to take tourists, until the relaxation benefit of a tourist is not affected by other tourists.

For the practical determining of such pressure, there are difficulties of course that relate to the strategies, as illustrated in the examples mentioned below.

At the end, the provider secures the product quality of his travel service by paying attention to these bounds of limitation. Even friendliness and openness of the locals is an important quality feature from the viewpoint of the guests.

In this context it should be examined too, if a concentration of the really damaging forms of tourism on the (already existing) main emphasis, should be focused. Or can artificially created holiday areas be an alternative to further development of natural destination areas ('under a glass roof', one think of the holiday parks of the enterprise Center Parcs).

Middle class companies often complain that due to the above-mentioned structure of the entire tourism system they have limited opportunities to influence their service providers. For a single tour operator there are opportunities of closer co-operation with a few service providers per destination region and this provides opportunities to have a greater influence. Due to long-lasting co-operation with selected service providers, the tour operator is more influenced in the risk too, which comes with an uncontrolled tourism development. Therefore the tour operator will support a long-lasting competitive destination region, different to a seasonal co-operation.

It could be that the tour operator agrees to longer lasting co-operation contracts with selected service providers (i.e. hotels), which gives the owner of the hotel a guaranteed purchase of accommodation capacity (i.e. of up to five years). Therefore the tour operator is in charge of the load factor risk. As a countermove, the hotel owner agrees to carry out necessary steps for the environmental protection (i.e. connection to a sewage plant, planting more green areas, etc.). The most extreme case would be an integration vertically as well as backwards, that means to build up own service providers or take them over. It would make a direct participation in environmental decisions possible.

The co-operation should not only refer to the direct service providers. In a further-reaching co-operation with the locals, as in friendship or culture societies, the German tour operator can initiate projects to preserve the natural environment or region / country specific cultural heritages. In this context a joint vote about the bounds of limitation could be agreed.

The overload of traffic can on an environmental basis only be solved through better flexibility of times of travelling. Obviously an individual tour operator cannot change or demand a more convenient European travelling season. However, due to their opportunities they can help to correct it 'in small standard' and with it they can try to fulfil the shown demand trend for their personal economical advantage. Therefore the second area of an environmental service creation is a more flexible travelling season. One can assume that from the demanding side there is inquiry for flexibility regarding the dates of travelling (for example departure times). It can be expected that a more flexible travelling duration will be especially inquired in the future. Both inquiries are directed to the flight tour operator – more flexible and more frequent charter chains.

Opportunities of influencing the behaviour of tourists

Tourists often offend local customs and norms due to ignorance and the natural environment is often damaged because of carelessness. By informing the tourists, tourism enterprises and destination agencies can help to avoid or limit any danger. The following steps could influence the behaviour of tourists:

- The general description of the destination region in a catalogue will be expanded; instead of changeable holiday clichés, realistic and typical information are given. A rubric 'you fit in this country / place if you . . . ' or 'This country / place would not please you if you . . . ' would be possible. By this means overrated demands of guests can be avoided which should have a positive effect regarding the numbers of complaints.

- Among the travel documents there can be a self-created small information brochure included, which should sensitise tourists for a social behaviour according to the society of the host country. This is especially important for long-distance journeys. The behaviour can be phrased in following the available work of the former team 'tourism with sense' and / or in co-operation with environmental protection committees in the framework of a 'Round table talk'.
- The tourist as well as the general public receive information about the problems which tourism companies have to deal with in destination regions by means of educational campaigns. Especially the limited opportunities of the influence of (middle class) companies on the (political) decision-makers in the destination regions as well as starting-points and steps already taken of an influence through their own company can be illustrated.
- Tour guides and entertainment officers are educated in 'socially tolerated tourism'. The tour guides are supposed to help by portraying a view and a sensitivity towards customs in a country and towards adapted behaviour.
- To develop internal environmental thinking in a company combined with an effective publication of the steps taken (next to marking the enterprise multiplication effects too!), tourism companies can name a representative for environmental protection in their own business, who is the representative to talk to and the co-ordinator for all political environmental protection (see above).

By taking such steps, middle class businesses can help consolidate such a problem awareness among tourists.

Financial steps for the preservation and re-establishment of the environment

There are already some examples how German tour operators due to a financial arrangement helped at least eliminating damage. Environmental projects in the destination regions get support (tropical rain) forests are planted or ski trails are made 'green' again.

Such attempts are useful especially if tourists can be persuaded successfully to have their own financial share. Due to the then higher involvement, a better sensitivity for their own behaviour can be reached. But it should not be suggested that a tourist could 'buy himself out' of any responsibility.

The 'Captive Dilemma': The Necessity and the Problematic Nature of an Industry Wide Environmental Strategy

Even if the initiation and realisation of sustainable tourism is an economic option for tourism businesses, the noticeable risks from a short-term perspective can be predominant. Many steps cannot be taken by a single business, but only be realised in co-operation with some or all enterprises of the same trade. Why, one could ask, are there no rules within the trade for the carrying out of sustainable tourism? Why do not all those responsible decide to do so, more or less at the same time? The answers to these questions as well as an explanation of the still wide observable passiveness can be given in regards to the so called 'Captive dilemma' model.

With regard to tourism, one starts with two strategic options for two competitors. For both competitors the conversion of sustainable tourism is effective and in principle desirable; but corresponding strategies lead to higher costs. Due to (short-term) economical reasons, ignorance of environmental protection seems to be the better alternative because consumers and the general public do not yet honour steps towards enough environmental protection. On a long-term basis the success of an enterprise can only be secured in view of the circumstances of the ecological and social targets.

If both competitors were to opt for an offensive environmental strategy, the common target of the environmental protection would be served. Also short-term and long-term success would be secured unchanged. But can either one of the tour operators be sure that the other follows this strategy?

If only one of the enterprises decides on an offensive strategy, it will have short-term competition disadvantages caused by higher costs. If on the other hand, one enterprise decides on passiveness, it will be (in the short-term) secured. But there might be passiveness on both sides – under the premise of a certain version of risk – which neither is sufficient with regard to the long-term objectives of both companies nor sufficient considering the social targets of sustainable tourism. Table 1 summarises this situation.

Table 1 Decision on a trade wide sustainable tourism as a 'Captive dilemma'

Tourism Enterprise A: / ***Tourism enterprise B:***	***Offensive*** = Following the targets of sustainable tourism	***Passiveness*** = Keeping up with the status quo / no reorientation towards sustainable tourism
Offensive = Following the targets of sustainable tourism	A and B both take care of the realisation of sustainable tourism. The position of power between A and B stays unchanged. Both secure their existence on a long-term basis.	A realises costs, and therefore profitability advantages, compared to B. The targets of sustainable tourism are slightly followed (only by B). The existence of A seems not to be secured on a long-term basis.
Passiveness = Keeping up with the status quo / no reorientation towards sustainable tourism	B realises costs- and therefore profitability advantages compared to A. The targets of sustainable tourism are slightly followed (only by A). The existence of B seems not to be secured on a long-term basis.	Neither A nor B have any influence on the realisation of sustainable tourism. The tourism problems even increase. The position of power between A and B stays unchanged. On a long-term basis the existences of both A and B are at risk.

Only if the demand for tourism service changes, the classical situation of a 'captive dilemma' will not be there anymore. It has to be in a way that the increased market acceptance of environmentally beneficial and socially tolerated forms of travelling lead to a clear and short-term realisation of competitive advantages due to an offensive environmental management.

Some years ago there happened to be such a situation in the framework of the tourism establishment in Turkey: at so called turtle bay, a giant hotel project was supposed to be realised which would have been the death for the turtles that regularly brooded there. The large German tour operators would have been the main buyers of this hotel project. This would have been a great opportunity for each individual tour operator to develop its tourism in Turkey. If only one tour operator would have done without it, it would have been an advantage for the others. If no tour operator would have done without it, a 'capacity balance' would have again been possible but the environment would have been gone. Owing to the pressure of the public opinion, caused by environmentalists, it was expected that each decision – supported by German tour operators – for the tourism development of this bay would have led to a lot of damage to the image. Finally all large tour operators went against this project. Without this expected and also economically effective character assassination, most of the tour operators would have decided to support this building project.

The previous considerations are enough to clearly show the difficulties of a general trade environmental strategy on the basis of individual and optional entrepreneurial decisions. As long as the demand development does not force the companies to take on the challenge of sustainable tourism offensively, general in the trade, environmental protection strategies can be realised only on the initiative of committees (one should not expect a lot of engagement of politics).

Nevertheless single enterprises within the trade – especially in the vertical value added chain as a result of co-operations or value added partnerships – can still come up with initiatives to realise an ecological and socially tolerated tourism.

For most German tour operators, the only option would be to take care of 'Goodwill' among the service providers and travel agents. For instance, maintain an intensive personal contact and establish special incentives for these market partners.

Further Attempts and Bounds of Limitation of Sustainable Tourism Programmes

There are no bounds of limitation to the inventiveness regarding possible steps to support sustainable tourism. But in many various ways, especially among really idealistic tourism critics, unrealistic demands and suggestions are established.

So in the 1990s the committee 'Naturfreundejugend Deutschlands' (NFJD) asked for alternatives to the ski tourism. 'Snow plays', 'theatre courses', 'juggling', 'mime' and similar 'soft' offers are named. The 'BUND' demanded at that time 'the turning away from the mass tourism and providing environmentally beneficial holiday opportunities among the tourism companies and to do without the usual – today still used – commercial meaning'. Environmentalists say that if tour operators and entire holiday destinations were to follow these demands, it would ruin them.

Due to such statements environmental protection committees gamble away their recognition by the tourism trade and therefore their possible positive influence on their strategies. In view of the positive effects of tourism, abolition cannot be the aim. Such an aim would be totally unreachable in a free social order, but economy and ecology have to be brought into accord usefully. Also 'imagination travels' which the computer simulates without moving away from the city where the traveller lives, or 'Esoteric holidays' with meditation, yoga and other forms of self-finding, are of interest for only a small minority. It can hardly contribute to bringing the mass under control.

It is also a hindrance that the (tourism specialist) publication seldom supports attempts for projects of a more sustainable tourism. The opposite is sometimes the case, if environmentally harmful travel offers (for example helicopter skiing) are sold as an 'insider tip'.

Generally it could be assumed that strategies of a more sustainable tourism give impulses of growth to tourism companies and tourism destinations only on a long-term basis. The more enterprises of a trade there are to carry on with eco-marketing, the more successful the individual will be. Pioneer profit can hardly be achieved with 'green marketing policy'. The opposite is the case. Pioneers have the risk of getting a 'boomerang effect' if they sensitise their potential customers. For many people, the striving for experience and adventure while on holiday is dominant and their environmental behaviour is limited due to a lack of willingness for personal sacrifices. Therefore the information in catalogues given by tour operators about ecological damage, damaging behaviour of tourists and so on, can lead to dissonance among consumers that make him/her susceptible to the 'safe world advertisement' of other providers. In this respect concepts of a more sustainable tourism are necessary in the long-term, but not a sufficient requirement for the expansion of an enterprise.

The case studies in the Bibliography are supposed to be examples and give stimulus of how in different countries and in different organisations the target to create a lasting, environmentally beneficial and social tolerated tourism on a long-term basis is followed.

Correspondence

Any correspondence should be directed to Prof. Dr Torsten Kirstges, Gutenbergweg 5, 26389 Wilhelmshaven, Germany (www.Kirstges.de).

References

Kirstges, T. (1993) Sanfter Tourismus: Modetrend oder strategische Herausforderung für Reiseveranstalter und Reisemittler? In D. Durlacher (ed.) *Pauschalreisemarkt im neuen Europa – Trends, Regulative, Umweltaspekte* (pp. 36–64). Vienna: ÖGAF.

Kirstges T. (1994) *Sanfter Tourismus* (2nd edn). München: Oldenbourg-Verlag.

Kirstges, T. (1996) *Expansionsstrategien im Tourismus: Marktanalyse und Strategiebausteine für mittelständische Reiseveranstalter.* Wiesbaden: Gabler-Verlag.

Kirstges, T. (1998) Skifahren und Umweltschutz – (k)ein Widerspruch. In T. Bausch and A. Schmölzer (eds) *Tourismus Forum 1998, Beiträge aus Forschung und Praxis des Wissenschaftszentrums der ITB Berlin* (pp. 135–41). Hamburg: Verlag TourCon/Niedecken.

Kirstges, T. (1999) Strategiealternativen von Reiseveranstaltern. In S. Gewald (ed.) *Handbuch des Touristik- und Hotelmanagement* (pp. 345–8). Munich/Vienna.

Kirstges, T. (1999) Tourismus im Zeitalter der Globalisierung – Fünf Thesen zu Trends im Tourismusmarketing des ausgehenden 20. Jahrhunderts und Konsequenzen für die Tourismuspolitik. *Tourismus Jahrbuch* 1, 139–43.

Kirstges, T. (2000) *Management von Tourismusunternehmen: Organisation, Personal- und Finanzwesen bei Reiseveranstaltern und Reisemittlern* (2nd edn). Munich/Vienna: Buch Oldenbourg-Verlag.

About the author

Prof. Dr Torsten H. Kirstges is Professor of General Business Management and Tourism (Tour operator/Travel agent) at the University of Applied Science in Wilhelmshaven. Main field of research: Tourism marketing; Tourism and environment; Middle class tour operators and Travel agents. Numerous publications and talks. Consultant for renowned enterprises and international institutions (Lufthansa, ITS, Deutsche Bahn, SITE, tourist regions).

Alternative Tourism Activities Management in the Argentinean–Chilean Great Lakes Corridor

Rodrigo González and Adriana Otero
Tourism Faculty, Universidad Nacional del Comquhe, Argentina

Tourist and recreational use of natural and protected areas in Argentine–Chilean Great Lakes Tourist Corridor has experienced a remarkable growth during last years. Although total amount of use is still within these areas admission capacity, problems arise derived from intensive use in certain places, as well as visitors management concerns in considered critical areas.

In this context, a research project was elaborated, approaching the problem of alternative tourism activites management, and focusing on aspects referred to their management and administration in the area of Binational Corridor. This paper refers to one of the dimensions considered in the project: alternative tourism activites demand in the Corridor.

Starting from the classification of sustainable tourism niches done by Eagles (1994), a segmentation matrix was prepared and applied. Such analysis has important research, planning and market implications and is critical to the development of suitable services as well as to the design of appropriate management strategies and techniques for those institutions in charge of tourism planning in wilderness areas. Results are not only valid for those activities mentioned in the area of study, but also for other outdoor activities management in the context of North-Patagonian protected areas.

Introduction

Tourist and recreational use of natural and protected areas in the Argentinean–Chilean Great Lakes Tourist Corridor has experienced a remarkable growth during the last few years, following the world-wide trend in tourism growth in this area. The well-known continual changes in demand, which are not only quantitative but also qualitative, influence the social variables (i.e. perceptions of the quality of visitor recreational experience) and physical/biological variables (i.e. composition and state of vegetal and animal species) that characterise these areas.

Although total use is still within the admission capacity of these areas, problems arise from intensive use in certain places and visitor management in those areas is considered to be a major concern. Considering the vertiginous increase in non-conventional tourism activities and its different forms (natural tourism, ecotourism, adventure tourism, low impact tourism) limiting development is a serious concern for managers and researchers working in these areas.

The expansion in the demand for tourist services leads us to such questions as: 'What kind of opportunities should be provided to tourists?' 'What should the role of each partner involved in this process (Park authorities, civil authorities, tourists and residents) be? 'What or who can satisfy these new and growing public needs in an efficient way'? 'How can we prevent unacceptable changes being brought about by the increase in recreational use?' These are only some of the questions that demand the adoption of strategies for action, based on planning and management approaches, that could respond to the complex and dynamic mosaic of situations in the management of tourism activities in these environments.

In this context, this research approached the problem of alternative tourism activities, focusing, in particular, on aspects of their management and administration in a bi-national Corridor. Specifically, guidelines for environmental management were developed for a set of activities presenting a notorious development in the Lakes Region: camping, rafting, trekking and hiking, mountain-biking and fishing, through case-studies in the Argentinean – Chilean bi-national circuit. The central idea was to develop management options based on public consensus, as well as to work on guidelines to promote public–private inter-institutional cooperation.

Objectives

The *general objective* was to develop management and control guidelines for rafting, camping sites, trekking, mountain-biking and fishing in areas considered to be critical which receive intensive use, within the Argentinean–Chilean Great Lakes Corridor.

The *specific objectives* were:

- to review the literature specifically devotoed to the characteristics of each activity, as well as the impacts which derive from their practice;
- to study the factors affecting the perception of the quality of the recreational experience by different tourist sectors visiting the Corridor; and
- to evaluate any management proposals for implementation feasibility.

Area of Study

The tourist Corridor is located in the Lakes Region in Chile, and in the south end and north-west of the Neuquén and Rio Negro Provinces in Argentina; between parallels 40° 38′ and 41° 20′ of south latitude and meridians 71° and 73° 10′ of west longitude.

The corridor includes the following tourist centres: San Carlos de Bariloche, Villa La Angostura in Argentina, and Osorno, Puerto Octay, Frutillar, Llanquihue, Puerto Varas, Puerto Montt, Ensenada, Petrohué and Peulla in Chile.

Methodology

Selection of activities to be studied

From the wide variety of activities developed in the corridor, those which present a current or potential conflict situation with implications for management and control were selected. Although many definitions exist around the concept of alternative tourism, for the present work, the focus was placed on those activities developed in a natural environment, with little structured programming in relation to conventional tourism activities, but which give the tourist a high level of independence in creating his/her own recreational experience.

The selected activities were camping, rafting, fishing and trekking in both countries. Later it was decided to incorporate the consideration of mountain-biking into the Argentinean sector, because of the importance that it is acquiring, and the trends that suggest a sustained growth for this sector in the short and medium term.

Analysis of demand, tourist operators and institutions in charge of visitor management in protected areas

In order to achieve an integrated approach, it was decided to focus the analysis on three dimensions: demand (tourists), tourist operators and institutions responsible for management and control in protected areas.

Analysis of the demand enabled user sectors and sub-sectors to be established, generating qualitative information that characterised their behaviour by considering different groups of variables: socio-demographics, activity-specific characteristics, market tendencies and environmental variables.

Tourist operators were studied to uncover the operating conditions and benefits derived from these tourist activities, as well as to discover the main sources of conflict in their practice.

Finally, the organisations in charge of tourism management in the National Parks included in the Corridor were analysed.

Data collection instruments

A variety of data collection instruments was used, including tourist surveys , non-structured interviews with government officials and private operators, participant and non-participant field observation and a review of the literature and documents relating to administration and visitor management in protected areas.

Demand analysis

Surveys of tourists practising the studied activities were undertaken. Different surveys were designed for camping, rafting and fly-fishing. Participants in fishing and rafting were observed. Key informants were interviewed, in order to corroborate the information obtained from the surveys. In-field observation was carried out, in order to experience the conflict situations resulting from tourists visiting the region.

Tourist operator analysis

Those tourist operators which had been in business the longest and were recognised by their own colleagues as the most appropriate for giving accurate information, both in San Carlos de Bariloche (Argentina) and Puerto Varas (Chile), were selected. A non-structured interview was designed, with a list of topics on which each interviewee would be examined.

Institutional analysis

At first, information was extracted from interviews with informants from different hierarchical levels, parks administrators, technical personnel and rangers – from both countries, made in advance by the research group. Later, another non-structured interview was undertaken with informants from the National Parks Administration (APN) in Argentina and the Forestry National Corporation (CONAF) in Chile, in order to obtain more detailed information about alternative tourism activities management and control.

Results

To achieve an integrated approach, it was decided to focus the analysis in three dimensions: demand (tourists), tourist operators and institutions in charge of visitor management and control in protected areas.

Description of analysed alternative tourism activities

As a result of surveys, interviews and field observation, information was generated relating to each of the activities considered in this study. In each case, the results are assigned to either the Argentinean or Chilean sectors. When not specified, the results refer to information presenting similar values in both sectors.

Sector analysis

The constant growth in alternative tourism activities has led to an increase in the complexity of demand composition. The market for sustainable tourism is large enough that specific sectors and sub-sectors could be best managed with their specific characteristics in mind. As Wight (1993) argues, sustainable tourism involves a spectrum of experiences, supply characteristics and market demands. A better understanding of each consumer sector will help in the design of management actions, and the ability to outline marketing strategies and techniques addressing each sector concerns. Mahoney (undated) points out that market strategies designed for the mass market result in products, prices and promotion that do not appeal to all potential customers. Thus, he suggests that recreation marketing must be based on market and target segmentation, in contrast to the idea of strategic actions designed for what has been called 'an average tourist'.

Such an analysis has important implications for research, planning and market and is critical to the development of suitable services as well as to the design of appropriate management strategies and techniques for those institutions in charge of alternative tourism planning in wilderness areas. This is valid for the activities mentioned in the area of study, considering the lack of appropriate information concerning alternative tourism activities.

Starting from the classification of sustainable tourism niches in Eagles (1994), a sector matrix was prepared. Four major variables were recognised, each including a number of specific variables depending on the activity considered: socio-demographic (place of residence, level of income, age, type of group, etc.), related to the practice of each activity (ability in its practice, previous experience, factors affecting overall satisfaction with a recreation experience, frequency of visit, etc.), environmental variables (environmental impact, resilience of recreation sites), market (growth tendency) and finally variables related to management concerns (use levels, key management issues).

The matrix was applied to all activities considered. Table 1 shows, as an example, the results obtained in the case of rafting.

The combination of variables can vary, depending on their suitability to describe each sector profile. It is important to note that the list of variables included in this study should not be considered to be definitive. New dimensions could be added in successive approaches, when considered necessary.

Table 1 Consumer analysis – rafting in the Argentinean–Chilean Great Lakes corridor

SEGMENT: RAFTING[(a)]	*SUBSEGMENTS*		
Variables	***Tourist practising rafting, both from Chile and Argentina***		***Foreign rafters, with previous experience***
	Without previous experience	With previous experience	
Socio-demographic variables			
Place of residence	Most important cities in Chile and Argentina (Santiago and Concepción in Chile; Buenos Aires, Córdoba, Rosario and Mendoza in Argentina)		North America, Germany, in minor proportion, from Canada, France and Spain
Level of income	Medium–high / High	Medium	Medium–high
Age	14 to 25 / 30 years old	22 / 25 to 35 / 40 years old	25 to 35 years old.
Type of group	Groups of friends Couples Father and son / s / Alone	Alone Groups of friends	Couples Father and son / s Alone
Activity-specific variables			
Ability / previous experience	Without previous experience	Previous experience in II or III class rivers	Previous experience in III, IV or V class rivers
Main motivation factor	* To live an enjoyable experience * To 'feel adrenaline' * To know the activity	* To know new rivers * To gain experience as rafters, increasing difficulty levels * To 'feel adrenaline'	* To know new rivers at distant places or exotic destinations, rather than increasing difficulty levels
Factors influencing overall satisfaction	* Practising the activity for the first time produces high satisfaction levels * Security conditions	* To raft in a river with higher difficulty level than those visited before, then gaining experience as rafters. * Security conditions	Service quality as a whole.
Frequency of visitation	It is common for visits to be repeated once or twice. Once they feel comfortable with a single river experience, they start thinking of visiting new rivers.	They intent to visit new rivers each time, in order to gain experience as rafters	Low frequency of visits, due to long distances from their homes
Tourist services requirements	* Quality of equipment * Guide skills	* Guide skills, to achieve new challenges in a safe way * Personnel attention * Security conditions related matters	Service quality

Table 1 (*contd*)

SEGMENT: RAFTING[(a)]	*SUBSEGMENTS*		
Environmental variables			
Environmental impacts	Low. However, indirect impacts can be identified, related to the possibility of getting to backcountry or remote sites, and then incrementing the risk of impacts on protected species.		
Market-related variables			
Market tendencies	Increasing, particularly for beginners		
Management-related variables			
Use levels	This is the sector presenting highest levels of use, with a sustained growing trend in the short term.	High, but with a lower increase than rafters without previous experience.	Even though it is important the number of foreign rafters have reached neither the magnitude nor the importance of the other two sectors.
Key management aspects	• Safety • Personal attention • Guide skills Considering safety and taking into account the increase, special attention must be paid to the establishment of a maximum number of tourists per boat.	Guide skills are essential Control of promoted services.	Service quality must be strictly considered, including general aspects and operation details. This sector's high experience level determines the need for high quality standards.

(a) Chile: Petrohue River / Argentina: Limay and Manso Rivers
Source: Own elaboration

The importance of such a process is linked not only to an accurate identification and description of each sector, but also to the possibility of setting a working methodology that could permit the authorities in national parks and other protected areas to develop further research on this topic, even extending this study to include other activities not considered in this work. The segmentation matrix presented here could also be useful in studying alternative tourism activities in other environments, by adapting the list of variables mentioned.

The most relevant findings for each activity are described in the following subsections.

Rafting. This is one of the activities that present a wide potential market, mainly because of the expanding demand. Both the tourists' *origin* (national and foreigners) and *previous experience* are the most relevant variables in determining this sector.

For all identified segments, *safety conditions* appears to be one of the most important components in the operators' selection of products. However 'Experience an adrenaline flow' was considered to be the main factor influencing visitor satisfaction.

The User's age range between 12 and 45/50 years. Group composition in relation to user age is heterogeneous.

The key management issues are clearly differentiated and determined by both *motivation* and *previous experience* in. For inexperienced tourists, management actions should address safety conditions during the excursion. For those with previous experience, observance of foreseen operating conditions should be assured.

Mountain-biking. Even though the actual activity volume is low, a trend towards sustained growth is recognised. The potential environmental impact of mountain-biking is high in the medium and long term, related to the relative ease with which it can be practised, cost of equipment, the current lack of controls, and the distance over which it can occur.

Tourist guides play a decisive role in visitor satisfaction, especially for those participants with little previous experience. They are also a decisive factor in controlling the impact on environment. Short journeys, with a low level of difficulty can suit whole family group interests.

Given these conditions, it is imperative to direct management actions towards the setting rules and normatives that could help sustain mountain-biking in the following years.

Fishing. *Capture objectives* and the *main motivation* of each group of participants influence the other variables characterising this activity: *satisfaction with recreational experience, loyalty to fishing places, requirements for recreational facilities and services and*, finally, *the key management aspects* for each identified micro-segment.

The manner in which *fishing* practised by each sportsman (or fishing modality) is influenced by his/her *previous experience* as a fisherman. Together, these provide two strong conditions for fishermen's environmental behaviour. Related to this point, the factors influencing recreational experience satisfaction differ for fishing modality, previous experience and motivation.

Recreational use is more concentrated in certain intensively used locations in Chile than in Argentina. In both countries, fishermen could be identified by fishing modality: fly-fishing, spinning or trawling. However, some important differences can be outlined:

- In Argentina, onboard fishermen (those who practise the modality 'trolling') use their own boats. In Chile, the majority of them hire boats for the trip through recognised guides in the area.
- It is important to highlight the recreational nature of the angling in the Chilean sector, which arises from the close proximity of the fishing sites in the corridor to the main cities in the region (Puerto Montt and Puerto Varas). This produces high loyalty levels with fishing sites, with those also angle fishing this area once or even twice during the summer high season.
- In both cases, a clear difference between the capture objectives for each group was noted. Anglers, with reduced capture objectives, look for *quality of fish* (in weight, size and ability to fight). They are extremely careful about natural resources. Onboard and recreational fishermen, in contrast, are characterised by moderate to high capture objectives, trying to obtain the highest number of fish, showing predator attitudes that endanger resource stability.

Trekking. This is the most practised activity within the Corridor but there is a notable difference in the practice of this activity in Chile and Argentina. In Argentina, trekking and hiking are associated with camping, and it is very diffuse, mainly because tourist circuits and attractions can be accessed from the camping areas. In Chile it is still incipient in the area studied, at least in its non-commercial form. Management actions should ensure transit conditions and safety for short- and medium-distance trails with a low level of difficulty.

Camping. In Chile, the demand for camping areas is clearly divided by *level of service and prices*. In Argentina, there are more alternatives for free camping, with good landscape conditions but these receive intensive use.

One of the most important differences in the demand is appear to have a *higher level in previous experience of Argentinean campers*. It could be argued that there is a *tradition* of visiting these mountain areas as a holiday destination; most of the tourists visiting these areas have a certain experience in this type of accommodation. In Chile, however, tourists have little previous experience in visiting camping sites, at least in this type of environment.

Related to this point, it is important to pay attention to the different *service requirements* of Chilean and Argentinean campers. Chilean tourists are very interested in good maintaining conditions, in particular at camping sites (conservation, maintenance, cleanliness, visual separation, access and privacy, interior space, etc). In the case of Argentinean campers, the main service requirements are linked to the existence of clean bathrooms, hot water, showers and small shops supplying necessary goods. Particular site characteristics did not seem to be relevant, even in cases where camping site conditions were clearly below the expected quality levels.

With respect to the variable *attachment to recreational settings*, most of the interviewees revealed that they had developed feelings of attachment of different magnitude and intensity to those places where they had camped, the most common being a sentimental bond. This can be called 'place identification'. Tourists feel proud to develop emotional bonds with certain places, as they pay repeat visits during a lifetime.

Bonds related to the ability a place offers for the development of certain activities were also mentioned, but these were only secondary to the emotional bonds.

Conflicts among users appears to be one of the factors that influence the satisfaction pattern, but always as a single element acting together with another variable in the process. Conflicts were attributed mainly to a lack of education for coexistence, as well as a lack of environmental conscience in many of the tourist groups visiting these areas.

As tourists increase their experience in a place and then become more attached to it, they develop 'growing exigency levels' toward the physical and social environment, by means of establishing personal evaluation patterns for the attributes of each area. In case of an *increase in a tourist's exigency level*, there is also an increase in the *perception of negative attributes toward the recreational experience*. These factors directly influence the *perception of the quality of the recreational experience*.

Analysis of institutions in charge of tourism management in protected areas within the Corridor

The interest in addressing the issues related to the institutions in charge of tourism management in protected areas within the Corridor was based on the fact that the use conditions offered by natural tourist attractions, as well as the way in which tourist activities are operated, are intimately related to the conditions imposed by those institutions regulating and controlling its public use.

The information summarised here is the result of a specific management document review, as well as interviews of key informants working in or related to the field of tourism management, in the following park authorities: Chile (CONAF, Forestry National Corporation) and Argentina (APN, National Parks Administration). Interviewees included park rangers, managers and administrators.

Planning and research

Management plans – tourism activities, political and programmes: Parks receiving the majority of tourist use within Argentinean Patagonia already have updated management plans. Management programmes and actions have been drawn up but in most of the cases they have not been implemented, although they are considered to be a part of the annual operative plan (POA). In Chile, all management units have modernised plans, which are supposed to be regularly updated every ten years. The execution of the plans, programmes and actions is controlled through a general revision of the whole plan, every three years.

Education and awareness programmes

Although there are no specific regulations or norms, in the past five years environmental education has begun to be seriously considered in the Argentinean Patagonian Parks. In Chile, environmental education is formally incorporated into public use management through education programmes, which is part of the Park Management Plans. However, in-field observation has demonstrated that such programmes for visitor education and awareness actions are rather rare and even non-existent at some critical sites.

Control management

In Argentinean Patagonian Parks, control systems are still in an early stage of development. Control activities are restricted to the mere adherence to certain practices, without any consideration of such aspects as service quality. Control tasks are carried out only by rangers. The main restrictions regarding control and surveillance refer to the lack of an appropriate norm to guide rangers, when they need specific solutions or even criteria for potential conflict situations.

In Chilean Parks, control and surveillance actions are included in each Management Protection Programme. Control is mainly the concern of the Ranger Corps, which is assisted by 'guards', local residents who are paid to reinforce the patrolling tasks entrusted to rangers. Nevertheless, a number of disruptions can be pointed to in the Chilean sector, most of them related to the lack of an appropriate number of control personnel working in conflict areas.

Legal and jurisdictional concerns

In Argentina, National Parks Law 22351 can be considered a useful, operative tool. Although a number of regulations can be cited (about tourism guides, tour operators, high mountain and trekking guides, fishing, camping sites, etc.), in fact they have a limited use at present, since they do not cover the wide variety of activities being offered un the Parks nowadays. It is also very important to consider an improvement in communication channels with concessionaires, in order to establish effective operative rules based on 'codes of conduct' and mutual agreement.

In Chile, Law 18362 of the Protected Areas National System has not yet been implemented. The lack of a protected-areas law has been recognised as one of the most severe restrictions that Park administrations have to face.

The conditions under which alternative-tourism-activities operate are regulated by an Alternative Tourism Regulation Act. This document, the product of a consent process between private operators and CONAF working together to find common solutions, establishes clear rules hence, diminishing or even eliminating potential communication conflicts among the involved parties.

This point confirms one of the most notable differences between the Parks administration in the two sectors within the Corridor. Communication between the interested parties seems to be one of the most important problems in managing tourism in the protected areas in Argentinean North-Patagonian national parks.

Finally, a number of serious deficiencies were found, related to the actual public use categories which are not allowed in the Protected Areas National System norm.

Another important aspect to point out is the administration of permits, licenses and concessions in the tourist services.

Management Proposals

Two types of management proposal were suggested. The first group was related to guidelines for structuring and implementing consent rules for each alternative tourism activity, based on common principles, regarding public–private cooperation in resource management and then of all interested parties in the planning process. The second group refers to specific management and control proposals for each activity, addressing particular conflict situations. Basically, they do not differ from management strategies and actions which already exist in other parts of the world.

This paper includes a description of guidelines to develop consent regulations, including steps to follow in order to reduce institutional and budget restrictions.

Rafting

The Petrohue River case study, in Chile, constitutes an antecedent that supports the idea that private–public cooperation in resource management can be possible. When management regulations are supported by each of the involved parties, they are respected, resulting in cooperative activity management. Given the success in rafting management in the Chilean sector, it was considered opportune to suggest capitalising on these experiences in rivers in the Argentinean sector.

Basically, it was proposed to maintain an open operation in rafting rivers within the area, establishing certain minimum rules for the operation of tourist services and the protection of the environment. Practical suggestions were then to observe the different components acting in the process – time of execution, specific instruments, communication techniques, and norms and rules promoting this type of cooperative work – to implement them in Argentinean sector.

Mountain-biking

Proposals were designed for two of the most important identified groups: tourists that book mountain bike excursions in San Carlos de Bariloche and cyclists visiting the area on their own. Management suggestions for the first group are included in the agreed regulation proposals already mentioned. For the second group, and considering the imminent explosive growth expected for this sector, suggested management actions refer mainly to the control of transit conditions, as well as communication strategies that could reinforce visitor satisfaction with the recreational experience.

(1) *Improvement of road signals*: In order to guide cyclists on their routes (distances to specific points, facilities and recommended services, camping sites near cycling trails, etc.) the road signals on main national routes in the area, need to be improved.

(2) *Implementation of a registration system for cyclists:* This is particularly important for those cycling on routes accessing and vehicular roads located inside the urban public space within tourist centres in the circuit. The purpose of this is to have updated information about cyclists transiting the area – number of cyclists, persons per group, probable route – as well as to prevent accidents or conflict situations by means of communication strategies based on personal contact. Inter-institutional coordination among municipalities, parks managers and main tourist operators in the area is essential at this stage.

    Although its practical implementation might seem difficult due to personnel and budget restrictions, an effort must be made to set the basis for appropriate management of this activity, for which sustained growth is expected even in the a short term.

(3) *Communication strategy*: An effective communication campaign should be developed, with the objective of informing cyclists about road conditions, recreational opportunities, visitation restrictions at certain places, practical suggestions, etc. In principle, two means of communication support were identified: brochures and visitor centres.

(4) *Settlement of cycling trail systems within urban areas* – in order to avoid accidents and reinforce cyclists' satisfaction. Again, interaction between the municipality of San Carlos de Bariloche and organisations linked to the activity (i.e. Mountain Guides Association at SCB) is essential. The Parks Authority should act as a consultant, advising on technical matters (width, length and design of suggested trails, signalling and other constructive aspects).

Table 2 Management strategies and techniques for intensive use camping areas

Strategies for techniques for the Argentinean sector	
Strategies	***Techniques***
Reduce use	Limit the number of visitors.
	Limit the length of stay.
Modify time of use	Encourage visitation out of high peak season.
	Increase entrance quotas at high peak season or when resources are more susceptible to impacts.
Modify location of use within critical areas	Avoid use outside camping areas or paths/trails already opened.
Maintain or rehabilitate the resource.	Eliminate use indications/Rehabilitate deteriorated places. Maintain paths and places which are used to avoid quick deterioration.
Modify type of use Control the application of visitor management techniques in critical areas.	Improve patrolling, contacts with visitorsand application of management rules.
	Implement an acceptable conditions control system by camping areas concessionaires.

Strategies and techniques for the Chilean sector	
Control of tourist services.	Separation of beach areas and camping sites near Puerto Varas.
	Control cleaning conditions in areas located far away from urban centres.
	For all camping areas studied in the Chilean sector: control of price level and product quality.
Maintain or rehabilitate the resource.	Review design, construction and cleanness of camping sites.
Modify location of use within problematic/critical areas.	Low-use camping areas promotion system.
	Coordinated camping site use system.
	For those camping areas registering spontaneous growth, set planning and management criteria that allow their correct operation in the current place, their relocation or even possibly their definitive closing.

Camping

Table 2 summarises proposals for managing camping in both sectors of the Corridor. Institutional restrictions and the cost for both the Parks Authorities and visitors were also investigated, in order to evaluate the possibilities for practical implementation.

Fishing

The proposals were aimed, for both sectors, at two main topics: protecting natural resources and ensuring fishing conditions.

Protecting natural resources at fishing sites. The system should focus on:

- strict control of the maximum number of allowed captures; and
- revised list of fishing conditions, especially for those fishermen who illegally practise this activity during night hours.

In-field operations should be coordinated and directed by the Ranger Corps, with assistance of a well-trained volunteers corps. A volunteer system would avoid higher personnel costs. Agreements with such institutions, as universities and private organisations would make this possible.

To ensure the fishing conditions for identified sectors

Here the actions are devoted to maintain and preserve fishermen satisfaction levels with a sport/recreational experience. In both sectors, trained personnel should be assigned near the main fishing sites, which should already be identified according to the existence of fishing resources and the affluence of fishermen. Although economic restrictions are important, the suggested actions could reinforce visitor satisfaction, especially for anglers, a sector which decreases significantly when an increase in the number of tourists occurs.

Trekking/hiking

The main proposal was oriented, as in the case of rafting and mountain-biking, towards the establishment of agreed regulations that set the operating conditions for the activity.

- For the Chilean sector, proposals will be guided to order the spontaneous character of this activity, introducing safety conditions on vehicular roads and routes.
- It was considered relevant to introduce an information system for tourists, mainly through targeted brochures, as well as personal attention at visitor centres and appropriate road signals.
- For those trails located within protected areas, control actions should be carried out by rangers or even a volunteer corps. Each sectional ranger should have appropriate information about trail conditions. An accurate registration of hikers/trekkers accessing trail systems should be encouraged.
- It is considered necessary to generate specific information for hikers/trekkers in order to promote the independent practice of this activity who would then respect the limits imposed by protected areas legislation.

Conclusion

A number of points, summarising the main facts emerging from this work are outlined here. They include management action suggestions, good practices to implement as well as topics for the discussion of those concepts related to alternative tourism planning and management in natural landscapes within the context of the Northern Patagonia Andes Region. Finally, the need for further discussion is emphasised, as the starting point for future research that could help to enrich the state of knowledge about certain matters linked to the development of alternative tourism activities in natural landscapes.

First, and closely related to alternative tourism activities management and control, it is considered very important to outline rules or norms for those activities that, up to date, have not been regulated, i.e. those which arecurrently practised spontaneously, causing actual and potential conflicts. This must act as the foundation for constructing policies addressing public use in protected areas.

In connection with the last point, it is essential to put in place valid consent mechanisms, capable of promoting greater coordination and communication between the public and private sectors interacting in the visitor management process. Park authorities, should be in charge of initiating an interactive dialogue that would permit the creation of action scenarios based on mutual work. An agenda should be drawn up. The process would build up to a meeting and group work schedule, devoted to the discussion of different aspects based on participative schemes. All involved groups should be invited and encouraged to participate. This would be helpful during the initial tasks of understanding each other's concerns and objectives. Norm derived from these work methodologies will encourage recognition of all involved parties.

The process can be structured through the following steps

(1) identification of tour operators working in the area (in charge of the National Parks Authority);
(2) Coordination between National Parks Administration and different operators, organisations and institutions, in order to design a work schedule and scheme for establishing consent management rules;
(3) Workshops – qualitative instruments designed with conducting meetings and organising emerging information; and
(4) design of each management rule taking into account each activity operator's opinion, concerns and objectives.

An agreed rules proposal as previously suggested could be a valid background. The vision guiding this work should be based in *being partners in common issues and solutions.*

One of the main conclusions arising from institutional issues related to the management of alternative tourism activities is the need to manage their development, paying special attention to similar cases in similar situations, which have proven to have relative success in their practical implementation. Analysing, understanding and even implementing processes, practices and specific actions developed by other institutions could be beneficial. This is linked not only to solutions of actual problems, but also as a practical way to start working togester with bi-national management of natural resources. It is possible to mention some examples: agreed management of rafting in Chile, as well as the previously mentioned Alternative Tourism Regulation Act can be an incentive to implement such strategies in Argentina. However, there is a growing professional approach in the tourism management field in Argentina, a gradual awareness of the importance of these activities within the context of the Northern Patagonia Andes area. This has been translated into a number of tourism graduates, working on this field. In Chile, CONAF authorities could consider the possibility of promoting tourism jobs within the organisation.

Alternative tourism management and control should be based on the fact that there is a trend towards a sustained growth in the number of tourists arriving in the region to practice these activities. This is the case, for instance, of mountain-biking and other activities, that are already creating overuse conditions and then conflict situations. A reflexive, conscious and serious position should be adopted in order to implement management criteria oriented towards solving conflicts in the near future.

Addressing this need, it is the authors' belief that the alternative tourism market analysis, the results of which have been given here, constitutes a research result itself. Based on this advance, segmentation methodologies and techniques must be constantly reviewed, adapted and even improved, in order to continue developing this type of analysis in coming years, as it has been found to be one of the best ways to deal with continuing changes in the alternative tourism activities scenario. Even with a constant growth in the amount of tourists motivated to practise alternative activities, antecedents of this type of research work were not identified in Patagonia. As previously mentioned, these advances impose the need for new research that brings further knowledge on these topics.

One of the most promising research fields is the one linked to in-depth studies addressing the direct and indirect environmental impacts derived from the practice of these activities. Although literature reviews have been carried out and the most relevant direct impacts have been outlined and characterised, it is considered extremely important to advance knowledge of those indirect impacts derived from the considered activities. Their proper analysis and approach would permit understanding of alternative tourism activity impacts as a whole, then designing and implementing more accurate guidelines and proposals for managing and preventing unacceptable conditions.

Correspondence

Any correspondence should be directed to Rodrigo González, Tourism Faculty, Universidad Nacional del Comahue, Argentina (rgonzale@uncoma.edu.ar).

References

Eagles, P.F.J. (1994) Understanding the market for sustainable tourism. In S. McCool, and A. Watson (eds) *Linking Tourism, the Environment, and Sustainability – Topical Volume of Compiled Papers from to special Session of the Annual Meeting of the National Recreation and Park Association.* General Technical Report INT-GTR-323. Ogden, UT: U.S. Departament of Agriculture, Forest Service, Intermountain Research Station.

Mahoney, E. (undated) Marketing parks and recreation: The need for a new approach. Unpublished paper on file at Michigan State University.

Wight, P. (1993) Sustainable ecotourism: Balancing economic, environmental and social goals within an ethical framework. *Journal of Tourism Studies* 4 (2), 54–66.

Analysis of the Visitors of Superagüi National Park, Brazil

Inge A. Niefer
Tv. Medianeira, 180/3, Boa Vista, 82210-040 Curitiba-PR, Brazil

João Carlos G.L. da Silva
Rua Lothário Meisner 3400, 80.210-170 – Curitiba-PR, Brazil

M. Amend
Rua Carlos Pradi, 167, Jardim das Amricas, 81530-180 – Curitiba-PR, Brazil

The present work consists of the analysis of the visitors' profile of the Superagüi National Park, located on the north coast of the State of Paraná, Brazil. During the season 1998/1999 94 interviews were analysed. It was verified that most of the visitors can be considered as 'ecotourists', because their profile fits the one commonly proposed in literature. Visitors' preferences related to activities and infrastructure and critics are valuable indicators for the park's future management.

Introduction

The Superagüi National Park is situated in South Brazil, in the Northern part of Paraná State, close to the border of São Paulo State (Figure 1). It was founded in 1989, with an area of about 21,400 ha. Currently (1999) it is being delimited, and the area has increased to 34,000 ha, including mainly the islands Ilha do Superagüi, Ilha das Peças, Ilha do Pinheiro, and Ilha do Pinheirinho. On the continent are included the valley of the river Rio dos Patos and the Varadouro canal, which separates the Island of Superagüi from the continent.

The National Park is part of the estuary complex formed by the Cananéia, Iguape and Paranaguá regions. In 1991 Unesco declared it a Biosphere Reserve (SPVS, 1992) and in 1999 a Natural World Heritage Site (Unesco, 1999). Under the viewpoint of alimentary supply, it is one of the most important areas of the country, because it is the 'cradle' of many maritime animal species.

The park includes bays, sandbanks, large areas of deserted beaches and coastal lowlands, several vegetation forms, including Atlantic coastal forest, salt marshes ('*restinga*') and mangroves.

The park provides a habitat for a range of significant animal species, some of them rare or threatened by extinction, such as the chauá parrot (*Amazona brasiliensis*), the black faced lion tamarin (*Leontopithecus caissara*) and the yellow crop alligator.

Currently the National Park has no organised touristic infrastructure and no management plan. There are four inns, one campground and three restaurants in Barra de Superagüi village where the research was conducted. Regular maritime transportation does not exist, and one must hire private boats.

Touristic demand is still relatively low, but because of the installation of electricity at the end of 1998 and the park's proximity to two large urban centres,

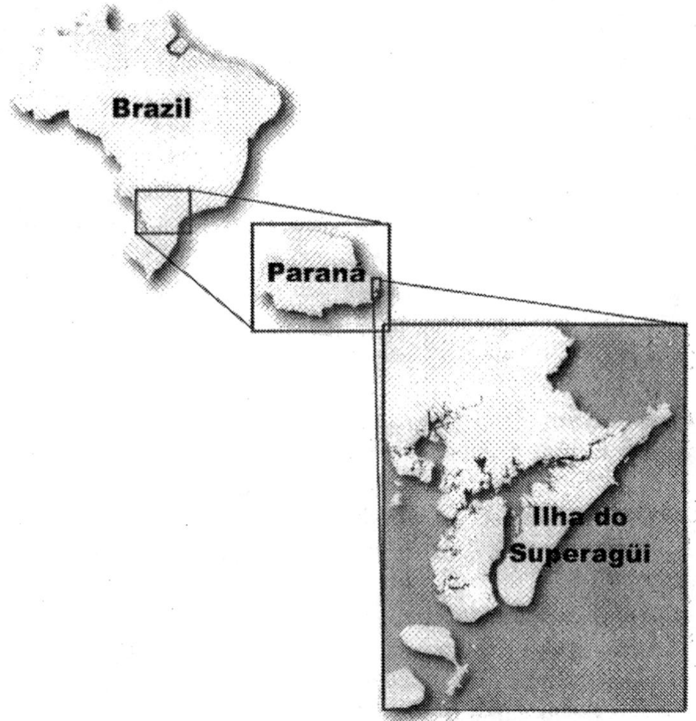

Figure 1 Location of Superagüi National Park

Curitiba and São Paulo, it is quite probable that demand will increase considerably in the near future.

Literature Review

Brazil's National Touristic Organisation Embratur (1994: 5) defines ecotourism as

> a segment of the tourist activity that uses in a sustainable way both the natural and cultural patrimony, motivating its conservation and fostering the formation of an environmental conscience, through the interpretation of the environment, promoting the well being of the involved population.

Valentine (1993) points out four qualifying components of ecotourism: it is based on relatively undisturbed natural areas; it is non-damaging, non-degrading, ecologically sustainable; it is a direct contributor to the continued protection and management of the natural areas used; and it is subject to an adequate and appropriate management regime.

Ceballos-Lascuráin (1998) believes that the term ecotourism should only be used if tourism activities take place in a natural environment, encourage conservation and help society achieve sustainable development.

Wight (1993), acknowledging that not all forms of ecotourism are sustainable, proposes that it is not the definition that is the most important feature, but the underlying principles and ethical values, regarding primarily conservation/sustainability and host communities.

According to the Office of National Tourism (1997), ecotourists generally appear to be seeking travel experiences that involve areas or attractions of natural beauty, small groups and being away from crowds, some level of interaction with the environment, interaction with other people (preferably like-minded and compatible), some degree of information and learning, and fun and enjoyment. Eagles and Cascagnette (1995) define an ecotourist simply as an adult who travels with the intent of observing, experiencing and learning about nature.

Weiler and Richins (1995) propose a three-dimensional model of the concept of who is an ecotourist: the model involves the level of environmental responsibility or impact; the level of intensity of interaction with the environment; and the level of physical difficulty or challenge of the experience. Ecotourists vary from minimal to extreme ecotourist according to the degree they assume at these levels.

There exist some studies about the profile of ecotourists, most of them limited to visitors of selected areas or origin. For example, Wight (1996a, b) analysed the North American ecotourism market. Experienced ecotourism travellers are found in all age groups, but most (76%) are between 25 and 54 years old. They have high educational levels and the genders are distributed equally. Most live in households without children, one-fourth as families and one-fourth alone; 61% like to travel as couples; 15% with family and 13% single. The most attractive activities are wilderness experience, wildlife viewing, hiking/trekking, rafting/canoeing/kayaking and casual walking. The North American ecotourists prefer camping and/or mid-range accommodation and their principal travel motivations are scenery/nature, new experiences/places, wildlife viewing, wilderness and uncrowded places.

Eagles (1992) and Eagles and Cascagnette (1995) investigated the motivations and profile of Canadian ecotourists. Results indicate that Canadian ecotourists have a high education level, can be of any age, but tend to be older and have an income higher than those of the general population. They like to learn about nature and to photograph, and the principal travel motives are wilderness, nature, and landscapes, which reveals an ecologistic attitude. The study also showed that the Canadian ecotourists do not require luxurious accommodation, food or nightlife and that they are willing to accept local conditions, culture and food.

Weiler and Richins (1995) studied participants of Earthwatch expeditions. The typical participant is female, single, between the ages of 26 to 35, well educated and well paid. She is not only environmentally responsible but also wants to enhance the environment visit, and has an intense level of interaction with the environment.

There is lack of extensive research on visitors' profiles in Brazilian protected areas. A hypothesis of the study was that visitors of Superagüi could be considered ecotourists, as defined in the literature.

Methodology

A questionnaire with 37 questions was designed to conduct a visitor survey. It was administered during December 1998 and January 1999 on the island of Superagüi, at the village Barra de Superagüi, as a pilot project of a larger research project involving three protected areas in Paraná State. Visitors were chosen randomly and interviewed personally; the average duration of an interview was about 30 minutes, and 94 interviews were conducted. The results were compiled, with average and standard deviations, where applicable.

Results

Age

Most of the visitors were over 20 years age, the biggest portion (50%) being found in the age group 20–29 years; 29% were between 30 and 39 years old and 15% between 40 and 49. Only 6% were younger than 20 (Figure 2).

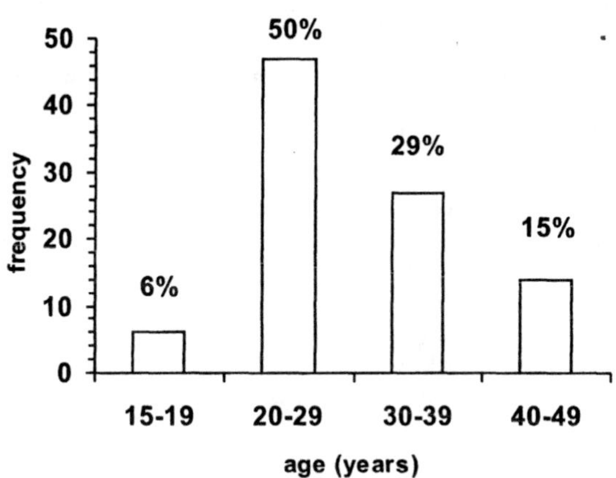

Figure 2 Age classes of visitors of Superagüi

Gender

Visitors were 51% male and 49% female, showing that there is no preference for visiting Superagüi National Park related to gender.

Education

The majority of respondents completed high school (36.17%) or graduated (44%). Only 10.64% had not completed high school or had a lower level of education (Table 1).

Table 1 Education of visitors of Superagüi

Education	*Frequency*	*(%)*
1st grade school uncom-pleted	1	1.06
1st grade school complete	4	4.26
High school uncompleted	5	5.32
High school completed	34	36.17
Graduated	44	46.81
Master degree	5	5.32
PhD	1	1.06
Total	94	100

Income

The average family income of visitors to the park is shown in Table 2. It is higher than the average in Brazil: 52.1% of Brazilians earn up to $R600, 21% between R$600 and 1200, 12.5% between R$1200 and 2400, and only 8.4% more than R$2400 (IBGE, 1997). However, the Brazilian Statistical Bureau IBGE uses a different scale for measuring family income, so it cannot be compared directly with the obtained results.

Table 2 Average monthly family income of visitors of Superagüi

*Family income (in $Real) per month**	*Frequency*	*%*
Up to 1000	21	22.34
1001 to 2000	34	36.17
2001 to 3000	19	20.21
3001 to 4000	6	6.38
More than 4000	14	14.89

Marital status

About 60% of respondents were singles and 34% were married, showing the predominance of singles among park visitors (Figure 3).

Party composition

As can be seen in Table 3, most visitors travel with friends (37%) or as a couple (35%). It is interesting that only 5% travel alone, although 61% of the visitors are single.

Origin of visitors

Most of the visitors (62%) are inhabitants of Paraná State, and 22% come from the neighbouring State of São Paulo. Table 4 shows the distance of cities of origin from Superagüi.

Purpose of trip

The main purpose of the trip to Superagüi was tourism, in 93% of cases. Some visitors came for tourism and research (4%), only research (2%) and tourism and work (1%).

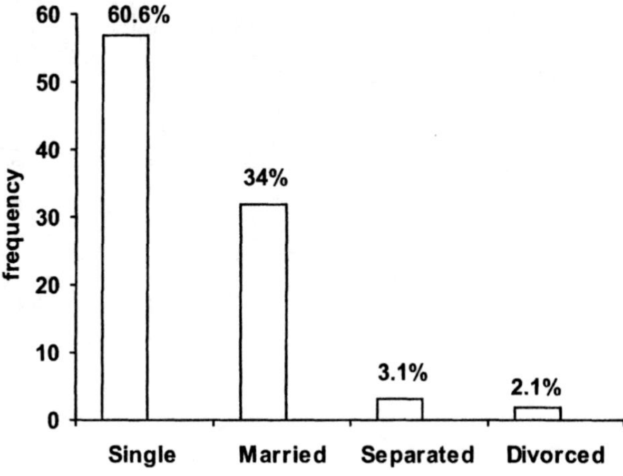

Figure 3 Marital status of park visitors

Table 3 Party composition of park visitors

Party composition	*Frequency*	*(%)*
With friends	35	37.23
Couple	33	35.11
With the family	11	11.70
With friends in a tour group	6	6.38
Alone	5	5.32
Tour group	2	2.13
Couple with friends	2	2.13

Table 4 Distance of cities of visitors'orgin from Superagüi

Distance from Superagüi	*Frequency*	*(%)*
Up to 200 km	53	56.38
201 to 500 km	4	4.26
501 to 800 km	21	22.34
801 to 1100 km	10	10.64
More than 1100 km	6	6.38

Expenditure

As Table 5 shows, the average expenditure per day / person was $R35.75 (1 $US 1.85 $Real). The cost of transportation was the biggest component of visitor expenditure. The high standard deviation for transport expenditure is explained by the different costs of transportation according to the distance from Superagüi.

Table 5 Visitors'expenditure / day / person in $Real

*Expenditure/day/person in $Real**	*Average*	*s*
Transport	16.21	19.27
Food	9.47	5.42
Accommodation	7.20	5.70
Others	2.46	3.79
Souvenirs	0.41	0.96
Total	35.75	23.96

* 1 $US ≈ 1.85 $Real

Travel characteristics

Sixty-nine percent of visitors knew about Superagüi from friends or family. Only 13% read about it in newspapers or magazines. Other sources of knowledge were travel guides (3%), radio / TV (2%) and others (13%), which included basically the Internet and tips while travelling. Only 2% of visitors used the services of a travel agency.

Seventy-three percent of tourists came directly from home and 27% had visited another destination before coming to the park; 72% returned home directly after the visit and 28% intended to visit another destination. This pattern can be explained by the origin of visitors who mainly came from nearby cities.

The average trip duration was about 7 days; 49% of visitors stayed 2–5 days, 37% 5–10 days and 11% more than 10 days. Only 3% stayed just one day. The trip duration is not representative of visits throughout the year, as the survey was conducted during the holiday season.

Forty-six percent of those surveyed visited the park for the first time. 38% had visited it already from two to five times, and 16% more than five times.

Accommodation

Most visitors stayed in inns (57%). Second preference was the campground (13%) and camping on the inn's area (13%). Others found accommodation in friends' or relatives' houses (11%).

Willingness to pay entrance fees

Most (96%) of the respondents knew that they were visiting a National Park. Asked whether they agreed with charging entrance fees for protected areas, using a scale from 1 (not correct) to 9 (absolutely correct) the average response was 8.41 (with s = 1.64), indicating a high disposition to pay entrance fees. About 47% of visitors would pay up to 5 Brazilian Reals (1$US 1.85 $R), 36% would pay $R5–10 and 14% would pay more than $R10 (Figure 4). Many respondents added 'if the money really would be applied for conservation of the protected area', probably because they think that the money would not be used adequately. The park currently does not charge entrance fees.

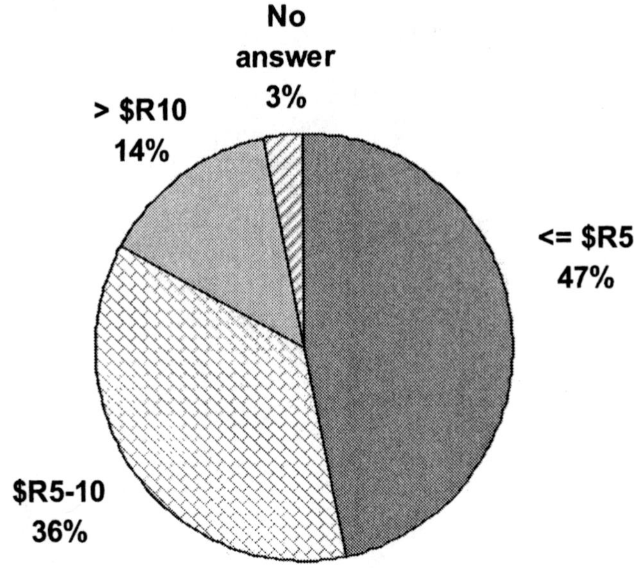

Figure 4 Value of entrance fees that visitors would be prepared to pay per visit

Willingness to obey rules of the park

Visitors were asked if they were willing to obey the rules regarding the protection of nature, even if this reduced their liberty. On a scale from 1 (No) to 9 (Yes), average answer was 8.8 (with s = 0.54), indicating that visitors have a strong environmental consciousness.

Importance of wilderness experience

Using a 5-point Likert-scale (1 = not important to 5 = very important), tourists were asked how important the wilderness experience is for them. The average response was 4.89 (s = 0.31). It is interesting that the respondents chose only the options 'very important' (95.7%) and 'important' (4.3%), which indicates that nature is one of the principal motives for a visit to Superagüi and that consequently conservation of nature is very important to visitors.

Environmental consciousness

Several questions were included to measure the environmental consciousness of visitors. The first group of questions concerned the use of environmentally sensitive practices, using a 5-point Likert-scale (5 = very important, 1 = not important). Next, the tourists were asked if they'd prefer an enterprise which uses these techniques and then if and how much more they'd pay for it.

The average value of importance for recycling was 4.87, for non-recyclable litter treatment 4.85, for use of alternative energies 4.4 and for sewage treatment 4.95, indicating that respondents give high importance to the use of these practices, which are not common in many areas of Brazil.

Most (94%) of respondents declared that they would definitely give preference to an enterprise that adopts these practices; 49% would pay up to 10% more for this, 32% would pay between 10 and 50% more, 5% would pay even more than 50%, 11% would not pay more, and 3% had no opinion.

Six items of the 'New Environmental Paradigm' scale (Table 6) were also used, as considered by Luzar *et al.* (1998). Possible scores ranged from 6 to 30, with a score higher than 18 (neutral) considered as an environmentally friendly attitude.

The average score of respondents was 26.9 with s = 2.65 and there was no score smaller than 18. The statistical analysis (using Cronbach's alpha) resulted in a not very satisfactory 0.4983 (the alpha should be higher than 0.5), which could mean that the 6-item-scale is not appropriate or that the sample was too small.

Table 6 The New Environmental Paradigm scale

	Strongly agree	*Agree*	*No opinion*	*Disagree*	*Strongly disagree*
The balance of nature is very delicate and easily upset.	5	4	3	2	1
Humans must live in harmony with nature in order to survive.	5	4	3	2	1
When humans interfere with nature it often produces disastrous results.	5	4	3	2	1
Humans are destined to rule over the rest of nature.	1	2	3	4	5
Plants and animals exist primarily to be used by humans.	1	2	3	4	5
Humans have the right to modify the natural environment to suit their needs.	1	2	3	4	5

Interest in information about special topics

Visitors were asked about their interest in obtaining information about some topics related to the environment and the park, using a 5-point Likert-scale (1 = not interested and 5 = very interested). Average results are shown in Table 7 and indicate that respondents are highly interested in these topics that are commonly associated with ecotourism.

Activity preferences

Respondents were given a list of possible activities in Superagüi and asked about their interest in practising in these activities, using a 5-point-Likert-scale (1 = not interested and 5 = very interested). The top rated activities were observation of landscape, and observation of flora and fauna, showing the visitors' high interest in nature (Table 8). Nightlife and surfing were the least interesting activities for respondents.

Table 7 Visitors' interest in learning about special topics related to the park

Topic	*Average*	*s*
Fauna	4.59	0.50
Culture	4.50	0.58
Flora	4.49	0.62
History	4.48	0.60
Social and environmental problems	4.40	0.80

Table 8 Activity preferences of park visitors

Activity	*Average*	*s*
Landscape observation	4.61	0.79
Observation of flora	4.57	0.77
Observation of fauna	4.55	0.78
Visit historical sites	4.43	0.87
Casual walking	4.41	0.87
Boat trips	4.35	0.84
Beach	4.33	1.05
Photography	4.31	0.98
Short trips (up to 2 hours)	4.27	0.96
Participation of local activities	4.10	0.86
Participation in research projects	4.09	1.08
Bicycle ride	3.95	1.22
Hiking with some difficulties	3.93	1.17
Swimming	3.80	1.27
Horse riding	3.69	1.34
Diving	3.61	1.50
Day hike (up to 1 day)	3.34	1.36
Fishing	3.31	1.48
Other water based sports	2.97	1.56
Long trips (more than 1 day)	2.88	1.58
Nightlife	2.22	1.42
Surfing	1.82	1.20

Problems met

Visitors were asked what kind of problems they encountered during their stay and how severe they judged the occurrence, using a 4-point Likert-scale (4 = Serious problem; 3 = Problem; 2 = Indifferent [it happened, but did not annoy] and 1 = No problem). As can be seen in Table 9 respondents considered problems related to cleanliness/sanitary conditions and lack of information as most severe. It is interesting that items like 'missing gastronomic services', 'poor access' and 'accommodations without comfort' did not annoy visitors too much, considering that all of the restaurants serve basically the same food every day, access is very difficult and the accommodations are quite rustic.

Table 9 Visitors' valuation of problems met

Problem	*Average*	s
Litter cans absent	2.62	1.25
Cleanliness of the place	2.18	1.14
Sanitary installations precarious	2.17	1.26
Missing or inadequate information	2.15	1.17
Missing signs	2.14	1.17
Public restrooms absent	2.06	1.22
Water unavailable	1.85	1.11
Missing gastronomic services	1.59	0.87
Poor access	1.57	0.78
Energy unavailable	1.57	0.84
Overcrowded	1.47	0.94
Doctor unavailable	1.46	1.01
Security during trip	1.37	0.79
Security	1.27	0.69
Poor gastronomic services	1.23	0.66
Accommodations without comfort	1.23	0.61
Vandalism	1.22	0.72
Conflicts with other recreation activities	1.07	0.45

Motivation

Visitors were asked about the motives for their visit to Superagüi and to indicate the degree of importance of some given motives, using a 5-point Likert-scale (1 = not important; 5 = very important). The three most important motives were observing Landscape/Nature, Rest and observing Wildlife. Average values of responses are shown in Table 10.

Table 10 Visitors' motivation

Motive	*Average*	s
Landscape	4.90	0.30
Rest	4.78	0.47
Wildlife	4.72	0.50
Adventure	4.00	1.06
Historical values	3.93	0.96
Cultural values	3.84	1.07
Social reasons	3.82	1.12
Solitude/introspection/meditation	3.80	1.21
Sports	3.34	1.14
Overcome one's own limits	2.37	1.32

Desired infrastructure

Visitors were given a list of items of infrastructure and asked how important they judge these items in Superagüi, using again a 5-point Likert-scale (1 = not important; 5 = very important). Average values for responses are shown in Table 11.

Table 11 Infrastructure desired by visitors

Item	*Average*	*s*
Information centre	4.12	1.24
Visitor centre	4.09	1.22
Inns	4.06	1.01
Trails with signs	3.68	1.20
Organised campground	3.63	1.20
Others	3.29	2.30
Shop with local handcraft	3.24	1.26
Guides	3.21	1.26
Regular maritime transport	3.19	1.52
Small commerce	2.97	1.21
Cabins	2.41	1.27
Hotels	1.61	0.95

It should be stressed that under the item 'Others' 62% of those interviewed mentioned a better medical supply, especially for the local population. Another point, which deserves attention, is the low ranking of 'regular maritime transportation'. Transportation to the island is quite expensive and difficult; nevertheless most people prefer it that way because it hinders a more intense visitation. A common comment was: 'It should be even more expensive/difficult, I do not want more people here.' Hotels and cabins were generally considered as not appropriate for the island and handcraft and guides should be local.

General evaluation

Asked about their satisfaction with their trip, 70% of the visitors responded 'Very satisfied' and 30% were 'Satisfied'. No one opted for one of the three other possible answers: indifferent, dissatisfied or very dissatisfied.

Regarding their intention to return, 83% of the visitors intend to return definitely, 14% would like to return and only 3% do not want to return, but the given reason was getting to know other places. Nobody chose 'indifferent' or 'definitely not'.

Additional comments

About 71% of visitors used the opportunity to make additional comments. The most frequent comments (61%) were something like: 'I do not want more visitors here', 'I want it to stay like it is', 'I do not want it to become another Ilha do Mel' (a nearby island, which is already suffering from excessive tourism).

Many of the comments showed also a concern about the inclusion of the local community in the planning process and a way to guarantee that locals take advantage of the touristic development and not outsiders.

Conclusion

The survey indicates that the visitors are mainly Brazilians between 20 and 39 years old, singles, well educated and with incomes higher than the average Brazilian. Most prefer travelling as couples or with friends.

As can be seen from the responses concerning 'problems met' and 'desired infrastructure', visitors are less demanding in terms of infrastructure for accommodation and food.

In all the items related to environmental concerns, visitors showed that they are conscious of the great importance of environmental protection. Activity preferences and motivations are strongly linked to nature and there exists a big concern with the social welfare of the local population.

All these characteristics, using commonly accepted definitions and known profiles of ecotourists, indicate that the visitors of Superagüi are ecotourists, and not 'common' tourists.

Although Superagüi National Park has been existing for 10 years, there is no management plan for the park. Therefore, one of the most significant results is the infrastructure desired by the visitors, because it provides bases for the formulation of management strategies for the Superagüi National Park, facilitating the combination of the goals for environmental preservation with the interests of both the local population and (eco) tourists.

It is to be expected that the number of visitors to the National Park will increase with the improvement of the infrastructure. Therefore, the zoning of areas which can be visited and which must remain untouched inside the park is as necessary as the control of the number of visitors.

The presented results are preliminary. The survey will be extended to two other protected areas, Ilha do Mel and Guaraqueçaba, where one expects to find a different visitor profile. Guaraqueçaba is a little city on the continent, with a large bay, but no beach; principal activities there are boat trips and hiking / trekking in the surrounding mountains. Ilha do Mel is a quite famous island which already attracts many visitors who do not respect nature.

Correspondence

Any correspondence should be directed to Inge A. Niefer, Tv. Medianeira, 180/3, Boa Vista, 82210-040 Curitiba-PR, Brazil (inge@superagui.net).

References

Ceballos-Lascuráin, H. (1998) Introduction. In *Ecotourism – A Guide for Planners and Managers* (vol. 2). North Bennington, VT: Ecotourism Society.

Eagles, P.F.J. (1992) The travel motivations of Canadian ecotourists. *Journal of Travel Research* 31 (2), 3–7.

Eagles, P.F.J. and Cascagnette, J.W. (1995) Canadian ecotourists – Who are they? *Tourism Recreation Research* 20 (1), 22–8.

Embratur (1994) *Diretrizes para uma Política Nacional de Ecoturismo*. Coordenação de Sílvio Magalhães e D. Hamú M. de la Penha. Brasília.

Ibge (1997) *Pesquisa Nacional por Amostra de Domicílios – Síntese de Indicadores 1996* (p. 163). Rio de Janeiro: IBGE.

Luzar, E.J., Diagne, A., Gan, C.E. and Henning, B. (1998) Profiling the nature based tourist: A multinomial logit approach. *Journal of Travel Research* 37, 48–55.

Office of National Tourism (1997) *Ecotourism Snapshot. A Focus on Recent Market Research*. Canberra, Australia: Office of National Tourism.

SPVS (1992) *Plano Integrado de Conservação Para a Região de Guaraqueçaba, Paraná, Brasil* (vol. 1). Curitiba, Brazil: SPVS.

Unesco Atlantic Forest Reserves (1999) On WWW at http://www.unesco.org/whc/sites/893.htm. Accessed 5.12.99).

Valentine, P.S. (1993) Ecotourism and nature conservation – a definition with some recent developments in Micronesia. *Tourism Management* 14 (2), 107–15.

Weiler, B. and Richins, H. (1995) Extreme, extravagant and elite: A profile of ecotourists on Earthwatch expeditions. *Tourism Recreation Research* 20 (1), 29–36.

Wight, P. (1993) Environmentally responsible marketing of ecotourism. In E. Cater and G. Lowman (eds.) *Ecotourism – A Sustainable Option?* London: Royal Geographic Society and Belhaven Press.

Wight, P. (1996a) North American ecotourists – market profile and trip characteristics. *Journal of Travel Research* 34 (4), 2–10.

Wight, P. (1996b) North American ecotourism markets: Motivations, preferences and destinations. *Journal of Travel Research* 34 (5), 3–10.

Supporting the Principles of Sustainable Development in Tourism and Ecotourism: Government's Potential Role

Pamela A. Wight
Pam Wight & Associates, Tourism Consultants, 14715-82 Avenue, Edmonton, Alberta, Canada T5R 3R7

This paper articulates the principles of sustainable development, sustainable tourism, and ecotourism, and their interrelationship, and explains the critical difference between growth and development, which are commonly confused. It discusses numerous activities during the course of the early 1990s, which arguably moved the government into a 'strong sustainability' mode, through its support of the principles of sustainable development, tourism, and ecotourism. The paper also briefly describes the reduction of government activities to support principles of sustainable development over the latter part of the decade, which moved the government to a weak sustainability mode. Supportive activities include integrated planning; cooperation and partnerships; public consultation; proactive research and education; environment protection and conservation; management of resources, impact and visitors; and green standards activities. The benefits for government support of principles of sustainability are briefly described.

The purpose of this paper is to articulate principles of sustainable development, sustainable tourism, and ecotourism, and to demonstrate how one level of government has chosen to support some of the key principles. The Province of Alberta is the selected case, which is particularly important, because in Canada, provincial governments have a major degree of control of natural resources. While it may be easily understood that different governments take different approaches, the paper shows that even one single government may vary in its degree and type of support over time.

Sustainable Development Principles

The term 'sustainable development' gained acceptance with the World Conservation Strategy and has since been expanded, applied and exploited in many ways. The World Commission on Environment and Development (WCED) made sustainable development its central theme, and emphasised that it is not a fixed state. Rather, it is 'a *process of change* in which the exploitation of resources, the direction of investments, the orientation of technological development, and institutional change are made consistent with future as well as present needs' (WCED, 1987: 9). The definition of sustainable development used by the Environment Council of Alberta (ECA) is 'management of resources in such a way that we can fulfill our economic, social, cultural, and aesthetic needs while maintaining the essential ecological processes, biological diversity, and naturally occurring life support systems within Alberta' (Public Advisory Committees, 1990: 5). The principles or objectives of sustainable development are:

(1) maintaining essential ecological processes;

(2) preserving biological diversity;
(3) sustaining use of species and ecosystems, some of which support important industries;
(4) developing diverse opportunities for non-material use (spiritual, recreational, aesthetic) of natural resources;
(5) maintaining and improving quality of life; and
(6) developing a long-term sustainable economy.

Other principles of sustainable development have been articulated, but most are based on these fundamentals. They provide a direction, or guiding framework, for other possible components of sustainable development, such as sustainable tourism, or ecotourism.

Sustainable Tourism and its Role in Sustainable Development

Sustainable tourism is not equivalent to sustainable development. Tourism is only part of the whole idea of sustainable development. *Tourism, as it relates to sustainable development,* is tourism which is developed so that the nature, scale, location, and manner of development is appropriate and sustainable over time, and where the environment's ability to support other activities and processes is not impaired, since tourism cannot be isolated from other resource use activities as a tourism-centric approach to sustainability. By contrast, *sustainable tourism* is tourism which continues to be viable over time. However, 'sustainable tourism' has become a form of shorthand for tourism that attempts to adhere to sustainable development principles, and it is used as such in this paper.

Characteristics of ecologically sustainable tourism, as expressed by the Commonwealth of Australia (1991: 42, 43), are tourism which:

- develops in accordance with the wisest use of environmental resources and services at the national, regional and local levels;
- operates within the biophysical limits of natural resources use;
- maintains a full range of recreational, educational and cultural opportunities across generations;
- maintains biodiversity and ecological systems and processes;
- develops in a manner which does not compromise the capacity of other sectors of the economy to achieve ecological sustainability.

These characteristics are closely related to the principles and objectives of sustainable development previously articulated. However, the characteristics may be somewhat fuzzy as a framework for tourism planning and operation. Principles for sustainable tourism that were developed in Britain may reflect more balance, and be clearer in their practical application (English Tourist Board *et al.*, 1991). In summary, these are:

(1) The environment has an intrinsic value and its long-term survival must not be prejudiced by short-term considerations.
(2) Tourism should be recognised as a positive activity, with the potential to benefit the community, place, and visitor.

(3) The relationship between tourism and the environment must be managed so tourism does not damage the resource, prejudice its future enjoyment, or bring unacceptable impacts.
(4) Tourism activities and developments should respect the scale, nature and character of place.
(5) In any location, harmony must be sought between the needs of the visitor, place and host community.
(6) In a dynamic world, some change is inevitable and can be beneficial, but adaptation should not be at the expense of any principle.
(7) The tourism industry, governments, and environmental agencies should respect these principles, and work together to achieve their realisation.

Not all tourism has been, or is, sustainable; nor has it always conformed to these principles. Sustainable tourism involves a challenge to develop quality tourism products without adversely affecting the natural and cultural environment that maintains and nurtures them. At the heart of sustainable tourism is a set of implicit values related to striving to integrate *economic, social and cultural* goals (Wight, 1993). This relationship may vary due to the need to adapt, over time, to changing social norms and ecological conditions, as well as the need to recognise that goals may change as the spatial scale of the systems are expanded from local to national or larger scales. As Burr (1994: 11) points out, 'approaches to sustainable tourism development and use . . . must fundamentally focus on equity and balance and integrative planning'.

Ecotourism and its Role in Sustainable Development

Just as tourism is only a part of the whole that is sustainable development, so ecotourism is only part of the whole which is sustainable tourism. It is, however, a leading-edge player in supporting principles of tourism sustainability, yet it has been subject to considerable criticism, often without constructive alternatives or solutions.

It has been stated that 'sustainable tourism will not be based on ecotourism; what we need is sustainable mass tourism' (Wall, 1992). While it is true that we need sustainable tourism at all levels and of all types, to look for one answer (such as sustainable mass tourism) may be a simplistic, if not impossible, quest. Any role that ecotourism plays in contributing to sustainable tourism would seem to be beneficial. It seems that ecotourism's influence is having far-reaching impacts towards extending principles of sustainability into other forms of tourism (Western, 1993; Wight, 1993).

It has been pointed out that not all products that purport to be ecotourism are sustainable. However, this is not the fault of ecotourism itself. Indeed, most of such products have been wrongly described as ecotourism, since they do not adhere to the principles of ecotourism. Ecotourism principles contribute to integrating social, economic, and environmental goals, and reflect the larger objective of sustainable tourism. They are (Wight, 1993) that ecotourism should involve:

- environmentally sound development, and no degradation of the resource;
- first-hand, participatory, enlightening experiences;

- all-party education (communities, government, NGOs, industry and tourists);
- recognition of the intrinsic values of the resources;
- acceptance of the resource on its own terms, recognising limits, which involves supply-oriented management;
- understanding and partnerships between many players;
- promotion of ethical responsibilities and behavior towards the natural and cultural environment;
- long-term benefits (economic and non-economic) to the resource, industry and the local community; and
- responsible conservation practices related to both internal and external operations.

Role of Government in Sustainable Development

Distinction between growth and development

The concept of sustainable development has been viewed as an oxymoron, because 'sustainable' is the language of balance and limits, and 'development' is the language of more (Illich, 1989). James *et al.* (1989) feel that the WCED definition emphasises growth, an economist's approach, and argue that there are other approaches to sustainable development.

It is necessary to distinguish between growth and development.

> Economic growth, which is an increase in quantity, cannot be sustainable indefinitely on a finite planet. Economic development, which is an improvement in the quality of life without necessarily causing an increase in quantity of resources consumed, may be sustainable. Sustainable growth is an impossibility. (Costanza, 1991: 75).

Growth means more of something – greater numbers or larger in size, while development involves differentiation, and results in an increase in complexity. Development normally makes possible specialisation and efficiency. Economic growth and human use of resources are not limitless; economic growth must be accompanied by development. The problems with a growth-oriented approach are that:

- growth may increase income, but increase the dependence of the economy on outside capital and technology;
- growth may increase jobs without raising the level of income;
- growth may use resources more efficiently, while depleting or degrading them to the point where the economy declines;
- growth does not ensure a developing economy; the latter is characterised by increased productivity and creation/expansion of a more diverse mix of businesses and economic activities.

Economic development means adding value to existing products or creating new products, using processes that are sustainable environmentally and economically, or applying new technology for more efficient production, use, and reuse. Tourism and economic development agencies are slowly shifting their positions on growth. Tourism Canada recognised, some years ago, that sustained growth was impossible. 'One of the constant strategies is the aim of zero product defect, not growth – growth cannot be infinitely maintained, and its continued pursuit conflicts with environmental responsibility' (Fyfe, 1992). This means that customers cannot always have whatever they want, with no regard to the consequence, and sometimes customers 'are not always right'. In other words, a market-driven perspective is not always the appropriate course of action.

In Alberta, Government's role has changed considerably over the last decade and more. This is partially reflected in the name changes (four names in five years), although the Department of Economic Development and Tourism (ED&T) will be the principal reference here. The paper will highlight some of the considerable progress which ED&T made towards sustainable tourism up to the mid-1990s, including ecotourism. It will also address how recent shifts in governmental and departmental roles have affected the sustainable tourism area.

Alberta's role in sustainable development and ecotourism

In Alberta, Government is not a developer; its primary role is to inform, assist and support industry, which develops tourism. However, in the early 1990s, the department took a proactive approach to obtaining the information the industry needed. Government and industry were partners in the challenge of sustainable tourism. The department encouraged all types of tourism to 'move' towards sustainability, and developed initiatives with broader relevance than to ecotourism alone. It recognised that the challenge in development and operation of Alberta's assets was that there should be minimum impact upon the natural environment. 'Our natural environment represents a capital resource – a bank account with nature that pays interest and dividends so long as the account is kept intact' (Alberta Tourism, 1990: 1).

The increasing move to sustainability was reflected in the key areas that became an Alberta Government focus: people, prosperity and preservation. These areas approximate to the sustainable development goals of harmonising society, economy and environment. The department implemented a series of projects, policies and initiatives, sometimes with other agencies, which were intended to contribute to sustainable development, through encouraging appropriate tourism development. Such activities included:

- contributions to environmental protection and resource management policies;
- integrating tourism into resource planning and decision making;
- advice and assistance to current and potential operators;
- consultations with stakeholders and the public;
- education and information dissemination;
- cooperative partnerships with communities, governments and others;
- research initiatives.

It is not possible to address all these activities here; those with particular relevance to ecotourism are highlighted.

Integrated Planning

ED&T worked with, and on behalf of, tourism project proponents, to improve the understanding and application of environmental planning, assessment and management. It worked beyond the single project level, in areas of high tourism potential. For example, it was the lead agency in an inter-agency 'Bow-Canmore Tourism Development Framework' adjacent to Banff National Park. This was not intended to be simply a regional land-use plan; it examined social, environmental, aesthetic and economic issues surrounding tourism development proposals, and was undertaken partly to ensure that development did not take place in an *ad hoc* manner (Wight, 1990).

The department has long participated in Alberta's Integrated Resource Planning (IRP) process, which takes an intersectoral approach to the sometimes conflicting demands of various sectors upon the environment. The IRP process, which was initiated in Alberta in the 1970s, initially focused upon public land-use management. In more recent attempts to reflect environmental realities, water and air-based components were integrated with land into the planning process and the new direction is Integrated Resource Management (IRM).

The IRM process reflects several of the principles of sustainable development, and of ecotourism, and comprehensive public participation is built into the process. While ED&T support opportunities for tourism and ecotourism, other sectors around the table also advance their positions, thus the process is one of collaboration. The result aims for a balance of resource use and protection. In many cases, development and use opportunities are strictly limited, or non-tourism sectors are given priority, since the goal is appropriate regional (rather than sectoral) planning.

Cooperation and Partnerships

ED&T has been a cooperative partner in many larger initiatives oriented towards sustainable tourism and ecotourism. In 1991, Alberta was a significant contributor to *Canada's Code of Ethics and Guidelines for Sustainable Tourism* (Tourism Industry Association of Canada, 1992). Unlike many codes, significant positive aspects of the TIAC document are that it includes:

- codes for both tourists and for industry;
- not only general codes, but also specific guidelines, at an overall level, and in detail, for five industry subsectors, including tour operators;
- natural environmental and also social and cultural perspectives;
- a comprehensive range of guidelines (including: policy, planning and decision-making; guests/the tourism experience; the host community; development; natural, cultural and historic resources; conservation of natural resources; environmental protection; marketing; research and education; public awareness; industry cooperation; and the global village).

In 1991 the department participated in a cross-Canada ecotourism workshop, oriented towards providing a consensus-built definition, and contributing to principles and proposed codes of ethics for ecotourism (Scace *et al.*, 1992). It was involved in the development of an interpretive wildlife viewing guide for the province, as well as a manual, *Developing your Wildlife Viewing Site* (Alberta Environmental Protection *et al.*, 1993). The manual is intended for landowners, municipalities, community groups and others. It guides, step-by-step, the development of a site, including: initial idea, research, interpretive planning, preparation of a site plan, implementation strategies and fund-raising, and facility construction and evaluation stages.

ED&T became involved in a community-based ecotourism initiative in 1995, involving various levels and sectors of government, community groups, NGOs, and landowners. This initiative examined the desire for ecotourism based on wildlife viewing at the community level, together with the issues, barriers, landowner perspectives, and potential partners. The intent was to develop a 'how to' document and a provincial strategy, with a pilot project approach (HLA Consultants and Pam Wight & Associates, 1997). Of particular value was the recognition that those who most obviously *benefit* from ecotourism (e.g. urban municipalities or commercial outlets) may not own or manage the resource base (e.g. rural municipalities or farmers), nor have the perceived or actual *problems* of ecotourism on these lands (e.g. access management or liability). Thus, the relationship between the resource manager (whether owner or leasee) and the other beneficiaries of ecotourism (e.g. neighbouring communities or agencies) is of particular focus. The equity principle of sustainable development is particularly supported here. The project expressly recognised that the primary objectives and benefits for each player will vary, and that social, economic, conservation and political goals need to be taken into account for the project to succeed.

Public and Stakeholder Consultations

The Government of Alberta has a strong tradition of public consultation. In 1991, it established a panel to address the need for a provincial tourism strategy. Tourism 2000 involved extensive consultations with a broad cross-section of Albertans, through symposia, industry/regional workshops, public open houses, public submissions, and a tourism impact monitoring survey (Alberta Economic Development and Tourism, 1993). These consultations were the key to the vision and objectives, to (1) increase tourism dollar receipts; (2) protect Alberta's biological diversity, the integrity of its landscape and the quality of its air, water and land; and (3) recognise and enhance the diversity of lifestyles in Alberta.

The environment was recognised as a natural advantage for Alberta. Some of the recommended activities included encouraging the ecotourism industry to adhere to TIAC's code for sustainable tourism, and ensuring the tourism industry achieves integration between use and preservation of natural assets.

Proactive Research and Education

One of the areas of greatest success for the department in the 1980s and early 1990s was its information programme, obtained through proactive research. Reports were sent to libraries throughout the province and beyond, to ensure adequate access to information by public and industry. If demand for reports by industry and others is any measure, success was enormous.

In the 1980s, the department began to commission studies to determine which provincial nature-based resources (if any) were of interest to tourism markets and were appropriate for ecotourism. ED&T cooperated with other government departments to undertake market research, which determined that local- and provincial-level markets were extremely interested in wildlife viewing and nature-based tourism (HLA *et al.*, 1990, Manecon, 1991), but international market and product potential was unknown. The research outlined below relates to both supply and demand side aspects of ecotourism.

Ecotourism product potential

One of the common perspectives on ecotourism, particularly as reflected in the literature, is that the focal destinations of interest to ecotourism markets are tropical and underdeveloped countries. ED&T commissioned a study to determine whether or not a northern, more developed destination (Alberta specifically) could have national and international ecotourism potential. The study presented a range of successful northern ecotourism product (HBT AGRA, 1992). ED&T stipulated the report presentation framework so that many aspects relevant to sustainability principles would be examined and highlighted. These included:

- location and resource description;
- product description;
- facilities;
- market information;
- marketing;
- approaches to incorporating environmental protection (including limits to growth, party size, restrictions, educational activities, codes of conduct, internal conservation measures, and local community);
- business and operational details; and
- relationships with local communities.

The study also examined various types of ecotourism programmes: government programmes (e.g. the McNeil River State Sanctuary, Alaska); government and private industry cooperatives (e.g. the polar bears of Churchill, Canada); private industry programmes (e.g. Ecosummer Canada), and private conservation programmes (e.g. the Community Baboon Sanctuary in Belize). The study concluded that each type of product fulfils a role that is appropriate within the local environment. It also concluded that there are, indeed, successful ecotourism ventures in more developed, non-tropical destinations. This was subsequently confirmed by primary market research.

Identifying locations potentially appropriate for ecotourism

Having determined *potential* as an ecotourism destination, the task was to determine which Alberta products were capable of sustaining ecotourism. This was in support of one of the principles of ecotourism – to enable *supply-based* management and planning for sustainable ecotourism to take place. ED&T commissioned a study where it was understood that ecotourism involves maintaining the quality of the natural environment on which the experience depends, as well as maintaining or enhancing the quality of life of the host community (Cottonwood *et al.*, 1992). Where the resource was considered too fragile to sustain ecotourism, *that area was excluded from further consideration*. This supported the principles of maintaining essential ecological process and preserving biodiversity – working towards environmentally sound development with no resource degradation.

A major objective was to develop criteria to assist in evaluating the locations identified as having ecotourism product development potential. It was understood that the resources upon which tourism depends may also have value to other sectors; thus an inter-governmental committee was formed, to ensure that many perspectives were incorporated into the evaluations. This was also assisted by interviews with industry operators and environmental groups.

Criteria of relevance were developed in an intergovernmental workshop. The criteria were listed on the Y axis of an evaluation matrix. Most of the 23 criteria had a number of subcomponents. There were a total of 22 geographic areas examined in five regions of the province, and these were listed along the X axis of the evaluation matrix. Areas were given points for each criterion. This exercise resulted in an Ecotourism Evaluation Matrix, which provided a series of total scores for each area. Table 1 shows the matrix and the major criteria, with actual numerical scores for Alberta's significant ecotourism product. Scores were not viewed as absolute, and were further interpreted based on team knowledge.

This approach has enabled industry and government to see just where areas of high ecotourism potential are located in the province. Selection of these areas was not intended to preclude future consideration of other areas, since scoring values and weighting of evaluation categories may change for different areas and in consideration of a number of factors (e.g. activities, product, market characteristics, and time). However, it is effort-effective to focus on the areas that have highest potential. The evaluation exercise and matrix established locations with ecotourism potential. It also took a supply-oriented perspective, which is one of the principles of ecotourism.

National and international ecotourism market potential

One of the principles of sustainable tourism is establishing harmony between the needs of the visitor, the place and the host community. However, ecotourism market needs were not well known prior to the mid-1990s. Although there were studies of international ecotourism markets from *operator* perspectives (Ingram & Durst, 1989; Yee, 1992), these studies tended to focus on group travellers and tropical destinations, had limited numbers of respondents (34 and 23 respectively), and provided no direct consumer perspective.

In order to obtain preliminary market information for Alberta, the department commissioned a survey of tour operators who had Alberta as a destination, and who were involved in nature, adventure, culture and educational tours (HLA, 1994). These operators included both National Tour Association members, as well as specialty operators. The study contrasted market preferences *between* types of operators, as well as integrating findings.

The biggest challenge was to obtain national and international ecotourism market information, to determine market needs, characteristics, trip and product preferences, changing demand, destinations of interest, and information to assist in marketing appropriately. This was known to be a costly and ambitious endeavour. To assist in solving this problem, the department collaborated with

Table 1 Ecotourism Evaluation Matrix

	Central Region							*Northwest Region*				*Northeast Region*					*Eastern Slopes*			*Rivers*		
Criteria	1	2	3	4	5	6	7	8	9	10	11	12	13	14	15	16	17	18	19	20	21	22
Biophysical/Cultural																						
1. Biogeography	2	2	1	1	2	2	1	2	2	6	3	1	2	3	1	4	3	3	4	2	1	1
2. Significant physical features	2	2	2	1	2	4	1	2	2	2	2	4	2	4	2	8	2	2	2	2	2	1
3. Significant biological features	8	2	2	2	2	2	2	8	2	8	8	2	4	2	4	8	8	8	8	8	4	2
4. Significant cultural features	2	2	4	2	2	2	4	4	2	2	2	4	2	2	2	8	2	1	2	4	2	2
5. Highly sought after species	10	6	8	4	6	4	4	10	4	10	4	8	8	4	4	10	10	10	10	4	4	4
6. Natural diversity	3	4	4	3	5	4	3	5	4	5	3	5	5	5	5	5	5	5	5	5	5	5
7. Topographic relief	2	2	4	2	4	2	2	4	4	4	4	4	4	2	4	4	8	8	8	4	4	2
8. Protected areas	2	2	8	8	8	8	8	8	8	8	8	8	8	4	8	8	0	4	2	8	8	8
9. Waterways	2	2	8	8	8	8	8	8	8	8	8	8	8	4	8	8	0	4	2	8	8	8
Subtotal	35	26	37	23	35	32	25	47	32	53	34	40	35	26	30	63	46	49	49	41	30	23
10. Land management conflicts	8	8	4	0	4	4	0	8	4	0	4	4	0	0	4	0	4	0	0	4	4	0
Land-use constraints																						
Subtotal	8	8	4	0	4	4	0	8	4	0	4	4	0	0	4	0	4	0	0	4	4	0
Other constraints																						
11. Weather	nr	nr	nr	nr	nr	nr	nr	nr	nr	nr	nr	nr	nr	nr	nr	nr	nr	nr	nr	nr	nr	nr
12. Biological hazards	nr	nr	nr	nr	nr	nr	nr	nr	nr	nr	nr	nr	nr	nr	nr	nr	nr	nr	nr	nr	nr	nr
13. Environmental sensitivity	nr	nr	nr	nr	nr	nr	nr	nr	nr	nr	nr	nr	nr	nr	nr	nr	nr	nr	nr	nr	nr	nr
14. Water quality and quantity	0	0	0	0	0	0	0	0	0	0	0	0	0	0	0	0	0	0	0	0	0	0
15. Physical capability/suitability	0	0	0	0	0	0	0	0	0	0	0	0	0	0	0	0	0	0	0	0	0	0
16. Recreation/tourism conflicts	–4	–4	0	0	0	0	0	–2	0	0	0	–2	0	0	0	0	–2	0	0	–2	0	0
Subtotal	–4	–4	0	0	0	0	0	–2	0	0	0	–2	0	0	0	0	–2	0	0	–2	0	0

	Central Region							Northwest Region				Northeast Region					Eastern Slopes			Rivers		
Infrastructure																						
17. Existing access	2	2	2	2	2	2	2	2	2	2	0	2	2	2	2	2	2	2	2	2	2	2
18.Existing accommodation/food	2	2	2	2	2	2	2	2	2	1	2	2	2	2	2	1	2	2	2	2	2	2
19. Utilities	2	2	2	2	2	2	2	2	2	2	2	2	2	2	2	2	2	2	2	2	2	2
20. Associated services/activities	2	2	2	2	2	2	2	2	2	2	0	2	2	2	2	2	2	2	2	2	2	2
Subtotal	8	8	8	8	8	8	8	8	8	7	4	8	8	8	8	7	8	8	8	8	8	8
Community interest																						
21. Ecotourism programmes	8	8	8	0	0	0	0	8	0	8	0	0	0	0	0	8	4	8	4	0	0	0
22. Diversity of ecotourism	8	4	0	0	0	0	0	4	0	4	0	0	0	0	0	4	0	8	0	0	0	0
23. Community interest	8	4	8	4	4	4	4	8	4	8	4	8	4	4	4	8	4	8	4	8	4	4
Subtotal	24	16	16	4	4	4	4	20	4	20	4	8	4	4	4	20	8	24	8	8	4	4
Grand total	55	38	57	35	43	40	37	63	40	80	38	50	47	38	38	90	56	81	65	51	38	35

Note: The numbers indicate the points given (out of ten) for each criterion.
nr = not rated

other governments (federal and provincial), and involved an industry partner. Alberta contributed significantly, in terms of project management, staff time, and participation in research activities. The first comprehensive international study of ecotourism markets resulted from this initiative (HLA/ARA, 1994) providing primary data directly from:

- North American travellers interested in ecotourism;
- experienced ecotourists; and
- the international ecotourism travel trade.

In a true spirit of cooperation, this study was shared at no charge with governments, industry and others around the world.

Involvement of industry and partners was an operating principle in that research programme. At the outset of the study, the provincial governments organised two workshops with industry and government in each of Alberta and British Columbia. Attendees were asked (1) what information was needed in the research, and (2) in what form they wanted the final product.

This front-end input proved invaluable. Once the study was complete, the department immediately initiated a series of day-long workshops with industry, in numerous locations around Alberta, including one especially designed for a remote, aboriginal community. This tailor-made workshop series supported principles related to adequate access to information and education, as well as being designed to assist industry and obtain feedback. In addition, all other departmental materials relevant to ecotourism and sustainable tourism were displayed and made available to attendees.

A large effort was made by ED&T to track down the contact details of the hundreds of ecotourism, adventure and related operators in the province who might benefit from the workshops. Attendees were private sector operators, communities and groups involved in ecotourism-related initiatives, as well as government resource managers. The workshops were custom designed to present study findings in a forum where there were also opportunities for questions, explanations, discussion of implications, opportunities and constraints, and industry needs.

One of the benefits to such a customised approach was the opportunity for players in the ecotourism industry to meet others with similar ideas or complementary products, in person. It was evident that a great deal of networking and future partnerships evolved at the workshops. This was partly because there had been no previous association or forum for those involved in ecotourism.

Environmental Protection and Conservation

Basic principles of sustainability include responsible conservation practices, promotion of ethics and recognition of the value of resources. In order to stimulate and promote responsible conservation practices, ED&T researched and commissioned information on alternative and environmentally sensitive technologies and techniques. These were intended to focus on *remote* areas, which are often the location of ecotourism facilities.

One study systematically examined conservation of water, energy and materials (product purchase and solid waste), and alternative sewage management techniques in tourism facilities (Nor'wester *et al.*, 1994). Not only were a range of technologies and operational practices discussed, but a comprehensive descriptive matrix was also developed. This matrix presented information on 22 practical components for every technology (Table 2). The findings of the alternative technologies research were not intended to be prescriptive, but to provide a range of optional approaches for actual and potential tourism lodge operators.

Table 2 Conservation technology components, summarised

- Fesibility
- Resource Appropriateness/Availability (Summer; & Winter)
- Compatibility with other technologies/practices
- Availability (inc. suppliers, services)
- Reliability
- Complexity
- Conformance to applicable codes, regulations
- Fuel/energy (requirements and savings)
- Life span
- Environmental consequences (aesthetics (visual, noise); biophysical; human safety, comfort)
- Benefits (economic; and non-economic)
- Order of magnitude costs (capital; and annual O&M)
- Payback period (where known)

Concurrent research was undertaken by department staff, to examine actual cases of remote lodges across Canada that had implemented conservation practices and technologies (Table 3), together with approaches, benefits and lessons learned (Alberta Economic Development & Tourism, 1994).

Together, the studies on conservation technologies and the actual cases have demonstrated that tourism accommodation/facility development does not have to take a 'business as usual' approach; that it is possible to plan, design and operate tourism facilities in a more environmentally sensitive and sustainable way. The studies were used by at least one operator planning an ecotourism lodge in a montane area (Rocky Mountain Escape). With departmental assistance, the operator, a biologist, developed a vision for the operation, as well as management based on sustainability principles. She ensured alternative approaches were considered by the planning team for site design, building and operations, and successfully gained planning approval for sensitive facility/operational development in a potentially fragile environment.

Integrating Environmental and Economic Decisions: Green Standards

It has been recognised that markets express support for environmentally sensitive travel operators (whether attractions, accommodation, transportation, food services, or tour operators). On average, travellers would spend 8.5% more for environmentally friendly travel services and products, and 87% of all US

Table 3 Alternative and minimum impact technologies, by facility

Remote lodges	*Site development and construction technologies*	*Energy technologies*	*Waste management technologies*	*Water quality and conservation technologies*
Wells Gray Park Backcountry Chalets, BC	X			
Sheep Mountain Visitor Information Centre, YUK	X	X		
Sorcerer Lake Lodge, BC	X	X		
Tarryall Lodge, ON	X	X		
Peterson's Point Lake Camp, NWT		X		
River Cove Campground, AB		X		
Mount Assiniboine Lodge, BC	X	X	X	
Selkirk Lodge, BC	X	X	X	
Boyne River Ecology Centre, ON	X	X	X	
North Knife Lake Lodge, MAN	X	X	X	
Arctic Watch Lodge, NWT	X	X	X	
Mistaya Lodge, BC	X	X	X	X
Purcell Lodge, BC	X	X	X	X
Alpine Huts, AB & BC			X	
Lake O'Hara Lodge, BC			X	X

Source: Alberta Economic Development and Tourism, 1994
Note: BC = British Columbia; YUK = Yukon; ON = Ontario; NWT = Northwest Territories Alberta; MAN = Manitoba.

travellers indicate that they would be likely or very likely to support or patronise travel companies that help preserve the environment (Cook *et al.*, 1992). Markets are also prepared to shun destinations or operators who are perceived to have negative environmental impacts (Goodno, 1993; Morton, 1993). Also, the hospitality industry has been a huge consumer of resources (energy, water and materials), and is responsible for large volumes of waste. Reducing consumption and waste production has the dual benefit of conserving resources and potentially reducing costs (Wight, 1998a).

In Alberta, tourism facilities and operations are listed in the Alberta Accommodation and Visitors' Guide. Each property has features of its operation listed on a summary matrix. Such aspects include: air conditioning, swimming pool, courtesy coffee, food services, price range, etc. In addition, there are quality ratings indicated by 1–5 stars (Canada Select) and a disabled access rating

(Access Canada, 1–4 levels). The ratings are established by an annual inspection at each property. The department conceived that it would be helpful to add a voluntary environmental rating. This could take the form of a minimum qualifying standard (like Denmark's Green Key programme), or a star-type system where the more categories are filled, the more stars are obtained (like Thailand's Green Leaves programme).

In 1994, ED&T initiated a Green Standards partnership project for the hospitality industry, intended to:

- educate and inform (visitors, communities, industry, and others);
- stimulate innovation (into appropriate technologies and practices);
- protect resources (through conservation practices);
- derive economic benefits (through cost savings and competitive positioning).

This project encompassed a wider realm than ecotourism, since there are opportunities for many players in the tourism industry to 'go green'. The initiative supported principles relating to partnerships and consulting stakeholders, marketing tourism responsibly, involving local communities, training staff, and reducing overconsumption and waste.

From 1994 to 1996, the Green Standards initiative was in the development and industry education phase. This involved informative articles being included in the newsletters of provincial hotel and motel associations, related to such focused topics as: energy, water or waste conservation. A key aspect was generating industry interest and 'buy in', using success stories from Alberta, and providing tips which were easy and low cost to implement. Further departmental activities were intended to include the development of specific industry standards, inspector training programmes, and 'how to' materials. It was expected that as the varied conservation and economic benefits of these Green Standards became apparent, the approach would percolate into other areas of the tourism industry, including Country Inns, bed and breakfast accommodation, guest ranches, lodges, tour operators, and other tourism operations.

ED&T also participated in hospitality industry conferences and trade shows to educate and inform. In addition, it worked with a prime tourism destination (the town of Banff) which hoped to include its own environmental standards in its *Official Visitor Guide*. ED&T participated in Banff's Environmental Committee, and conceived of and assisted Banff with a 'Conservation Expo' for industry and public, to communicate a range of benefits and cost-effective conservation activities for its facilities.

Unfortunately, due to government cutbacks and reorganisation, implementation was never realised. The groundwork was laid for implementation, but the initiative was dropped. There have been subsequent national-level moves in this direction, and Alberta has lost its leadership potential here.

Management of Resources, Visitors, and Impact

There have been numerous calls in the literature for carrying capacity to be determined, in order to appropriately plan, manage and control the direction and consequences of tourism and other activities (e.g. Card & Vogelsong, 1994;

World Tourism Organisation *et al.*, 1992). Unfortunately, however, while the *concept* of carrying capacity is appealing, it has had limited success outside the field of wildlife management, and cannot deal with the complexity and diversity of issues associated with recreation, tourism and ecotourism. Although the concept is attractive, in practical tourism terms it is not applicable (McCool, 1991; Wight, 1994, 1998b; Williams & Gill, 1991).

Sustainable development does imply limits; not absolute limits, but limitations imposed by the present state of technology and social organisation on environmental resources, and by the ability of the biosphere to absorb the effects of human activities (Burr, 1994). Research and programmes are now focusing on managing the resource, the visitors, and the impacts, rather than carrying capacity (Cole *et al.*, 1987; Commonwealth of Australia, 1991; Hennessy, 1991, Wight, 1996, 1998b).

ED&T was concerned that potential future growth and impact of tourism development be managed appropriately, particularly in sensitive environments. It commissioned research into carrying capacity and related concepts, providing the consultants with much of its own internal growth management research findings, which are found throughout the report (Williams & Gill, 1991). The subsequent report provided direction towards growth management approaches, and highlighted some of the problems inherent in aiming to determine carrying capacity. Particularly, problems include unrealistic expectations (e.g. that there is a technique that can provide a specific number, limit or threshold), and untenable assumptions (e.g. that there is a direct relationship between visitor use and impact, and that limiting use limits impact).

In Alberta, Beaverhill Lake Natural Area is an internationally recognised bird staging and migration area, and is an IUCN Ramsar site. This large, shallow lake has long been a popular destination for naturalists, particularly birdwatchers. It has grown in popularity through its recognition as a provincial watchable wildlife site. In 1993, the local community of Tofield initiated the annual Snow Goose Festival, listed in the North American Directory of Birding Festivals. The increase in attendance at the festival (over 6000 people in one weekend in 1995) and the potential for growing tourism visitation at other times, gave rise to concerns that the site would not be able to accommodate the visitors interested in the area. Locally, there was the idea that determining 'the number' of visitors, or carrying capacity, would solve problems.

The department recognised that one approach to resource management concerns may not be appropriate; after all, limiting the number of visitors is only one tactic of many, in a range of possible management strategies (Wight, 1996). With the assistance of department staff and consultants, it was demonstrated that, rather than establishing carrying capacity, a visitor management plan was needed. Together with government, NGOs, and municipal and community partners, the department commissioned a pilot study which examined the Beaverhill site, with a view to enabling lessons and principles to be applied elsewhere in the province (HLA *et al.*, 1995).

This visitor management plan has become a critical component in appropriate nature-based tourism development for the area. The plan aimed to maintain the integrity of the resources upon which the visitor experience is based; optimise visitor satisfaction within the constraints of the destination environment; and address the preferences of the nearby landowners/communities. It established appropriate site access, orientation, circulation, paths, viewing mounds, and behaviours of visitors. Elements addressed in the plan included visitor impact indicators, monitoring guidelines, and facility development and management strategies to minimise the impact on landowners and the environment.

The plan established a model approach to developing an effective strategy involving participation of all stakeholders. The approach is a good example of shared stewardship, and allowed important wildlife habitat to be preserved, while at the same time supporting economic development through nature-based tourism opportunities. This reflects the sustainability principles of striving for harmony between the needs of the visitor, the place and the host community.

Changing Government Roles through the 1990s

Alberta Economic Development and Tourism was at the forefront of ecotourism and sustainable tourism initiatives for many years, and contributed significantly to work on issues relevant to ecotourism, both at the provincial, national, and international scale. It has been the research, education, and policy development roles which have been most emphasised. These roles have required understanding and incorporating many principles of sustainability.

As part of overall government requirements for departments to measure their achievements, in the mid-1990s there was considerable emphasis given to one realm of the sustainable development model – economics. This included considerable focus on growth, as has been evidenced by Alberta's recent 'Growth Summits'. Unfortunately, the Alberta Government has not recognised that it is impossible to maximise one goal without adversely impacting the others. Government could have had even greater success in contributing to sustainable development if there was a greater ability among departments to build more balance into their measures of success, to reflect greater balance among the goals of sustainable development. Separation of environmental conservation and economic development is one of three obstacles to sustainable development (World Conservation Union *et al.*, 1990).

Virtually all of the initiatives described in this paper were completed before 1996, or truncated abruptly at that time. Between 1990 and 1999, the department had four names, six ministers, and multiple reorganisations. Massive departmental cutbacks and layoffs, as well as role reorganisation, have resulted in current tourism responsibilities being only minimal core functions.

Hinch and Slack (1997) provided an excellent description of the restructuring of tourist organisations, using Alberta as a case study. In describing the privatisation of public-sector activities, they describe how, with respect to tourism, the explicit rationale for government and tourism agencies had been primarily economic; however, in the early 1990s, government advocated the protection of the social and physical environments in which tourism operates and upon which its attractions are often based (ED&T, 1993). The following summarises Hinch and Slack's further points:

- the tourism portfolio began to be shuffled through a range of departments and ministers in the early 1990s, giving rise to questions about changing government priorities for tourism;

- by 1993, the Alberta Government had begun to severely reduce funding for a variety of tourism programmes;
- new organisational frameworks were developed for tourism with the move to a private sector led marketing organisation, the Alberta Tourism Partnership Corporation (ATPC);
- 'the provincial government … has ceased or severely curtailed tourism functions related to basic market research, community-based tourism planning support, product standards and inspections, and tourism business consulting. With the exception of marketing and some basic market research, these functions have not been assumed by the ATPC' (p. 277);
- while previous departmental staff numbered around 90, ATPC's staff was about 25, and the department's Tourism Development Agency (TDA) was reduced to nine;
- the TDA's 'orphaned status puts them at risk in a bureaucracy that may face further budgetary cutbacks' (p. 279).

In summary, Hinch and Slack stated, 'to the extent that peripheral areas are by definition at an earlier stage of tourism development than the core areas, this decrease in public-sector resources represents a significant challenge' for the independent operators, who are burdened with much of government's transfer of responsibilities (Hinch & Slack, 1997: 279). Ecotourism opportunities in Alberta are mostly in peripheral regions. To a large extent, current and potential ecotourism and related tourism operators have suffered as a result of this government role change, with some explicitly citing this as a reason for them going out of business.

Table 4 illustrates the changing role that the government department responsible for tourism has assumed. Vertical columns represent general principles of sustainability discussed in the text, together with the main years when these were evident in departmental activities. The absence of initiatives after 1995 eloquently speaks to the changing role of government related to tourism.

Criticisms of sustainable development within the context of tourism have been that approaches are 'extremely tourism centric', and thus partly divorced from the main principles of sustainable development (Hunter, 1995). He suggested that there are four different approaches to sustainable development based on four types of sustainability (Hunter, 1997). These approaches are: Very Weak, Weak, Strong, and Very Strong.

When the changing role and activities of the Alberta department responsible for tourism are examined, there is some parallel with Hunter's four types of sustainability within tourism. Figure 1 illustrates the relationship of the type of sustainability evidenced by government over the last decade, which is very pronounced when examined together with ministry reorganisations, and the activities shown in Table 4. During the 'Strong' sustainability period (shown in Figure 1) it would be fair to indicate that while environmental matters were a strong focus, tourism was not 'environment-*led*' as Hunter indicates it would be in a 'Strong' scenario. The 'Very Strong Sustainability' scenario has never been present in Alberta. The most recent 'Weak' and 'Very Weak' scenarios (1996–1999) are not only weak, they have not even focused much on tourism, due to reduced government responsibilities.

Table 4 Alberta's Tourism Department initatives supporting sustainable development[1]

Name of department	Year	*Principles supporting sustainable development:* *Integrated planning*	*Cooperation and partnerships*	*Public consultation*	*Research and education*	*Environment protection and conservation*	*Management of resources, impact, visitors*	*Green standards*
Tourism	1990	X	X TIAC		X		X	
Tourism	1991	X	X CEAC	X Tourism 2000	X Compar-ables		X Growth Manage-ment	
Tourism, Parks & Recreation	1992	X	X AEP		X N. Alberta		X	
ED&T	1993	X	X Wildlife		X	X	X	
ED&T	1994	X	X Demand		X Tour Operator	X Alt. Techno-logies	X	X
ED&T	1995[2]	X	X NAWMP	X Special Places[3]	X Accomm odation		X VIM Beaver-hill	X Banff, AHA, MAA
ED&T	1996[4]	X						
Economic Development	1997							
Economic Development	1998							
Economic Development	1999							

1. X = Years when supportive principles are most evident. Descriptions are found in the text which correspond to departmental activities.
2. A move to privatisation in tourism began, together with massive departmental staff and budget cutbacks.
3. Government of Alberta (1995).
4. IRP became Integrated Resource Management, but with a move to devolve plans to the regions, and has largely languished since 1996.
5. TIAC = Tourism Industry Association of Canada. CEAC = Canadian Environmental Advisory Council. AEP = Alberta Environmental Protection. NAWMP = North American Waterfowl Management Plan. VIM = Visitor Impact Management. AHA = Alberta Hotal Association. MAA = Motel Association of Alberta.

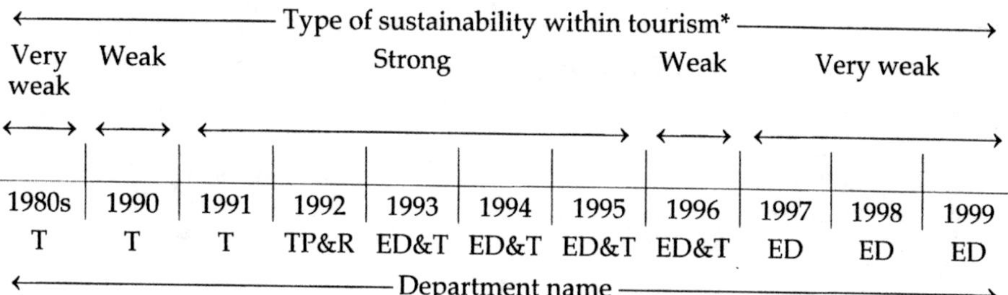

* Hunter's (1995) four types of sustainability are: Very weak: tourism imperative scenario; Weak: product-led tourism scenario; Strong: environment-led tourism scenario; Very strong: neotenous tourism scenario

T = Tourism; TP&R = Tourism, Parks & Recreation; ED&T = Economic Development & Tourism; ED = Economic Development

Figure 1 Alberta Government tourism responsibility: types of sustainability

This paper has focused on one level of government (provincial), a critical one for sustainable tourism due to provincial responsibility for natural resources. However, there is wider relevance to this case study. A number of benefits emerged from the Alberta Government selecting initiatives that supported principles of sustainability in the early 1990s. These were particularly in contributions to environmental protection and resource management policies (maintaining essential ecological processes); consultations with stakeholders/publics (which led to initiatives to preserve biological diversity and sustain species and ecosystems); research and educational initiatives (highlighting diverse opportunities for non-material use of natural resources); and integrating tourism into resource planning and cooperative partnerships (maintaining and improving quality of life, supporting a sustainable economy and preserving biological diversity).

The activities listed above have been selected to highlight certain of the principles of sustainable development (in brackets), but actually, any one initiative tended to support more than one principle. Non-tourism government departments, with different core mandates, also contributed strongly to such areas as resource management. The areas where ED&T has been most effective, from this author's perspective, is in leadership research, covering a gamut of topics, including at the 'enterprise level' for environmental protection and resource management. From this case, it seems that it is in the area of research that governments (particularly departments responsible for tourism) have a large opportunity for support. Such appropriate research goes far beyond conventional exit survey activities, and is particularly appropriate for topics that are beyond the scope or capability of the tourism industry. However, it is also useful to note that government initiatives which themselves are not sustained, may have an adverse effect. In addition, renewed primary emphasis on economic and growth perspectives can have negative ripple effects on the priorities and directions of all departments and industry, and thus on communities and the environment.

Clearly, while the Alberta Government was responsible for many ground-breaking ecotourism initiatives up to the mid-1990s, its role has since changed dramatically. By mid-1999, the time when this paper was written, this had reverted to the economic development imperative, with essentially no initiatives in support of sustainable development principles, which has virtually paralleled the privatisation initiatives of government. However, this is not to negate the leadership work conducted up to then; in fact, it points to the critical role that governments can have in supporting the principles of sustainable development.

Correspondence

Any correspondence should be directed to Pam Wight & Associates, Tourism Consultants, 14715-82 Avenue, Edmonton, Alberta, Canada T5R 3R7 (pamwight@superiway.net).

References

Alberta Economic Development and Tourism (1993) *Tourism 2000 – A Vision for the Future – a Strategy for Tourism in Alberta*. Edmonton: Author.

Alberta Economic Development and Tourism (1994) *Environmentally Sensitive Facilities: Remote Tourism Case Studies*. Edmonton: Development Services Branch.

Alberta Environmental Protection, Community Development and Economic Development and Tourism (1993) *Developing your Wildlife-viewing Site*. Edmonton: Author.

Alberta Tourism (1990) *Sustainable Development and Tourism. Hotline* (pp. 1–2). Edmonton: Alberta Tourism Pulse.

Burr, S.W. (1994) Sustainable tourism development and use: Follies, foibles, and practical approaches. In S.F. McCool and A.E. Watson (eds) *Linking Tourism, the Environment, and Sustainability* (pp. 8–13). Papers compiled from a session of the National Recreation and Park Association, Minneapolis, 12–14 October. General Technical Report INT-GTR-323. Ogden, UT: USDA, Forest Service.

Card, F.A. and Vogelsong, M.J. (1994) Ecotourism as a mechanism for economic enhancement in developing countries. In S.F. McCool and A.E. Watson (eds) *Linking Tourism, the Environment, and Sustainability* (pp. 57–60). Papers compiled from a session of the National Recreation and Park Association, Minneapolis, 12–14 October. General Technical Report INT-GTR-323. Ogden, UT: USDA, Forest Service.

Cole, D.N., Petersen, M.E. and Lucas, R.C. (1987) *Managing Wilderness Recreation Use: Common Problems and Potential Solutions*. General Technical Report INT-230. Ogden, UT: USDA Forest Service.

Commonwealth of Australia (1991) *Ecologically Sustainable Development Working Groups: Final Report – Tourism*. Canberra: Government of Australia.

Cook, S.D., Stewart, E., Repass, K. and US Travel Data Center (1992) *Discover America: Tourism and the Environment*. Washington, DC: Travel Industry Association of America.

Costanza, R. (1991) The ecological economics of sustainability: Investing in natural capital. In R. Goodland, H. Daly and S.E. Serafy (eds) *Environmentally Sustainable Economic Development: Building on Brundtland* (pp. 72–79). Environment Working Paper No. 46. Washington, DC: World Bank.

Cottonwood Consultants, Gaia Consultants and HLA Consultants (1992) *Ecotourism Potential in Northern Alberta*. Edmonton: Alberta Tourism, Parks and Recreation.

English Tourist Board, Rural Development Commission and Countryside Commission (1991) *The Green Light – A Guide to Sustainable Tourism*. Edmonton: Author.

Fyfe, D. (1992) The challenge of changing markets and expectations relative to the environment. Paper presented to the Tourism Stream of GLOBE'92 conference, Vancouver, BC, 15–20 March.

Goodno, J.B. (1993) Leaves rate Thai hotels on ecology. *Hotel and Motel Management* 208 (8), 52.

Government of Alberta (1995) *Special Places 2000 – Alberta's Natural Heritage*. Edmonton: Alberta Environmental Protection.

HBT AGRA Earth and Environmental Group (1992) *Ecotourism Comparables Study*. Edmonton: Alberta Tourism.

Hennessy, M.B. (1991) Limiting use in wilderness areas: Internal and external controls. *Western Wildlands* 16 (4),18–22.

Hinch, T.D. and Slack, T. (1997) Restructuring tourist organizations: Implications for peripheral regions. *Journal of Applied Recreation Research* 22 (4), 276–92.

HLA Consultants (1994) *Tour Operator Market for Alberta Ecotourism Experiences*. Edmonton: Alberta Economic Development and Tourism.

HLA Consultants, Gaia Consultants and Cottonwood Consultants (1990) *Marketing Watchable Wildlife Tourism in Alberta*. Edmonton: Alberta Tourism and Alberta Forestry, Lands and Wildlife.

HLA Consultants and Pam Wight and Associates (1997) *Alberta Community Wildlife Viewing Initiative: A Strategy Document*. Edmonton: North America Waterfowl Management Plan Centre.

HLA Consultants and ARA Consulting (1994) Ecotourism – nature, adventure culture: Alberta and British Columbia market demand assessment. Prepared for Canadian Heritage, Industry Canada, BC Small Business, Tourism and Culture, Alberta Economic Development and Tourism, and the Outdoor Recreation Council of BC.

HLA Consultants, Butler Krebes and Associates and Gaia Consultants (1995) *Beaverhill Lake Visitor Management Plan*. Edmonton: Alberta Economic Development and Tourism.

Hunter, C. (1995) On the need to re-conceptualize sustainable tourism development. *Journal of Sustainable Tourism* 3 (3), 155–65.

Hunter, C. (1997) Sustainable tourism as an adaptive paradigm. *Annals of Tourism Research* 24 (4), 850–67.

Illich, I. (1989) The shadow our future throws. *New Perspectives Quarterly* 6 (1).

Ingram, C.D. and Durst, P.B. (1989) Nature-oriented tour operators: Travel to developing countries. *Journal of Travel Research* 28 (2), 11–15.

James, D.E., Nijkamp, P. and Opschoor, J.B. (1989) Ecological sustainability and economic development. In F. Archibugi and P. Nijkamp (eds) *Economy and Ecology: Toward Sustainable Development* (pp. 27–48). Boston: Kluwer Academic Publishers.

Manecon Partnership (1991) *Wildlife Viewing in Alberta: A Survey of Interests and Involvement*. Edmonton: Alberta Forestry, Lands and Wildlife, Alberta Tourism, Alberta Recreation and Parks.

McCool, S.F. (1991) Limits of acceptable change: A strategy for managing the effects of nature-dependent tourism development. Paper presented at Tourism and the land: Building a common future conference. Whistler, BC, 1–3 December.

Morton, T. (1993) Veneto hoteliers heed environment's call. *Hotel and Motel Management* 208 (8), 44.

Nor'wester Energy Systems, MPE Engineering and Willow Root Environmental (1994) *Alternative and Minimum Impact Technologies for Remote Tourism Developments*. Edmonton: Alberta Economic Development and Tourism.

Public Advisory Committees to the Environment Council of Alberta (1990) *Alberta Conservation Strategy: Framework for Action*. A draft for public discussion. Edmonton: Environment Council of Alberta.

Scace, R.C., Griffone, E. and Usher, R. (1992) *Ecotourism in Canada*. Hull, Quebec: Canadian Environmental Advisory Council.

Tourism Industry Association of Canada (TIAC) (1992) *Code of Ethics and Guidelines for Sustainable Tourism*. Ottawa: TIAC and National Round Table on Environment and the Economy.

Wall, G. (1992) *Key Challenges – What do they Mean to the Industry?* Panel discussion, Tourism Stream of GLOBE'92 conference, Vancouver, BC, 15–20 March.

Western, D. (1993) Defining ecotourism. In K. Lindbergh and D.E. Hawkins (eds) *Ecotourism: A Guide for Planners and Managers* (pp. 7–11). North Bennington, VT: Ecotourism Society.

Wight, P.A. (1990) Tourism-recreation EIAs in Alberta: A need for an integrated approach in legislation, environmental assessment, and development planning. Paper presented at the 12th International Seminar on Environmental Assessment and Management, Centre for Environmental Management and Planning, Aberdeen.

Wight, P.A. (1993) Sustainable ecotourism: Balancing economic, environmental and social goals within an ethical framework. *Journal of Tourism Studies* 4 (2), 54–66.

Wight, P.A. (1994) Limits of acceptable change: A recreational tourism tool for cumulative effects assessment. In A.J. Kennedy (ed) *Cumulative Effects Assessment in Canada: From Concept to Practice* (pp. 159–78). Papers from the 15th Symposium held by the Alberta Society of Professional Biologists, Calgary.

Wight, P.A. (1996) Planning for success in sustainable tourism. Invited paper presented to Plan for Success Canadian Institute of Planners National Conference, Saskatoon, Saskatchewan, 2–5 June.

Wight, P.A. (1998a) Greening of remote tourism lodges. In M.E. Johnston, G.D. Twynam and W. Haider (eds) *Shaping Tomorrow's North: The Role of Tourism and Recreation* (pp. 148–64). Thunder Bay, ON: Lakehead University.

Wight, P.A. (1998b) Tools for sustainability analysis in planning and managing tourism and recreation in the destination. In C.M. Hall and A.A. Lew (eds) *Sustainable Tourism: A Geographical Perspectives* (pp. 75 – 91). Harlow: Addison, Wesley Longman.

Williams, P.W. and Gill, A. (1991) *Carrying Capacity Management in Tourism Settings: A Tourism Growth Management Process*. Edmonton: Alberta Tourism.

World Commission on Environment and Development (1987) *Our Common Future*. WCED. New York: Oxford University Press.

World Conservation Union (IUCN), United Nations Environment Programme and the World Wide Fund for Nature (1990) *Caring for the World: A Strategy for Sustainability*. Gland, Switzerland: IUCN.

World Tourism Organization, United Nations Environment Programme and IUCN (1992) *Guidelines: Development of National Parks and Protected Areas for Tourism*. Technical Report No. 13. Madrid: WTO/UNEP.

Yee, J. (1992) *Ecotourism Market Survey: A Survey of North American Ecotourism Operators*. San Francisco: Intelligence Centre, Pacific Asia Travel Association.

NGO-Community Collaboration for Ecotourism: A Strategy for Sustainable Regional Development

David Barkin
Universidad Autónoma Metropolitaria-Xochimilco, Calzada del Hueso 1100, 04960 Coyoacán, DF, Mexico

Carlos Paillés Bouchez
Centro de Soporte Ecológico Bahias de Huatulco Costa de Oxaca, Bahia Sta Cruz, 210, Bahidas de Huatulco, Oax 70989, Mexico

An inappropriate mega-tourist project dramatically threatened the communities and ecosystems at Bahias de Huatulco, a beautiful site on the Pacific coast of Oaxaca, Mexico. The indigenous communities in the neighbouring highlands suffered, first as their forests were logged, and then by the economic pressures and cultural onslaught from globalised tourist development. An environmentally sensitive programme to emplace an infrastructure to provide ecotourism services, supported by the traditional beach-front tourist industry, offers a mechanism to strengthen the social organisation and the economic base of the participating communities. Together with complementary activities to rehabilitate and better manage the forests, to introduce artisanal activities and create a local wildlife reserve, ecotourism is stimulating conservation efforts and sustainable management and production practices. By introducing these alternatives to the marginal economic opportunities offered by the beach tourism, the local peoples enjoy a higher quality of life and are better insulated from the cyclical swings in the national and international economy that are taking a high toll on peoples elsewhere.

Introduction

In 1984, a mega-resort, designed to attract beach tourism to international hotels, was initiated on the south Pacific coast of Mexico in the state of Oaxaca. Known as the Bahias de Huatulco, the spectacular setting, in a previously isolated region, is home to about 50,000 people from four different indigenous groups living in some 150 subsistence communities widely dispersed over 700,000 hectares in the surrounding highlands and a number of small fishing villages. The new mega-resort and the accompanying infrastructure integrated the region into the international market, sparking a self-reinforcing cycle of speculation and investment that accelerated the process of social and spatial polarisation, impoverishing the native populations and raising tensions throughout the region; the destruction wrought by hurricane Paulina in October 1997 suddenly intensified the problems of poverty and environmental destruction. Even before the disaster, a local non-governmental organisation (NGO), the Centre for Ecological Support (CSE, for its Spanish initials), created in 1993 to promote regional development, had begun to implement a resource management programme for sustainable development, by channelling domestic and international resources to attack these problems with a series of productive programmes designed to stem environmental degradation and strengthen the economy.

The isolated existence of the indigenous people who lived in the Huatulco region was violently transformed when the narrow coastal strip (about 30 km) was expropriated by the Mexican Tourist Development Fund (FONATUR) in the early 1980s for a transnational beach tourism project. After pushing them from their small fishing villages, little thought was given to the local population; construction attracted workers of all sorts along with other people seeking their fortunes from other parts of Mexico. For more than 10 years, social tensions rose as five large hotels and many smaller installations were built; menial jobs were offered to the natives who had taken refuge in the larger settlements dispersed in the surrounding mountain communities or in the shanty towns that sprouted to attend to the demands of the new industry. The prevailing pattern of polarising development characteristic of the rest of Mexico became firmly entrenched in this area, with a small, prosperous beach-front community coexisting alongside makeshift facilities for the service workers; the local communities increasingly found themselves in dire straits, as national policy discriminated against rural production in general and poor, small-scale farmers in particular.

In this article we will examine the creative role of a local NGO in promoting an alternative approach to development that might contribute to reconciling the conflicting interests in the region. By explicitly recognising the special role that NGOs can play in facilitating community participation, the CSE has facilitated the interaction of groups from different cultural backgrounds and social classes in what promises to be an innovative programme of diversified development in which environmental tourism will play a fundamental part.

The River Basins around Bahias de Huatulco

In 1958, the landscape of the coast of Oaxaca, seen from the peaks of the Sierra Sur, was that of multiple greenish tones, contrasting with the multiple bluish tones of the Pacific Ocean. In the river basin feeding the coastal aquifer, minor breaks of less than 5% in the tropical dry forest included traditional fields of corn, beans and fruit trees. The coffee areas were covered by the canopies of shade trees. Forty years later, the forest coverage had been reduced by 50%; only 20% resembled its former condition, while the rest suffered from a partial extraction of its timber resources. During the past 15 years the rate of deforestation doubled that of the previous 25 years.

These tropical dry forests are one of the most fragile ecosystems in the world and are rapidly disappearing. Historically, the inherited culture of forest management within the coastal communities has been eroded by an antiquated and venal commercial structure. In spite of sustained demand for tropical hardwoods and attractive prices for species such as rosewood and lignum vitae, a complex and costly system of intermediation discouraged communal planting and conservation and forced more intensive exploitation by drastically reducing local prices. Tourist development induced a heavy flow of migrants from the central highlands and other regions to the coast, overwhelming communal management practices that defined and restricted access to the forests.

Two thirds of this destruction is due to the 'walking milpa' (the system of slash- and burn-cultivation that encroaches on the forest for the short term planting of corn and associated crops) and agrochemicals. The other third is mostly due to the illegal cutting of trees encouraged by developers of the tourist corridor from Huatulco to Puerto Escondido. Devastation of the forests has been followed by the erosion of the soil and the final result is critical: the water supply to the Bahias de Huatulco tourist development area will be exhausted by the year 2020, unless some regeneration programme is implemented.[1]

Most people in the region are still not even aware of the depths of the impending crisis. International integration assures regular supplies of lumber and food at prices that do not reflect their real costs: producers are poorly paid, water wasted and the environment despoiled. Consumers have become accustomed to these subsidies from the poor, from a clientelist political structure and from nature; in the process, peasants have been forced to eke out an existence, dismembering their communities and devastating their environment. So absurd is the process that the new hotels elected to import rolls of carpet grass from the centre of the country rather than seed new lawns in Huatulco, as if the region's abundant natural and human resources were not relevant. Even water appears as a gift from heaven: in Huatulco, urban consumers receive it free and, although they complain, the hotels are charged only a fraction of what they would pay in other international resorts. Underpriced resources for the privileged urban population are yet another signal discouraging peasant society from continuing its arduous task of environmental management, truncating its time-honoured commitment to assure water for their children and their grandchildren. In the end this combination of factors contributes to a self-devaluation within peasant society, a seemingly irreversible loss of self-esteem.[2]

To add insult to injury, in 1997, hurricane Paulina destroyed six or seven million trees, increasing desertification in the river courses by 80% and damaging two thirds of the peasant homes. But it also instilled a renewed sense of responsibility towards nature in most of those communities that had been able to maintain communal organisations. This is the basis for the growing enthusiasm of the communities to participate in the regeneration activities.

Communal Organisation and the CSE: A Complex History of Accommodation for Development

Unlike many other groups in Mexico and Latin America, the communities in this part of Oaxaca have strong communal organisations. In spite of having origins in four different ethnic groups, each with its own language and cultural patterns, all of the native peoples in this region share a tradition of strong collective roots based on the collective ownership and management of their land, their abiding support for local forms of communal organisation and well-engrained cultural patterns that reinforce the traditional mechanisms of decision making, known as 'uses and customs'. These communities have struggled through the centuries to defend their homelands against outside invaders, be they other Meso-American groups, the Spanish conquerors, or the new powers from a modernising nation. Even as they developed relationships with these outsiders, they managed to defend substantial areas of community life and decision making from attempts to dictate the terms of their submission or fuller integration into alien societies.

When the government decided to create the resort development, the Oaxacan natives were rudely shunted aside. Expelled from their coastal communities, even the meagre compensations promised for expropriations were rarely paid. Uncomprehending and without alternatives, many of those who resisted were slaughtered in the unrelenting drive to push forward with the programme. Developers moved in with impunity, backed by military might and a political commitment to forge a beach-front paradise. It is no wonder, then, that as the hotels were inaugurated and menial employment offered, many in the region chose to remain in their communities while a few migrated further afield in search of better opportunities. Traditional authorities and elders counselled against integration, moving to reinforce local options.

The CSE was created sometime after the first large hotels were inaugurated in the new resort. Cognisant of the underlying conflicts that permeated the region, the NGO carved out a niche for itself: working with the native communities to regenerate some of the smaller river basins in the region as part of a broader effort to promote community welfare, through the rehabilitation of the tropical dry forests, replanting denuded areas with native species of trees with cultural and commercial value. It started to work with the communities to implement a diversified development programme in which the forests would play a central role, but where complementary activities would offer an essential economic underpinning to ensure its economic viability and guarantee sufficient opportunities to persuade people to remain and strengthen confidence in community governance and management capabilities.

The complementary activities envisioned in the CSE programme included ecotourism, a renewed emphasis on production of basic foods for local consumption, and commercial production of goods and services for local and specialised foreign markets. The new strategy was anchored in a carefully designed programme to use reforestation as the centre of a programme to rebuild the deteriorated watershed that would be the foundation of a stronger productive system in the region, a prerequisite for supporting the local communities and their cultures. This approach was designed to create a favourable environment to attract visitors who might be interested in a variety of ecotourism offerings; these would be owned and managed by the indigenous communities participating in the programme and sensitive to the natural heritage that they were rescuing and preserving.

The CSE's initial diagnosis of the local ecosystems confirmed its early analysis that the unusual tropical dry forests presented a unique challenge for rehabilitation and conservation. The early decision to organise the work on the basis of water basins proved crucial, as the nurseries and new plantings required regular flows of water or irrigation; pruning and other cultivation practices were implemented through a process of joint administration in which outside experts shared their knowledge with the natives who applied their inherited learning about the region. A new diversified mixture of species began to thrive with unexpectedly high growth rates. From the very beginning, bungalows were constructed as part of the programme, creating an opportunity for offering some ecotourism services as part of an effort to demonstrate that the local cultures were also of interest to people from far afield, and that local practices for managing and conserving the environment were valued by others who would be willing to pay for the privilege of visiting the area.

The CSE participates in these programmes through a series of trust funds that are administered through a tripartite structure. The indigenous authorities charged with the management of community property and local political representatives join with the NGO to implement decisions about how governmental programmes and outside assistance will be applied within each community. One of the programmes that has been in operation longest illustrates how the process works: the Magdalena River Programme includes a broad series of activities that include the monitoring of aquifers, protection of the integrity of river beds and banks from erosion, reforestation through new planting, soil stabilisation and protection, water conservation, sustainable agriculture, reuse of agricultural and forest waste products, infrastructure for environmental tourism, and community environmental education. A long period was required to implement this programme, developing the mechanisms for communication with the communities and overcoming the historical pattern of paternalism by which outside assistance was transferred to such groups in return for political support without a corresponding opportunity for local participation and without any meaningful consultation about the programmes' design or implementation.

The devastating hurricane Paulina hit the region in autumn 1997. It proved to be a turning point, demonstrating the effectiveness of many of the CSE programmes and identifying design weaknesses of some of the conservation and construction practices. The storm destroyed millions of trees, accelerating the process of desertification while demonstrating the urgency for increasing the scale and intensity of the rehabilitation and diversification programmes. The tragedy catalysed the communities, leading to the consolidation of more communal assemblies that began to demand assistance, effectively transferring the initiative from a lethargic bureaucracy to the local groups anxious to initiate their own programmes with the resources that might otherwise have been siphoned off by ineffective governmental agencies.

Although the destruction wreaked in the highland communities was serious, it turned out that the crisis on the coast would prove more worrisome in the long term. As a result of the hurricane, and the river basin approach adopted by the CSE, the NGO began to examine the coastal aquifer closely, revealing a serious shortfall that would leave the tourist economy without local supplies of drinking water in less than a quarter of a century if corrective measures were not implemented. This alarming finding was denied by the official water agency, but most other official organisations joined in supporting the CSE efforts to broaden the scope of its programme to prepare to confront the impending crisis.

The Forging of a Sustainable Development Strategy

With the disaster, the CSE perceived an opportunity to undertake a more ambitious programme for the region as a whole. (The principles of sustainability on which this project is based are discussed at length in Barkin (1998).)Federal agencies quickly took advantage of the Centre's presence and capabilities to charge it with intermediate-term responsibilities for reconstruction, once the emergency disaster relief programmes were terminated. A history of bureaucratic bungling placed the NGO in a favourable position to complement the river basin project with a far more ambitious reforestation programme that would replant target areas with a view to restoring biodiversity, a concern of people within the communities, while ensuring that some of the species serve the demands of the marketplace. The forestry programme was conceived of as part of a broader programme for regional development and environmental protection. Because economic and social viability was a criterion from the beginning, technological innovations associated with existing market opportunities will allow wood products and derivatives rather than raw trees to be marketed, creating more employment and generating greater value for the communities. This is a fundamental feature of the programme, since these communities have suffered from unfavourable conditions for their products for decades – if not centuries as the market works to exacerbate the discrimination imposed by society against indigenous groups and peasants, placing a low value on their labour, their resources and the products of their work.

The reforestation programme differs dramatically from similar programmes elsewhere. The first round of plantations resulted in germination rates exceeding 90% for the several species and replanting brought the effective rate to virtually 100%. The selection of varieties, the techniques used and the anticipated marketing opportunities are creating an extraction profile that will allow the first harvest of smaller trees only five years after the initial effort. In the meanwhile, the planting of other areas, the construction of bungalows, and other activities will assume increasing importance in the region.

The organisational structure is also innovative. The CSE is a constitutive part of several local trust funds that integrate governmental agencies, the communities and the private sector into the programme. Although some local business groups have made contributions to local public relations efforts, only the Sheraton Hotel has offered substantial direct support for the conservation activities; it is remarkable that the other international chain, ClubMed, has resisted participating even in promotional activities. The operating Trust Fund, charged with the eventual coordination of the individual enterprises that are being established by the communities themselves (including a pure water bottling plant and the ecotourism project) has established a formula that attempts to create a solid foundation for future activities: prices for goods and services, while remaining competitive, must be sufficient not only to cover the direct costs of production, but also contribute to a fund for additional activities in the community and environmental programmes in the region as a whole; at present, the division is a third going to each part. This is the essence of the international 'fair trade' movement.

During the initial stages, the communities have displayed a remarkable capacity to integrate these programmes into their existing structures. The assemblies where the initiatives are discussed reveal that their forefathers regularly engaged in such activities; we discovered that forest protection and replanting brigades used the same seed collection techniques and planting methods that are now being (re)introduced. This same process of interaction with the regional supervisors reveals the importance of water management and protection activities in the communities in past epochs, tasks that have been neglected as discriminatory governmental policies have forced the peasants to search for income and employment in nearby towns or even in the USA to ensure the viability of their communities and the survival of their families.

The present programme envisages an eventual charge to the coastal communities to cover part of the costs of the environmental services being provided through the regeneration of the river basin. At present, this cannot be implemented because the water system is controlled by the government tourism agency which has not been able to fulfil its promises to deliver a high-quality product; compounding the problem, the hydraulic infrastructure is not well maintained. In fact, at present the local Chamber of Commerce considers the lack of an adequate water supply to be a major obstacle blocking the construction of at least a dozen new hotel projects in the area. Once the communities have demonstrated their ability and willingness to maintain their systems, as well as their effectiveness in reducing the damage from seasonal rains, it is expected that the local authorities will be able to include a charge for these environmental services for large-scale users. In the interim, other mechanisms are being explored as a way of explicitly integrating the coastal beneficiaries into the programme. They are expected to provide some support for the ecotourism activities; future programmes include reserves for native flora and fauna, with the possibility of areas for larger mammals, once common in the zone. The communities will shortly begin developing a dependable capacity to supply fruits and vegetables to the hotels, and contracts that will compensate the communities correctly for the real costs of production, including fair wages for the workers and a charge for the environmental services that are normally not included by the market. The opening of channels for regional discussions of activities that will increase the overall attractiveness of the area for visitors in a sustainable fashion is a fundamental part of the collaboration among dissimilar groups, and essential for the long-term consolidation of the CSE agenda.

The Role of Ecotourism

From the very beginning, it was clear that tourism might play an important part of the resource management programme. The communities would be able to offer a variety of nature tourism and similar activities as part of a diversified regional development effort. The CSE initiated preparations by designing bungalows that could be built by the communities. Local promoters were already helping people to integrate this type of activity into community life, encouraging women to think about preparing traditional meals, and helping men to improve their skills to ensure that the construction would offer a quality service. When the hurricane struck several of the buildings were destroyed or collapsed, forcing design modifications that produced a more solid and attractive structure.

If this activity is to be successful, however, many more cottages will have to be built throughout the larger river basin. Careful thought is being given to the carrying capacity of each area within the region, and the ability of the people in the communities to provide the range of services that will be offered to the visitors, without threatening the structure of local life and production. Some of the local tourist promoters (including one of the hotels) have agreed to participate by channelling some of their own clients into these facilities on attractive terms that will assure the communities a steady flow of income and gainful employment consistent with strengthening local institutions.

The CSE is proceeding cautiously. The tropical dry forest ecosystem is a fragile environment: its preservation and protection require an infrastructure to assure healthy growth; visitors will have to be carefully guided through the region, constructing trails and training local people on how best to share their knowledge with the visitors. Once initiated, the temptation to attract large groups presents a permanent threat to the project, the ecosystem and the communities themselves: the steady progress in incorporating the communities into the development of a variety of smaller enterprises is part of the long-term process of creating appropriate conditions for the communities to begin direct control the activities.

Today's efforts to rehabilitate the region and create the foundations of a basic infrastructure are being financed with development assistance funds from the national government and international sources. The move to a commercial stage will require different sources of capital: there is no lack of outside investors interested in financing this project. Here the CSE again views its role as more than that of a promoter; it is not simply attempting to create opportunities so that the communities can take advantage of a potential market. The local hotels have expressed their willingness to support the implementation of the overall resource management programme through the ecotourism activities. Some of the more visionary hoteliers have begun to realise that this offering can complement rather than detract from their own markets and have accepted the position of the CSE that community ownership and control is an essential building block to ensure the viability of the overall reconstruction programme. The main challenge will be to control this development so that it is a complementary part of the larger programme, rather than one that dominates and subsumes the communities and their ecosystems to the short-term demands of a sometimes fickle market.

A review of many ecotourism projects in Mexico and Central America reveals their destructive impacts on local processes of sustainable advance. In fact, one of the areas that attracts the largest number of nature tourists in Mexico, the reserve of the monarch butterfly, is actually in the throes of a process of impoverishment because the local population has not been allowed to participate directly in creating adequate facilities to offer the more than 200,000 visitors who visit the area during the four-month period when the lepidopters nest there (Bartin, 1999). Other projects offer crass distortions of the concept, like the site advertised as 'Nature's Sacred Paradise'; it displaced local Mayan communities, dynamited sacred wells, and illegally keeps endangered species in captivity, to attract visitors to its lucrative 'ecotourism' theme park in Quintana Roo. The difficulties of combining local participation with a socially and environmentally balanced programme that also produces a profit create a constant tension that provokes conflicts among groups with the best of intentions.[3] The CSE model on the coast of Oaxaca offers a promising alternative, by inserting an ecotourism component into a broader project of community-directed regional resource management, that offers essential environmental benefits to every social group in the area.

Correspondence

Any correspondence should be directed to Prof. David Barkin, Universidad Autónoma Metropolitana-Xochimilco, Calzada del Hueso 1100, 04960 Coyoacán, D.F., Mexico (barkin@cueyatl.uam.mx).

Notes

1. Data collected from the battery of wells that supply water to the coastal areas showed a 26% decline in the levels of the aquifers between 1986 and 1992. Extrapolation of this trend leaves insufficient water for cost-effective pumping in less than a quarter century.
2. The uprising by the Zapatista Army of National Liberation in January 1994 is dramatic testimony to the depths of this process and the latent reserve of pride in this endangered heritage.
3. Ron Mader's recent tourist guides to Mexico and Honduras (Mader, 1998a, b) are a testimony to the variety of efforts and the difficulty of finding the ideal model. His constructive comments are an excellent contribution to help visitors make the most of their ecotravels.

References

Barkin, D. (1998) *Wealth, Poverty and Sustainable Development*. Mexico: Editorial Jus.

Barkin, D. (1999) The economic impact of ecotourism. Conflicts and solutions in highland Mexico. In P.M. Godde, M.F. Price and F.M. Zimmerman (eds) *Tourism and Development in Mountain Arias* (pp. 157–172). London: CAB International.

Mader, R. (1998a) *Adventures in Nature* (Mexico). Santa Fe, NM: John Muir Publications.

Mader, R. (1998b) *Adventures in Nature* (Honduras). Santa Fe, NM: John Muir Publications.

Endangered Visitors: A Phenomenological Study of Eco-Resort Development

W. Glen Croy

Department of Tourism, School of Business, University of Otago, Dunedin, New Zealand

Lise Høgh

School of Tourism and Hospitality, Waiariki Institute of Technology, Rotorua, New Zealand

With the growing awareness of eco-tourism and the development of infrastructure at attractions, it has become necessary to use best practices to reduce the impact of increased visitor numbers. It has been noted that many of the past and current developments of eco-tourism infrastructures have been made in an improvised manner resulting in unsustainable practices. This study highlights the current planning trends in the ad hoc development of eco-resorts through a phenomenological approach. The methodology applied qualitative research methods to examine university students' understanding of eco-resort development and best practice. The use of an eco-resort development exercise on a fictional Peruvian site was the basis of analysis. The content of planned developments by the respondents and their experience of eco-tourism formed significant results. Results showed a difference between a theoretical definition and the application in practice, which could lead to eco-tourism being defined out of existence.

Introduction

In recent years, enjoying and learning about the natural environment has become increasingly popular as a tourist motivation.

> The idea of visiting and experiencing high quality natural environments and also protecting them from harmful impacts is now an acceptable and marketable one. (Orams, 1995: 3)

The rise of interest in the ecological estate has increased as tourists are looking for alternative quality experiences that are educational and cultural (Collier, 1996). However, 'a large number of travellers all over the world cause different kinds of physical and social impacts on the environment' (Lück, 1998: 154). Because of this increasing popularity, many eco-friendly businesses have emerged to cater for the demand. Unfortunately, many businesses are not always totally environmentally aware (Wight, 1993). Whilst organisations have their business in an environment that is highly susceptible to impacts, there may be infrastructure or management systems in place that are not environmentally friendly. For example, ecologically untrained tour drivers in Amboseli National Park, Kenya, have been allowed to dictate their own viewing patterns. This has contributed to a pattern of off-road vehicular traffic that has created massive environmental impacts in the park (Environmental Tourist, 1991; Weaver, 1998).

Eco-tourism could be regarded as the most sustainable tourism venture through the eyes of the tourist. This is because, in theory, eco-resorts practise sustainability through careful management to reduce the impact of visitors on the site and environment. This paper discusses the best practices of eco-tourism. It begins with definitions of eco-tourism, green holidays, eco-resorts, and will then discuss the benefits of eco-tourism and planning in the environment. The authors will also discuss the best practices for eco-tourism, applying a study of university students' planning and development of an eco-resort in Peru.

Eco-tourism has been studied intensively over the years (for example, Budowski, 1976; Ceballos-Lascurain, 1991; Lindberg & Hawkins, 1993; Orams, 1995; Ross & Wall, 1999; Warren & Taylor, 1994). These authors have discussed what eco-tourism is and have come up with various answers denoting the difficulty in establishing a standard definition. However, they all have in common the tourist experiencing the natural environment and the need to protect it from the impact of those visitors. Eco-tourism is in its infancy, it is a new trend, a fashion, and is now becoming a huge money earner whilst attempting to sustain and protect the natural environment for future generations. Indeed, many eco-resorts and eco-tourist operations have started up in the last 10–15 years, as the demand for a 'green holiday' has become more popular.

Collier (1996: 276) suggests 'A green holiday ... is nature orientated, active, educational and tucked away harmoniously in the countryside; it emphasises environmental education and protection.' Many tourists are partaking in some sort of eco-friendly activity while on holiday (Simon, 1991). The green holidayers could be partaking in an eco-tour to look at wildlife, undertaking bush-walks and nature walks to learn about the flora of the area or sailing to places that people have had little contact with. For example, visiting the Royal Albatross Colony at Tairoa Head near Dunedin, New Zealand, picking up rubbish at Mount Everest Base-Camp in Nepal, or diving off the coral reefs of Belize.

Eco-resorts are where the tourist is offered the whole eco-experience. Not only is the sightseeing eco-friendly, but their accommodation, transport and cooking methods are also eco-friendly. Using solar heating, having bio-toilets, and using transport systems more efficiently are all eco-friendly examples put to use to reduce the effect of people on the environment. This, however, is difficult to achieve. Indeed many eco-resort operators advertise that they are eco-friendly, yet they have components in their business that may be questionable (Bottrill & Pearce, 1995; Lawrence *et al.*, 1997).

The eco-tourists' travel motivations to visit these resorts have also been studied extensively in the literature (Crossley & Lee, 1994; Eagles, 1992; Fennel & Smale, 1992; Kretchman & Eagles, 1990). Motivations include to learn about nature, to be physically active, to meet people with similar interests, experience new lifestyles, be daring or adventurous, to escape from everyday life and to learn and experience native culture. Nevertheless, any visit to an environmentally susceptible site will have impacts.

The impacts of eco-tourism

Many authors have discussed the costs and benefits of eco-tourism in depth (Briassoulis, 1992; Gilbert, 1997; Lindberg, 1991; Lindberg & McKercher, 1997; Ross & Wall, 1999; Weaver, 1998; Wood & House, 1992). Weaver (1998) divides the costs and benefits into three groups: environmental impacts, economic impacts and socio-cultural impacts. The main focus of eco-tourism is the environment. Environmental impacts of eco-tourism have been stated as both positive and negative. The positive environmental benefits include preserving natural and semi-natural environments and restoring and converting modified habitats back to their original state. The negative environmental impacts include the danger that carrying capacities will be unintentionally exceeded due to rapid growth rates, and fragile areas may be exposed to less benign forms of tourism resulting in the loss of species. Because of this, sustainable management procedures have to be introduced.

Sustainable eco-tourism management

> Many tour operators have contended themselves with buying up tracts of forest where they can build a lodge, locate a few jungle trails, hire a few locals and then claim that they are doing their share to save the rain forest and, ... it can be called eco-tourism. (Moore, 1991: 563)

The need for planning is becoming more important as increasing numbers of people become interested in the natural environment and are, therefore, having an impact on this environment (Andersen, 1993; Barnao, 1994; Boyd & Butler, 1996). Where a narrow dirt track may have sufficed earlier, a wider, gravel or tar-seal track may be required. Camping sites that were previously appropriate, may have to be upgraded to include permanent accommodation, toilets, water facilities, and regular clean-ups may be required in places where there was little previous impact. In effect, the attraction may become endangered to the extent that species may be lost, and the area loses its appeal to visitors (Boyd & Butler, 1996; Davis & Harriott, 1996; Krippendorf, 1982; Lawrence *et al.*, 1997). Therefore, 'considerations for sustainability need to be taken for the protection and preservation of the resources as well as for the experiences and benefits visitors demand from the site' (Croy, 1998: 14)

The aim of eco-tourism is to be sustainable and protective of the natural environment. 'Tourism has the potential to act as a force to conserve natural resources' (Budowski, 1976: 27). However, it is difficult to do this when just one person can have an immeasurable negative effect on an environment. Protected areas are becoming more important worldwide as native forests dwindle (Environmental Tourist, 1991). There is an imperative need to protect the flora and fauna or lose them forever as species become extinct. Protected areas can keep species flourishing, whilst teaching visitors, readers and viewers about the special flora and fauna in them, for example, the Gannet colony at Cape Kidnappers, New Zealand, or the rainforest in Belize. The increasing popularity of eco-ventures in protected areas are attracting more people, who are demanding quality infrastructure.

> If eco-tourism is to contribute favourably to conservation in general and protected areas in particular, there must be a much greater emphasis on managing the natural resource which is the basis for it. (Moore, 1991: 564)

Management systems need to be put in place to educate visitors for the aim to protect these areas (Croy, 1998). Managers of the protected areas, tourism operators, local authorities, community members and government need to develop co-operative management strategies to plan for the sustainability of these areas (Croy, 1998; Daniels *et al.*, 1996; Moore, 1991; Joppe, 1996; Selsky, 1991, 1997;

Weaver, 1998; Wendt, 1991). Boyd and Butler (1994) outlined a model that combined all stakeholders and decision-makers in an eco-tourism situation. The model included members from the tourism industry, resource-based industry, private agencies, local communities and political authorities.

Managers and planners need to consider many questions concerning accessibility, concessions, permissible activities, zoning, carrying capacity, education, safety and types of infrastructure when developing and managing an eco-resort. Numerous authors have discussed strategies to sustain eco-tourism in environmental areas (Boo, 1993; Duffus & Dearden, 1990; Holmes, 1993; Moore & Carter, 1993; Orams, 1996). Moore and Carter (1993) discuss various management options that result in the protection and sustainability of resource areas. A long-term strategic plan is necessary to integrate the most appropriate management systems and operational plans for the subject area (Croy, 1998; Moore, 1991). Finding the 'best practice' for these management systems can take a long time. However, it is worthwhile to keep the area in a relatively pristine condition for future generations to enjoy (Krippendorf, 1991).

Tour operators must also have a plan to reduce the impact of visitors to eco-resort areas. Sirakaya (1997) outlines the Eco-tourism Society's (1991) guidelines for nature tour operators. These include: first, preparation of travellers before departure to minimise their negative impacts while visiting sensitive environments and cultures; second, minimising visitor impacts on the environment by offering literature, briefings, leading by example and taking corrective actions; third, for resort managers to be a contributor to the conservation of the region being visited; fourth, the use of adequate leadership and maintaining small enough groups to ensure minimum group impact on destinations; fifth, avoid areas that are under-managed and over-visited; finally, offer site-sensitive accommodations that are not wasteful of local resources or destructive to the environment. Accommodation that also provides ample opportunity for learning about the environment and sensitive interchange with local communities is recommended. Oastler (1994) also discusses what the eco-tourist should look for in an operation using the term 'eco-tour' with similar findings to the aforementioned research.

Various authors have discussed the 'best practices' of eco-tourism (Commonwealth Department of Tourism, 1995; Dowling, 1997; Inskeep, 1987; Ioannides, 1995; Kusler, 1991; Orams, 1995; Ross & Wall, 1999; Tisdell, 1996). Many note that it is difficult to achieve total eco-practices in application. They also discuss what management systems should be put into practice but few discuss how. One of the exceptions is *Best Practice Eco-tourism: A Guide to Energy and Waste Minimisation* (Commonwealth Department of Tourism, 1995) which discusses eco-friendly practices in detail, covering areas such as transport, energy supplies and toilets to washing methods, recycling and refrigeration. The analysis of an eco-resort development exercise follows, using the above literature as a basis for the investigation.

Methodology

The methodology illustrates the phenomenological approach used, a background to the research area, the analysis of results and the results expected from the research. This research exercise was situated at a fictional inland Peruvian site, at the meeting of the Ghazali River and the Musa River. The major international recognition for this site is that it is the habitat of five endangered species in the Ghazali–Musa Swamp area. Another major attraction in the area is the Fly Falls waterfall, on the Ghazali River, a 30-metre waterfall, with the main section descending 20 metres.

The phenomenological approach used in this research reflects a study undertaken by Masberg and Silverman (1996) into students' experiences at heritage sites. The current research was developed to understand or discover the phenomenon of eco-resort planning and development, which seems to happen in an *ad hoc* manner at present. As in previous research (Beeho & Prentice, 1995, 1996, 1997; Croy, 1998; Masberg & Silverman, 1996; McIntosh, 1997a, 1997b), this research developed a phenomenological approach to meet the needs of the study: a method was adopted that allowed respondents to offer their own interpretations and explanations of both eco-tourism and eco-resort development. This divorced the study from a quantitative analysis, so typical of tourism studies, as it involved the evaluation of the exercise based on the individual's subjective interpretation of their experiences that applied. Although this research assembled individuals into random groups, the individual elements of interpretation are nonetheless exemplified in the results. The exercise involved a 'free hand' to the eco-resort development. Some infrastructure observations were made, but the inclusion, if at all, and placement was at the discretion of the 'developers'. Also, to reiterate this point, previous phenomenological studies have relied on standard circumstances. For example, Croy (1998) relied on the built heritage environment as a common theme throughout the analysis, and Masberg and Silverman (1986) presented a set list of open-ended questions to elicit results. As in previous investigations, the current research provided the information to develop an open-ended interpretation of a common theme.

Student respondents were selected as their environmental planning and development background was a purposeful attempt to replicate the 'layman's' eco-resort design training and reflect many eco-resort management structures within New Zealand and around the world. The respondents had been given six lectures on management of physical and human culture resources, including two on eco-tourism specifically. Additionally, all the respondents viewed a video (Environmental Tourist, 1991) of an ineffective example of an eco-resort, namely Amboseli National Park, Kenya, and a proactive management example of an eco-marine resort in Belize. Also, a reading on *Best Practice Eco-tourism* (Commonwealth Department of Tourism, 1995) was made available to respondents prior to the commencement of this exercise.

For this research, respondents were provided background information in the form of an information sheet (Croy & Høgh, 1999) and a map of the area (Croy, 1999, Figure 1). The information sheet described economically, socially and politically the country in which this exercise took place, namely Peru. The background information to the specific site was then introduced. This information gave a summary of the current usage, about 250 hunters and anglers by permit, plus walkers. A description of the location's scenery, spatial location, infrastructure and environmental importance was also contained. A brief background for the reasons to develop the eco-resort was also given. The key reasons given were the economic development for the local area, discontinuation of corrupt control by local government and the protection of the internationally important species in the area. The species, the Peruvian Alligator, the Pink Throated Mud Frog, the Limbani Swamp Fowl, the Piebald Pizarro Snake and the South American Mud Pike, all needing distinct yet analogous habitats. The congregation of these species was in a swamp area identified in the middle of the map provided (Figure 1). The significance of the swamp area was explicitly stated. Another reason given for the development was that the international image of Peru would be strengthened with the protection of this area. A brief summary of needs for an eco-resort was provided at the end of the information sheet. This summary was as follows:

> Facilities need to be designed and placed in the area for the tourist market. The consideration of the habitat and eco-friendly development will also be needed. Facilities that are needed include accommodation and eatery, toilets, information boards, picnic areas, viewing areas, recreation facilities, access, energy supply and so on. (Croy & Høgh, 1999)

As can be seen from the above excerpt, specific types of facilities were not mentioned. The respondents were given 15 minutes to develop their eco-resorts based on previous experience, curriculum and background information provided. This exercise was concluded with a presentation to the class, in which the developers explained their interpretations, explanations of the exercise and the eco-resort they had designed.

The results of this research analysed the placement and type of infrastructure on the map used by respondents. The map was first transposed onto a grid. The placement of infrastructure could then be analysed by specific areas. The placement of accommodation, toilets, information boards, picnic areas, viewing areas, recreation, access, energy sources and so on, were analysed separately to gain a greater insight into the development of the eco-resort. Types of recreation provided, extra access and energy sources were also analysed based on placement and impact that these expansions would create. The final analysis would provide the total placement of infrastructure for the interpretation of a 'layman's' design of an eco-resort, including facilities used and placement of these. This final analysis was compared to a 'best practice' of eco-tourism as covered in tourism literature (Commonwealth Department of Tourism, 1995; Dowling, 1997; Ioannides, 1995; Kusler, 1991; Orams, 1995; Ross & Wall, 1999; Tisdell, 1996).

Demographic questions were also asked, which were analysed separately, as group make-up was not as important as the respondent's comprehension of eco-tourism. These results included experiences in or of eco-tourism, which were analysed for individual respondent's interpretation of what is eco-tourism, rather than as a basis of appreciation of elements effecting eco-development.

The expected results from this research were not prejudged, and phenomenological research was performed in a manner wherein the authors could not predetermine scrutiny. This approach was used to gain insights and develop interpretation of a previously under-researched area of eco-tourism. This was undertaken in the view that 'with the implementation of the right tourism management strategy, the area will be sustainable and provide for the preservation, community and economic development, which are the main objectives ...' (Croy, 1998: 28) With this in mind, this research expected the results to offer an insight into management strategies currently prevalent in

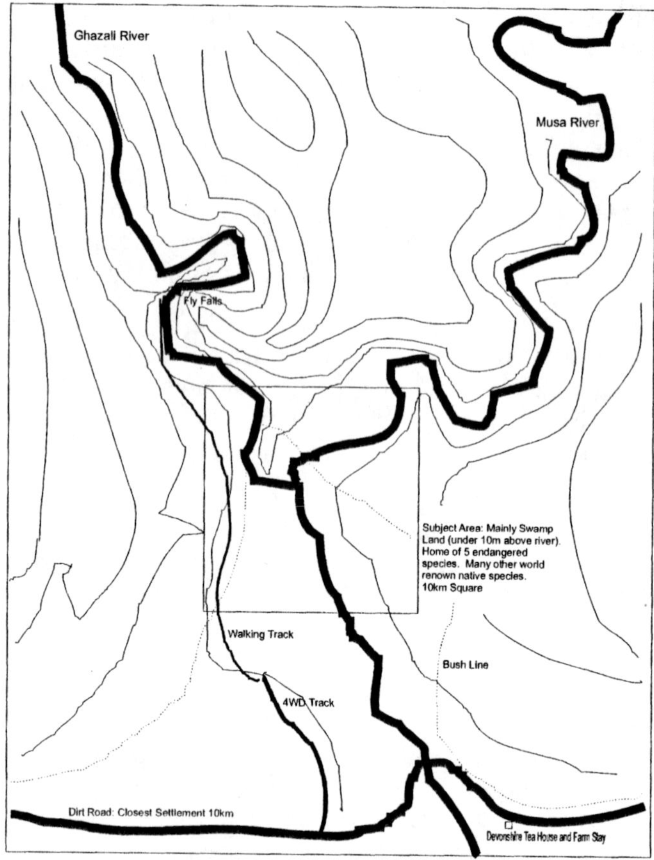

Figure 1 Map of the fictitious Ghazali River and Musa River site, southeast Peru near the Bolivian Border, including the Ghazali–Musa swamp area (boxed centre) (Croy, 1999)

eco-tourism. This would then provide a starting point for future research and the promotion for the adoption of eco-tourism standard practices in development and planning. As there are such standards existing, it is the contention of the authors that these are not fully utilised by or available to developers.

The map was at full A4 size for the exercise. The contour lines are at 10 metre intervals above the rivers. The area below the bush line is largely grass plains, the bush is rain forest. The subject area (boxed area in centre) is 10 kilometres wide.

Results

Respondents and demographics

A sample of university students studying undergraduate tourism was selected to elicit a phenomenological response to an eco-resort design exercise. The subject area for the placement and development of the eco-resort, as described previously (Figure 1), includes a region of immense international importance as it is the habitat to five endangered species. The analysis of the development of the subject area was administered to compare respondent's results to 'best practice' eco-resort development and planning.

There were 186 respondents in all, making up 53 groups of 'developers'. This collection of developers comprised of 82 males and 104 females. Just less than 90% (166) of the respondents were aged between 18 and 21 years inclusive. The range of ages was between 17 and 39 inclusive. The mean (21), median (19) and mode (19) are highly centralised as the sample was taken from an undergraduate university tourism course: 90% (167) of respondents were New Zealanders, with the remaining 90% coming from countries throughout the globe.

This profile gives an insight into who the respondents were. Although there is a high concentration of age, the eco-background was the foremost justification for the selection of this sample, as discussed earlier.

Eco-tourist experience

Thirty-seven percent (69) of the respondents stated that they had no previous experience of eco-tourism, and another 22% (42) did not answer this question. Consequently, nearly 60% (111) of respondents did not state any eco-tourism experiences. Thirteen percent (25) of the respondents had had more than one eco-tourist experience, with one respondent citing 11 experiences. This gave a total of 145 responses to this question, not including no-experience and non-response. Three respondents had worked in the eco-tourism industry and two stated specifically that they had been to eco-resorts. All of these respondents did not say exactly where these sites were or what they did, so the interpretation is left open to industry definitions. Twenty-nine respondents cited tramping, hiking or walking as one of their eco-tourism experiences. Twenty-eight respondents stated walking tracks that had been completed. Overall 40 of the responses were place specific rather than experience or activity explicitly. Fourteen respondents stated animal related activities; including visiting a zoo, swimming with dolphins and safaris in Africa. Seven respondents had had course related experience of eco-tourism excluding the current paper, ranging from Energy Management to Geography to History. Other experiences in or of eco-tourism that were mentioned mainly comprised adventure activities (7); such as skiing and white water rafting, and nature experiences (6); for instance, nature walks or visiting reserves, totalling only 9% of responses (18). With the ambiguous nature of some of the responses to this open question, it is hard to position answers under any title, especially eco-tourism. The preponderance of usable answers would not be termed in the speciality of eco-tourism as defined in the introduction to this paper. This leads to the assumption that, even with an understanding of eco-tourism and eco-practices, the definition in practice is quite different to that in theory. This also reflects the paradigms that Orams (1995) detailed, that there is a continuum of responses, from all tourism (involved in natural locales *per se*) being eco-tourism, to responses of more nature orientated, but not necessarily eco-friendly tourism.

Placement of infrastructure

In the development of the site as an eco-resort certain factors needed to be taken into consideration. These factors include the reasons for developing the resort, functions of the resort, the future sustainable management of the resort, and finally the host community. First, the reasons for developing the resort were for the economic sustainability of the local community and the protection of the endangered species to create a better international image for Peru. Second, the functions of the resort include the conservation of the flora and fauna in the area and entertaining visitors whilst creating a profit. Third, the sustainable management of the resort is an ongoing practice that needs constant contemplation, and therefore should be strategically entrenched into all management plans. Fourth, the needs of the host community's cultural and access priorities for the area have to be respected. It must be noted that access has been confined to permit holders in the recent past.

In consideration of the first and second factors, international image and economic prosperity, the prospective visitors would be internationally renowned and affluent. This is in contemplation that to minimise impacts, it would be ideal to minimise visitors whilst maximising economic return, and therefore create a sustainable area.

The management of the area needs to take a long-term strategic role in the providing of all four factors. Sustainable management practices should be able to integrate the objectives of the area. Eco-management practices will also need to be put into place for ecological protection. Significance of the subject area, which habitats the five endangered species, would be crucial to the management strategy.

The integration of the community in planning and managing the eco-resort is needed for the success of the venture in relation to all the factors. Community support is vital for the success of any tourism undertaking, particularly in this situation, as one of the objectives is the economic sustainability of the community. Also of concern to the local community would be the development of the site and the cultural, economic and environmental impacts this would create.

The infrastructure used on the site would have to accommodate the needs of the visitors, whilst complementing the surrounding environment. The avoidance of impacts, in the subject area especially, needs to be compromised for the economic gain from visitors accessing and viewing the site. Mitigating strategies can be put in place to reduce impacts caused through the access of visitors. The main mitigating strategies that could be used are educating and monitoring visitors on correct behaviour, and the creation of barriers, both physical and visual, to limit the access to susceptible areas. Infrastructure deemed necessary, by the authors, in the development of the site as an eco-resort, include accommodation and eatery facilities, access, education and information facilities, viewing areas, picnic areas, toilet facilities, and recreational facilities.

Respondents' placement of infrastructure in the mapped area was very enlightening. Most of the developments were close to the existing infrastructures; specifically, the farm stay cattle ranch, the dirt road, the four-wheel drive track and the walkway. The additions to the existing infrastructures were really dependent on the items the respondents thought necessary for an eco-resort. The types of infrastructure put in place by the respondents were generally standard development of accommodation, access, information facilities, viewing facilities, and toilets. Additional development of recreation areas and facilities, as well as energy supplies were also fashioned by some of the respondents.

Initially, the subject area, the area in which the five endangered species inhabit, was of key interest to respondents, as it was the reason for developing the eco-resort. Sequentially, the subject area was largely left untouched by most respondents. This was interesting from two points: first, the protection of the area is paramount to sustaining the attraction; second, the species habituated the area and so to see them, the main attraction, an intrusion into the area would be needed. This was a strategic decision from which most respondents chose the first point disregarding the second. If the second option was taken, it usually disregarded the first point of conservation. There were exceptions though that appeared highly interrelated with other developments.

The eco-resort was principally shaped relative to where the main accommodation facilities were placed. Accommodation was largely concentrated to the area directly surrounding the four-wheel drive track and the dirt road four-wheel drive track entrance with 29 accommodation facilities placed in this area by respondents. Respondents also placed a significant number (15) of accommodation facilities at the end of the walking track, at the base of the Fly Falls. The majority of the other 29 accommodation placements were situated along the walking track in the form of tramping huts. There were some huts also placed on newly developed walking tracks in the areas to the right of the Musa River and above the Ghazali–Musa swamp area. The accommodation blocks surrounding the dirt road and the four-wheel drive track were generally the main accommodation for the resort with other facilities including an eatery, toilet and shower blocks and information centres. Thirteen respondent groups had two or more accommodation facilities within their eco-resort development.

In endorsement of prevalent placement of infrastructure by respondents, the placement of infrastructure on site needs to be close to the attractions at the site, whilst at the same time mitigating possible impacts to the attractions. The main accommodation, bathroom, toilet and eatery facilities would have been placed at the start of the walking track by the authors. This would be to have the visitors close to the attractions, whilst still far enough away to reduce random excursions to the subject area. The placement of these facilities also helps in the management of visitors as they are on site, in contrast to some respondents who accommodated visitors in the neighbouring community or at the nearby farm-stay. Because of the creation of additional access routes, such as long hiking tracks, the construction of other accommodation facilities would also be needed.

Respondents principally maintained the original access routes in their current states for the eco-resort development; however 133 changes were made for access. Forty-two changes were made in the upgrading of the current access ways and the expansion of boat access up the Ghazali and Musa Rivers. Forty-nine new developments of access, from boating to bridges, from walking tracks to floating viewing platforms, were developed in the subject area. Thirty-three of these were interrelated, for example, a walking track, over a bridge, to a viewing platform. There were 13 developments of road or walking track access leaving the dirt road before the four-wheel drive track, either going to accommodation facilities or for more direct access to the Fly Falls. In two-thirds of these cases (nine), this was in consideration of the subject area and a need to restrict access to minimise the impact of developments to it. For further exploration and additional recreation for visitors to the eco-resort area, respondents created other tracks. These other tracks generally created a loop-walking track adjacent to the subject area incorporating the original walking track. The authors would also make modifications to current access comparable to those of respondents. The four-wheel drive track to the start of the walking track would be upgraded for easier access to the accommodation facilities. Additional walking tracks would also be put in place for easier viewing in the subject area. Other recreation-related tracks, such as mountain bike tracks, would be added clear of the subject area and conditional on conduct of visitors.

Information facilities were placed on the site to inform of attractions, and advise appropriate conduct to visitors. The 53 development groups placed 135 information sites in the area. Of these, respondents constructed seven interactive information sites, such as museums and information centres. These were all situated with accommodation at the start of the walking track. Information amenities were located at the start of the walking track (28), near the Fly Falls (26), at the entrance to the subject area (10) and at the exit of the subject area (8). The other 67 information sites were dispersed throughout the area. It is noted, however, that there were more information boards at the Fly Falls than all the information boards in and around the subject area, the area most prone to significant impact because of the endangered fauna in the area. This arrangement could be off-set by the information boards placed at the start of the walking track. The authors commend the inclusion of an interactive educational facility erected with the accommodation facilities. Other educational facilities should be placed at strategic points throughout the area, with special notice taken of the subject area, the Fly Falls, focal cultural places of folklore and interest, and other significant fauna and flora in the locality.

The respondents developed 89 viewing facilities on the mapped area. Viewing sites were generally specified as raised platforms made from wood. In the swamp area, floating platforms were also used by some respondents. As with the information sites, these viewing areas were popularly located at the Fly Falls. The 53 groups purposefully placed 37 viewing platforms in the Fly Falls area, compared to 32 viewing sites within the subject area. Of these 32 viewing sites within the subject area, 21 were on or above the bush line, which would limit the viewing of the swamp based endangered fauna. This may have been a misinterpretation by respondents that would not normally happen in the field; however, the respondents were explicitly informed of the bush line. Also, most of these viewing areas above the bush line were situated on the existing walking track, which could be a consideration to limit development in the subject area. The other 20 viewing sites were distributed adjacent to the subject area, on the point above the Ghazali–Musa swamp area and at the start of the walking track. In consideration of the viewing sites adjacent to the subject area, it must be noted that the viewing area is 10 kilometres wide, so specific viewing of fauna may be limited. The authors generally concur with the placement of viewing facilities, but furthermore necessitate additional focus on the subject area and development in conjunction with the local community for location of culturally prominent sites.

Respondents created 73 picnic areas. Picnic areas were perceived as comprising tables and cooking facilities. The most popular spots were the Fly Falls with 22 picnic sites and the start of the walking track (19). The other 32 picnic sites were dispersed throughout the area. Eighteen picnic areas were placed in the subject area. All but six of these were purposefully placed off the existing walking track, creating unnecessary impacts to the subject area. For the conservation of the subject area delimitation of unnecessary development must be encouraged.

The placement of toilets was largely dependent on other infrastructure in the area. Respondents developed 107 toilets on the site. Of these two were specified as dry or composting toilets. The popular points for accommodation received high attention; the Fly Falls (29), the start of the walking track (23) and the four-wheel drive track (10). Seventeen toilets were placed inside the subject area, which would be of high concern for the eco-system of the fauna and flora at the site. The other 28 toilets were placed along the existing tracks and alongside newly developed tracks and facilities. The authors, as with respondents, would construct toilets in the area together with picnic sites and accommodation facilities.

Recreation facilities were deemed necessary by the authors to prolong the stay of visitors in the effort to gain additional financial remuneration. Recreation activities needed to fit in with the image of the eco-resort and the requirements and expectations of the visitors. These activities would have to be environmentally sustainable, not necessarily ecologically friendly. Activities such as mountain biking, hiking, kayaking, boat cruises and hunting were thought of as fitting this definition by the authors. These activities are on differing scales of 'friends of the ecology', and zoning of activities would be needed to delimit impacts. The subject area would be closed to all recreational activity outside the practice of viewing the significant fauna and flora in the area. Mountain biking and hiking would need specifically created areas, and be confined to these areas. Kayaking would be limited to outside the subject area. The demarcation of areas below the subject area would be adequate for this activity. Boat cruises are one avenue to viewing the fauna in the subject area. The type of boat used is of specific importance in order to minimise impacts to the area. Finally, hunting would be for culling purposes only, by permit, and following strict guidelines in specific areas.

Thirty-three of the respondent groups put in place 69 recreation facilities. The recreation activities that would be organised for the eco-resort visitors comprised hunting, fishing, kayaking, boat cruises, helicopter rides, jet boat rides, bungy jumping, golf, a gym, gondolas, water skiing, general water related recreation, walking and hiking, an explorers area, rafting, jetty facilities and a spa. All the higher impacting activities, such as hunting and fishing, rafting, water recreation, excluding boat cruises, were restricted to specific areas. Gondolas were made use of by two groups as a low impacting viewing device in the subject area, and also as a method of transporting visitors to other areas without encroaching too much into the significant subject area. Whilst these activities fit the requirements of the visitors, their development may not complement the image of an eco-resort and be considered eco-antagonistic, for example the development of a golf course or jet boat tours.

The management of waste and the creation of energy were the two crucial aspects for the sustainable management of the area. Waste management practices are intricately intertwined with resource usage; resource requirements need to be limited to limit waste. Considering the ecology and the visitor, some compromises will need to be made, but none that should negate the sustainability of the area. The use and emphasis of waste reduction strategies and recycling help, but disposal is also necessary. Disposal needs to be carried out in an ecologically friendly way, even if this means total extraction of the waste from the area. Seven respondent groups mentioned these pertinent factors, describing rubbish and waste management practices. These waste management practices included type of toilet facilities and disposal of waste.

The creation of energy is also an ecologically sensitive topic. Energy types and sources have assorted effects on the surrounding environment. First, a programme of minimisation of energy usage is essential, and then second, ecological friendly sources can be implemented. The prominent energy sources for selection at this eco-resort were solar energy and gas. A solar energy source would be selected, since it is largely non-intrusive on the locale, as it is on top of existing buildings and is quiet. Gas would be selected as a back-up energy source for its properties of low auditory output and its environmentally friendliness when compared to alternative sources.

The transport energy sources are the most complicated to assert. The land transport needed would transfer all visitors, their luggage and site supplies, from the nearby community airport (that would be built if one does not already exist) to the accommodation. A diesel two-wheel drive vehicle, was selected, as diesel is more fuel efficient than a petrol vehicle and the four-wheel drive access would be modified to accommodate a more fuel efficient two-wheel drive vehicle. For the water recreation usage, boats would be diesel powered and fuel efficiently designed. The design of the boats and propulsion devices would also have to accommodate the susceptible environment they would be travelling into.

Thirty-one of the development groups put energy supplies in their eco--resorts, five had more than one power source. Energy types used included water turbines on the river, windmills on the hills, diesel generators, solar power, LPG generators, electricity lines from the neighbouring settlement (25 kilometres away) and a hydro dam. Non-river damming water turbines (9) and unspecified generators (8), were the most preferred. Interestingly power lines from the nearest settlement were selected six times as the energy source for the resort. The use of a hydro dam was selected only once. The dam was placed on the upper reaches (on the map) of the Musa River, above the Ghazali–Musa swamp area. General portable gas burners or LPG generators were typically preferred as power sources for the tramping huts. Respondents situated three power sources in the subject area, two unspecified generators and one series of power lines. All of these power sources in the subject area were placed above the tree line, near the edges of the subject area. The use of impacting energy supplies is of concern in the designation and management of the site as an eco-resort.

Respondents made other comments as to management of the eco-resort. Twenty-six groups made 47 management practice notes for the eco-resort. The 47 comments were divided into 31 particular categories of explanation, so there were numerous practices recommended. The most common management recommendation was limiting access to the subject area, with eight groups recommending that only guided groups being allowed, to banning access altogether, to access only allowed to paying visitors, to limits of numbers of people in the area at a time. The provision of an interactive information service was also popular, noted by seven of the respondent groups. Three groups also recommended limiting the type of people allowed by measures of fitness. Other recommendations ranged from removal of all access tracks into the area to develop a wilderness experience, compared with the development of sealed direct access to the Fly Falls. Two groups also mentioned the selection of guides and access by these guides into specific parts of the area. One group specified five star accommodations. The other recommendations included the minimisation of impacts, visually, ecologically, audibly and physically. Two notable mentions were the use of locals in the managing of the eco-resort and as guides.

Summary

The inference of these results is the difficulty of defining 'eco', a label that has had definitional problems, not only in the literature, as exemplified in the introduction to this paper, but more so in the actual practice of eco-tourism. This has been epitomised in the respondents' application of eco-theory to this practical case.

The majority of the respondent groups did not pay necessary attention to the reasons for the eco-resort development: they focused on minimal infrastructure requirements and paid considerable attention to the Fly Falls relative to the subject area, as is exemplified in infrastructure placement. Whilst most respondents placed accommodation facilities in ideal places, the development of facilities to which travelling through the subject area was needed, would be deemed unsatisfactory for the conservation of the area.

Information facilities were satisfactory, but the attention on the Fly Falls site by respondents diverted the significance of the subject area in the attraction of visitors. Moreover, the lack of attention to the subject area may create a perception of insignificance, so visitors may not feel the need to monitor their own behaviour to the same extent. Respondents' initial wave of signage at the start of the walking track may mitigate the lack of information in the subject area.

Viewing facilities also were not focused on the subject area, although, as mentioned previously, this could be a strategic move by respondents to limit impacts in the subject area. However, with the factors for the creation of the development, an intrusion is necessary for the viewing of the fauna and flora at the site.

Placement of picnic areas appeared *ad hoc*. Other than assignment of areas at the Fly Falls and the start of the walking track, positioning at random intervals along the tracks was prevalent.

The placement of toilets was generally good, though the exceptions were noteworthy. Placement of toilets in the subject area would certainly be an incompetent initiative, as the impacts to the ecology could be non-reversible. Comparatively, types of environmentally friendly toilets recommended by some respondents were encouraging.

The energy sources used by respondents were also deluding the factors encouraging the eco-resort development, specifically the conservation of the existing natural environment. The impacts to the area would be, in some cases, monumental, especially damming the river or running electricity lines from the neighbouring settlement, which, in this second world country, may not have an effective electricity supply of its own. A number of the respondents implementing energy supplies did make use of more environmentally friendly devices such as non-damming water turbines and solar panels.

The majority of respondent groups made use of recreation activities in the area to prolong the stay of visitors, although the use of appropriate activities sometimes eluded the groups. The use of jet boats could cause devastating ecological effects caused by the wake, noise and turmoil in the water created by the motors. The penchant for other unrestricted water activity also gave concerns for the sustainability and security of the fauna and flora at the site. Although a third of respondents did not include any additional recreation activities or facilities, this in itself possibly could be detrimental to the eco-resort and the objective factors. The sustainability of the area and the local community would hinge on the gains at the eco-resort. Though there were exceptions, the general overview of the eco-resorts designed by respondent groups highlighted incompetencies in the application of theory to a practical case.

Conclusion

The mode of eco-resort developers, using this sample as an explorative definition, is in a state of idle regression. Even with in-depth coverage of the subject of eco-tourism and sustainable management, respondents' application of comprehension to a case scenario was limited. The definition, as found through respondents´ experiences, is expansive and deceptive compared to the definitions given in the literature and instruction they received. From the definition used in the respondents´ experiences, the eco-resorts they developed were not appreciably divergent from standards. With the consideration of the application of expansive definitions, as in this case, the proposal of eco-tourism existence is quite presumptuous and even misleading. This investigation outlines the differences between best practice theory and application in an eco-resort developer's procedure. The study of 'eco-resorts' really needs a standard base definition to which a development either fits or does not. The paradigms of eco-resorts (Orams, 1995) are thriving, not only because of marketing needs, but because developers are using these expansive definitions as a source or keystone to their development. The use of these definitions as a basis for development sequentially condones the naming of such a resort an eco-resort. This outlines the following needs for the future development of resorts. Standards of development need to be fashioned to grade the eco-resorts in criterions of sustainability and conscientiousness to their ecology. Also, there are needs for these resources and training in application to be made proactively accessible to developers.

In conclusion, the differences between theoretical and practical application of definition are so considerable in some cases that eco-tourism may define itself out of existence. The universal or common definition shall contaminate the category and invalidate the term 'eco-tourism' as defined in the literature. The sustainability of eco-tourism, as a practice, is not probable with a lack of standards to define the application of the term to resorts and people. The supposition from this is that the genus of eco-tourist is in danger of extinction through a lack of a sustained definition. The paradox: 'eco-tourist' – the endangered visitor.

Acknowledgements

The authors would like to acknowledge the help of tutors and students in undergraduate tourism studies at the University of Otago.

Correspondence

Any correspondence should be directed to W. Glen Croy, Lecturer, School of Tourism and Hospitality, Waiariki Institute of Technology, Rotorua, New Zealand (glen.croy@waiariki.ac.nz).

References

Andersen, D.L. (1993) A window to the natural world – the design of eco-tourism facilities. In K. Lindberg and D.E. Hawkins (eds) *Eco-tourism – A Guide for Planners and Managers.* Bennington, VT: Ecotourism Society.

Barnao, P. (1994) NZ tourism future lies 'with nature'. *Otago Daily Times* (18 April). Dunedin, New Zealand.

Beeho, A.J. and Prentice, R.C. (1995) Evaluating the experiences and benefits gained by tourists visiting a socio-industrial museum: An application of ASEB grid analysis to Blists Hill Open-Air Museum, The Ironbridge Gorge Museum, UK. *Museum Management and Curatorship* 14 (3), 229–51.

Beeho, A.J. and Prentice, R.C. (1996) Understanding visitor experience as a basis for product development: ASEB grid analysis and the Black Country Museum in the West Midlands of England. In L.C. Harrison and W. Husbands (eds) *Practising Responsible Tourism:'International Case Studies in Tourism Planning, Policy and Development'* (pp. 472–94). New York: Wiley and Sons.

Beeho, A.J. and Prentice, R.C. (1997) Conceptualising the experiences of heritage tourists: A case study of New Lanark World Heritage Village. *Tourism Management* 18 (2), 75–87.

Boo, E. (1993) Eco-tourism planning for protected areas. In K. Lindberg and D.E. Hawkins (eds) *Eco-tourism: A Guide for Planners and Managers* (pp. 15–31). Bennington, VA: Ecotourism Society.

Bottrill, C.G. and Pearce, D.G. (1995) Eco-tourism: Towards a key elements approach to operationalising the concept. *Journal of Sustainable Tourism* 3 (1), 45–54.

Boyd, S.W. and Butler, R.W. (1994) *Geographical Information Systems: A Tool for Establishing Parameters for Eco-tours Criteria.* Report for Department of Natural Resources / Forestry, Ministry of Natural Resources. Canada: Ministry of Natural Resources.

Boyd, S.W. and Butler, R.W. (1996) Managing eco-tourism – an opportunity spectrum approach. *Tourism Management* 17 (8), 557–66.

Briassoulis, H. (1992) Environmental impacts of tourism: A framework for analysing and evaluation. In S. Briassoulis and J. van der Straaten (eds) *Tourism and the Environment: The Netherlands* (pp. 11–22). Kluwer Academic Publishers.

Budowski, G. (1976) Tourism and conservation – conflict, coexistence or symbiosis. *Environmental Conservation* 3, 27–31.

Ceballos-Lascurain, H. (1991) Tourism, eco-tourism, and protected areas. In J.A. Kusler (ed.) *Eco-tourism and Resource Conservation: Selected Papers from the 2nd International Symposium: Eco-tourism and Resource Conservation* (vol. 1) (pp. 24–30). USA: Omnipress.

Collier, A. (1996) *Principles of Tourism: A New Zealand Perspective* (3rd edn). Auckland: Longman Paul.

Commonwealth Department of Tourism (1995) *Best Practice Eco-tourism: A Guide to Energy and Waste Minimisation.* Canberra: Commonwealth of Australia.

Crossley, J. and Lee, B. (1994) *Eco-tourists and Mass Tourists – A Difference in Benefits Sought.* Travel and Tourism Research Association Conference Report. Washington: TTRA.

Croy, W.G. (1998) The management of heritage – the application of an ASEB grid analysis for a visitor focused management strategy at the Harbour Street – Tyne Street Built Heritage Site, Oamaru, North Otago, New Zealand. Unpublished dissertation, University of Otago, Dunedin.

Croy, W.G. (1999) Ghazali and Musa river area map. Unpublished. University of Otago, Dunedin.

Croy, W.G. and Høgh, L.K. (1999) The Ghazali and Musa rivers eco-resort, information sheet. Unpublished. University of Otago, Dunedin.

Daniels, S.E., Lawrence, R.L. and Alig, R.J. (1996) Decision-making and ecosystem based management – applying the Vroom-Yetton model to public participation strategy. *Environmental Impact Assess Revue* 16 (1), 13–30.

Davis, D. and Harriott, V.J. (1996) Sustainable tourism development or a case of loving a special place to death. In L.C. Harrison and W. Husbands (eds) *Practicing Responsible Tourism – International Case Studies in Tourism Planning, Policy and Development* (pp. 422–44). USA: John Wiley and Sons.

Dowling, R.K. (1997) Plans for the development of regional eco-tourism – theory and practice. In C.M. Hall, J. Jenkins and G.W. Kearsley (eds) *Tourism Planning and Policy in Australia and New Zealand: Cases, Issues and Practice* (pp. 110–26). Australia: Irwin Publishers.

Duffus, D.A. and Dearden, P. (1990) Non-consumptive wildlife-oriented recreation – a conceptual framework. *Biological Conservation* 53, 213–31.

Eagles, P. (1992) The travel motivations of Canadian eco-tourist. *Journal of Travel Research* 31 (2), 3–7.

Environmental Tourist (1991) *An Eco-tourist Revolution.* A co-production of the National Audubon Society, TBS Productions and WETA.

Fennell, D.A. and Smale, B.J.A. (1992) Eco-tourism and natural resource protection. *Tourism Recreation Research* 17 (1), 21–32.

Gilbert, J. (1997) *Eco-tourism Means Business.* Wellington: GP Publications.

Holmes, J. (1993) Loving nature to death. *New Zealand Science Monthly* (April), 6–8.

Ioannides, D. (1995) A flawed implementation of sustainable tourism – the experience of Akamas, Cyprus. *Tourism Management* 16 (8), 583–92.

Inskeep, E. (1987) Environmental planning for tourism. *Annals of Tourism Research* 14 (1), 118–35.

Joppe, M. (1996) Sustainable community tourism development revisited. *Tourism Management* 17 (7), 475–9.

Kretchman, J.A. and Eagles, P. (1990) An analysis of the motives of eco-tourists in comparison to the general Canadian population. *Society and Leisure* 13 (2), 499–508.

Krippendorf, J. (1982) Towards new tourism policies – the importance of environmental and socio-cultural factors. *Tourism Management* 3 (3), 142.

Krippendorf, J. (1991) Towards new tourism policies. In S. Medlik (ed.) *Managing Tourism.* London: Butterworth-Heinemann.

Kusler, J.A. (1991) Protected area approaches and eco-tourism. In J.A. Kusler (ed.) *Ecotourism and Resource Conservation: Selected Papers form the 2nd International Symposium: Eco-tourism and Resource Conservation* (vol. 1) (pp. 14–23). USA: Omnipress.

Lawrence, T.B., Wickins, D. and Phillips, N. (1997) Managing legitimacy in eco-tourism. *Tourism Management* 18 (5), 307–16.

Lindberg, K. (1991) *Policies for Maximising Nature Tourism's Ecological and Economic Benefits.* Washington, DC: World Resources Institute.

Lindberg, K. and Hawkins, D.E. (eds) (1993) *Eco-tourism: A Guide for Planners and Managers.* Bennington, VT: Ecotourism Society.

Lindberg, K. and McKercher, B. (1997) Eco-tourism: A Critical Overview. *Pacific Tourism Review* 1, 65–79.

Lück, M. (1998) Sustainable tourism – do modern trends in tourism make a sustainable management more easy to achieve? *Tourismus Jahrbuch* 2 (2), 141–57.

McIntosh, A.J. (1997a) The experience and benefits gained by tourists visiting socio-industrial heritage attractions. Doctorial thesis, Open University, Queen Margaret College. Edinburgh.

McIntosh, A.J. (1997b) ASEB grid analysis – understanding the value of heritage to its visitors. In *Trails in the Third Millennium* (pp. 221–36) Conference Proceedings. Cromwell.

Masberg, B.A. and Silverman, L.H. (1996) Visitor experiences at heritage sites: A phenomenological approach. *Journal of Travel Research* 34 (4), 20–25.

Moore, A.W. (1991) Planning for eco-tourism in protected areas. In J.A. Kusler (ed.) *Eco-tourism and Resource Conservation: Selected Papers form the 2nd International Symposium: Eco-tourism and Resource Conservation* (vol. 1) (pp. 563–73). USA: Omnipress.

Moore, S. and Carter, B. (1993) Eco-tourism in the 21st century. *Tourism Management* 14 (2), 123–30.

Oastler, P. (1994) Eco-tourism. *Wilderness News* (November).

Orams, M.B. (1995) Towards a more desirable form of eco-tourism. *Tourism Management* 16 (1), 3–8.

Orams, M.B. (1996) A conceptual model of tourist–wildlife interaction: The case for education as a management strategy. *Australian Geographer* 27 (1), 39–50.

Ross, S. and Wall, S. (1999) Eco-tourism: Towards congruence between theory and practice. *Tourism Management* 20 (1), 123–32.

Selsky, J.W. (1991) Lessons in community development – an activist approach to stimulating inter-organisational collaboration. *Journal of Applied Behavioural Science* 27 (1), 91–115.

Selsky, J.W. (1997) Developmental dynamics in non profit sector federations (2nd revision). Unpublished working paper. University of Otago, Dunedin.

Simon, D. (1991) Putting the tourist to work for you. In J.A. Kusler (ed.) *Eco-tourism and Resource Conservation: Selected Papers from the 2nd International Symposium: Eco-tourism and Resource Conservation* (vol. 1) (pp. 134–47). USA: Omnipress.

Sirakaya, E. (1997) Attitudinal compliance with eco-tourism guidelines. *Annals of Tourism Research* 24 (4), 919–50.

Tisdell, C. (1996) Eco-tourism, economics, and the environment: Observations from China. *Journal of Travel Research* 34 (4), 11–19.

Warren, J.A.N. and Taylor, C.N. (1994) *Developing Eco-tourism in New Zealand* Christchurch/Wellington: New Zealand Institute for Social Research.

Weaver, D.B. (1998) *Eco-tourism in the Less Developed World*. United Kingdom: CAB International.

Wendt, W.W. (1991) Providing the human and physical infrastructure for regulating eco-tourism use of protected areas. In J.A. Kusler (ed.) *Eco-tourism and Resource Conservation: A Collection of Papers* (vol. 2) (pp. 520–8). USA: Omnipress.

Wight, P. (1993) Eco-tourism: Ethics or Eco-Sell? *Journal of Travel Research* 31 (3), 3–9.

Wood, K. and House, S. (1992) *The Good Tourist* (1992 edition). Great Britain: Mandarin Paperbacks.

Latin American Ecotourism: What is it?

Ron Mader
Alcala 902-Bis, Centro, 68000 Oaxaca, Oaxaca, Mexico

Defining – and agreeing upon a definition of – the word 'ecotourism' poses a challenge. This is especially true in Latin America where the buzzword remains a vague term used to market anything related to nature or environmental tourism. 'Proyectos ecoturisticos' sell everything from community development projects to jet skis. There are pros and cons in using any specific viewpoint – if we insist on high environmental standards and minimal impacts, the costs skyrocket. This places the services and destinations into a 'luxury class' tourism – sometimes without the amenities to which those who pay high-end prices are accustomed. These five-star operations often run into conflict with more humble, grassroots operations. At risk are rural and/or indigenous guides who do not have the financial resources to take part in established guide training programmes – not offered in the field, but usually in the capital city. Good intentions lie behind guide training and accreditation, but if governments or agencies do not empower rural guides and tourism operations, the absence of 'local participation' betrays one of the main components of ecotourism.

Introduction

Defining – and agreeing upon a definition of – the word 'ecotourism' poses a challenge, particularly in Latin America where this buzzword remains a vague term used to market anything related to nature or environmental tourism. 'Proyectos ecoturisticos' sell everything from community development projects to jet skis.

The lack of a standard terminology has resulted in a myriad of definitions. In a comparative study of ecotourism policy in the Americas, Steve Edwards, William McLauglin and Sam Ham found that of the 25 government tourism agencies that chose to define 'ecotourism', 21 preferred to create their own home-made definition (Edwards *et al.*, 1998).

Moreover, international organisations, such as the International Union for the Conservation of Nature (IUCN), the Sierra Club and the American Society of Travel Agents (ASTA) have each created their own guidelines promoting eco-friendly travel.

'A few years ago I stopped using the word 'ecotourism' to describe our operations', says Amos Bien, owner of Costa Rica's Rara Avis Lodge, a pioneering effort with inscrutable ethics on how one creates a touristic enterprise precisely to save the surrounding rainforest. Bien now uses the term, explaining that tourists are starting to understand the nuances in the definition and that Rara Avis sets an example when it comes to showing how tourism can benefit the environment (Bien, 1999).

In Latin America anything and everything 'Eco' boomed in the 1990s, particularly after the Rio de Janeiro Earth Summit in 1992. In Costa Rica the most questionable example was the country's 'Eco-Rent-A-Car'. Mexico boasts 'Eco Taxis', 'Eco Cines' and an 'Eco Estacionamiento' – or an 'Eco Parking Lot' because of a few trees planted around the perimeter.

So what is 'ecotourism?' For Bien and other pioneers, implementation and action was more important than definition. The next stage of ecotourism development may include the concept of 'ecotourism certification', a popular topic now within international institutions and national governments throughout the Americas. However, for all of its merits, the idea of certification should be scrutinised as much as the operations themselves.

Certification requires infrastructure, coordination and financial resources that are lacking not only in the developing world, but also globally. Moreover, the lack of a standard definition of ecotourism may not be easily overcome without creating additional problems for those who might best benefit from the concept, namely campesinos and residents of rural areas that abut or coincide with protected areas. That brings us back to the question what ecotourism is.

Evaluating Ecotourism

While the details vary, most definitions of ecotourism come down to a special form of tourism that meets three criteria:

(1) it provides for conservation measures;
(2) it includes meaningful community participation; and
(3) it is profitable and can sustain itself.

Imagine these goals as being three overlapping circles (Figure 1).

If a project or service meets all three criteria, it can be unmistakably called ecotourism. But what about the projects that are just a little off the mark? Are they genuine ecotourism projects? Moreover, if they are not, does the lack of accreditation generate a move toward ecotourism or a dismissal of the entire process? These three components of ecotourism are difficult to accomplish individually, let alone as a package. They are also difficult to measure or quantify. Assuming one wants to know which are the 'best ecotourism destinations', how is one to judge?

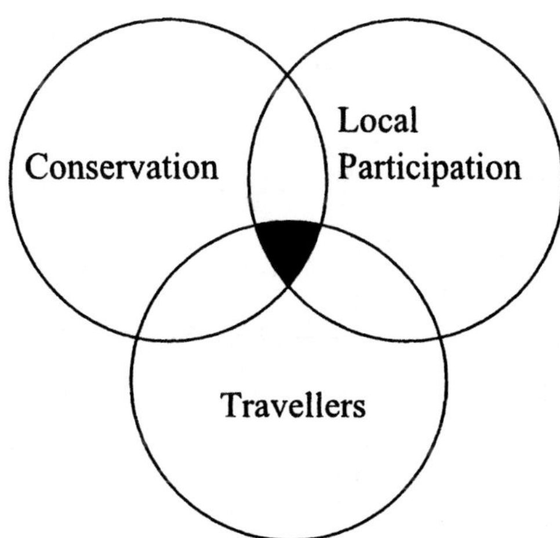

Figure 1 The goals of ecotourism

Membership in organisations, such as 'The International Ecotourism Society' (TIES) or 'Partners in Responsible Tourism' requires only the payment of a membership fee. For example, TIES does not certify a member's compliance, nor does it endorse any member's product or organisation. Instead, the society requires members to sign a pledge stating that the member will be a 'responsible traveller or travel-related professional who conserves natural environments and sustains the well-being of local people'. (TIES, 1999)

While this ethic sounds good and this self-regulatory system boasts the best of intentions, any types of audits are missing. There is no system of double-checking the information and no 'teeth' in which members are judged or penalised for misconduct. The absence of accreditation programmes has prompted some to suggest the creation of a third-party organisation, such as the firms that measure and certify organic coffee for the world market. However, ecotourism is not only a commodity, it is a social process that is exceedingly difficult to measure or regulate successfully.

Point of View

The lack of a common definition results in multiple interpretations. Even if they agree on the big picture, conservation groups and tour agencies have decidedly different interpretations of what constitutes ecotourism. And if they agree on the basic criteria, they weight the components differently. For example, projects heralded by conservation groups may have good conservation strategies, but tend to lack marketing savvy and knowledge of the tourism industry. The lack of such knowledge frequently causes these projects to go out of business. Conversely, some large tourism businesses offer nature tours that are highly profitable but that include little or no community partnership or conservation assistance. Consequently, very few nature tourism projects can meet all three criteria.

The creation of an independent evaluation programme for tourism guides or services seems like a great idea to ensure high quality. But whose standards are we to use? Ecotourism's success or failure depends on the eye of the beholder. Conservationists will measure the merits of a project by its contributions to the local environmental protection. Travel agencies will focus on the bottom line – are they making a sufficient profit? Each traveller comes to an ecotourism destination or provider with their own personal experience and bias.

There are pros and cons in using any specific viewpoint. If we insist on high environmental standards the costs skyrocket. This places the services and destinations into 'luxury' class tourism – sometimes without the amenities those who pay high-end prices are accustomed to. This also conflicts with more humble, grassroots operations.

Is the best example of ecotourism a rustic, community lodge or a foreign-owned, eco-friendly hotel? Too often architects and consultants promote high technical standards and luxurious eco-lodges because they have a personal stake to certify those businesses that can pay them well. Also at risk are rural and/or indigenous guides who do not have the financial resources to take part in established guide training programmes, which are usually not offered in the field, but in the capital city. Good intentions are behind guide training and accreditation, but if governments or agencies do not empower rural guides, 'local participation' in ecotourism is absent.

The Ecotourism Market

Many of the traditional means of measuring the tourism market by itself are deceiving. Who are the ecotourists? The short answer is that even statistics about regular tourism are suspect. It is difficult to freely check data produced by the World Tourism Organisation (WTO), which in the early 1990s estimated that the annual arrivals growth would be around 7% and global receipts expected to rise to US$527 billion in 2000. The figures sound great, but independent audits of the data are missing (Ceballos-Lascurain, 1996).

In Mexico, SECTUR, the country's tourism secretariat, reported that the country received 21 million visitors in 1997. Most, however, are day-trippers and family members returning home, leaving 7.5 to 8.5 million visitors a year as 'authentic tourists' spending roughly $550 per trip. This figure includes business as well as recreational travel (Barkin, 1999).

The necessary first step for understanding the tourism market is deflating and questioning these figures. What also has to be called into question is the acquisition of ecotourism statistics. Polls of 'eco' tourists have been garnered at international airports and rarely in the field. Can these figures adequately depict what people would or would not do in rural areas? It is inadequate to label anyone an 'ecotourist' just because they visit a park or protected area.

Ecotourism in Mexico

In many Latin American countries officials intrigued by the promise of 'ecotourism' have attempted to promote and/or regulate this niche market. In each case, the first challenge has been uniting energies of the tourism and environmental departments. There have been more failures than successes here as government departments prefer sole control of a project.

Mexico should be the case example of things done right. It is one of the few Latin American examples in which the secretariats of tourism (SECTUR) and Environment (SEMARNAT) signed an agreement to collaborate on ecotourism development. This took place in 1995. However, while the offices are officially working together, there have been few results, perhaps because the liaison personnel in both offices have been in great flux. The lack of continuity threatens the coordination. Too much emphasis by officials is placed on the 'paper agreement' between the two institutions. However, not all is bleak. While government officials move in and out of their office quickly, some private entrepreneurs have set up their own group – Mexico's Association of Adventure Travel and Ecotourism (AMTAVE). Aided by some initial funding provided by the SECTUR, AMTAVE now raises most of its funds via membership fees. This private group boasts members throughout the country, although most of them base their operations in Mexico City. This association does review members, and not everyone who applies is accepted. But this is not to say that everyone who offers nature or ecotourism in Mexico are (or want to be) members of AMTAVE. Many simply work out from environmental ethic and the knowledge that travellers are receptive to eco-friendly hotels and services.

'People talk about ecotourism, but the fact is that the tourism industry is always looking for a quick buck', said hotelier Doug Rhodes, owner of Hotel Paraiso del Oso in Cerocahui, Chihuahua. 'Hotels throughout the Copper Canyon still lack waste treatment facilities. Some of the garbage is thrown into the canyon or disposed near community wells' (Rhodes, 1998). Rhodes said that tourists are willing to pay for such environmental guarantees and added that the technologies are not that expensive; it is just a matter of will.

In July 1999, the country hosted its first annual trade conference on ecotourism and adventure tourism in Mexico City's World Trade Center. States with a keen interest in promoting their natural wonders, namely Veracruz, Oaxaca, Michoacan and Morelos, purchased exposition space, alongside rafting companies, natural history tours and regional airlines. It is important to add that these states offered discounted or free space at their booths to community-run projects, such as the Museos Comunitarios de Oaxaca or the Nuevo San Juan Parangaricutiro project near the Paracutin Volcano in Michoacan.

Other Latin American Examples

Private ecotourism groups have also been set up in other countries, though unfortunately many have been created in government conferences, often at the urging of international development agencies. Few show a long-term commitment to national ecotourism development. USAID, for example, funded and promoted several ecotourism associations throughout Central America, most of which existed solely on paper. Like 'paper parks', 'paper ecotourism organisations' give the illusion of action and coordination, but lack substance and continuity.

The tourism industry can be a leader, though recent history throughout the region is a series of battles between traditional tourism and those who promote 'alternative tourism'. There are, however, some bright spots. In Belize, members of the Belize Tourism Industry Association (BETA) set up the Belize Ecotourism Association. 'We in the private sector have a tremendous opportunity to do something for conservation in conjunction with the government', said ex-BETA President Jim Bevis (Mahler, 1997).

Ecuador also has a nascent organisation, the Ecuadorian Ecotourism Association, though it has been criticised by those who do not live in Quito for not adequately addressing the needs of the Amazon or Pacific regions of the country.

Costa Rica is the country with the best reputation for ecotourism practices and destinations, but it does not have a formal ecotourism group. Bien, the owner of Rara Avis Lodge, says:

> The origins of ecotourism in Costa Rica can be traced to the La Selva field station, Monteverde, Corcovado, Tortugero and Rara Avis. We've always been too busy to start a national ecotourism association, preferring to work within the sub-commissions of one Environmental Secretariat or the Costa Rican Tourism Institute instead (Bien, 1999).

The Role of Information

Travellers interested in nature want to know how to get to where the 'wild things' are and how to do so in a responsible manner. Unfortunately, governments rarely provide quality up-to-date information for the general public. One missing ingredient is maps. The tourism institutes of both Costa Rica and Honduras publish country maps with information on protected areas. Mexico once published such a map, but it quickly went out of print. Other Latin American countries lack publicly available maps of their national parks. Ecotourism conferences are offered throughout the region, but with few exceptions, they are either closed to the general public or too expensive. Again, international development groups as well as international governmental conferences prefer the closed-door sessions. They should provide access to the conference materials and lists of participants. This rarely occurs. Trade conferences do offer access, but at a high cost. There should be more alternatives that can take advantage of the growing interest within the region.

Development agencies, foundations and environmental groups have combined forces to promote ecotourism in the region, with some success. Information about these efforts in the planning stage or analysis, or project reports afterwards could be placed on the World-Wide-Web for global access, but are notable for their absence. International environmental groups (for example, The Nature Conservancy, Conservation International, World Wildlife Fund) are culpable of hoarding information. Scholarly dissertations on regional ecotourism may cite the 'unpublished reports' but few readers have access to them. Policy information is desperately needed, not only to know what has been done well, but also what has failed. These experiences need to be thought of an experiment that we can learn from. Unfortunately, environmental groups are loath to discuss, let alone divulge, instances of failure.

One of the best places for travellers to find information about ecotourism destinations is not from government offices or environmental groups, but from regional guidebooks. There is a clear role for guidebooks in the development of true ecotourism in the region. Guidebooks offer a holistic vision of a country or a region and are publicly accessible. The author freely crosses political and/or vocational borders to provide a manual of use to travellers from a variety of backgrounds. One good example is Joe Cumming's 'Northern Border Handbook' (Moon Publications), the only guidebook that focuses on Mexico's frontier with the United States. Another key text that deserves to be recommended is 'The New Key to Costa Rica' (Ulysses Press), one of the first guidebooks that explained the concept of ecotourism and sustainable development and promoted the hotels and lodges that were working toward environmental protection. These books contrast with more traditional guidebooks that either belittle the 'friendly people' or focus solely on more popular coastal resorts. Both have been instrumental not only in directing travellers *where* to go, but also *how* to go.

For ecotourism planners or hoteliers, international organisations such as The Ecotourism Society do provide a great deal of information and resources for their members. In this sense, membership offers the benefits of coming up to speed in the field as well as ongoing networking and information sharing with other members and the host organisation.

Conclusion

Achieving ecotourism is not so much hitting a stationary target, but taking part in a dynamic process. The success of ecotourism depends on being able to coordinate activities and share information with people who do not come from a similar background. Rather than elaborating about the definition, more attention needs to be spent on the application of ecotourism. It is better when evaluating ecotourism to view these services not with a yardstick, but using a more fluid approach. Given the three categories that are widely accepted as components of ecotourism, it is wiser to measure the three in balance with one another as well as the tendency of a given project or service to move toward the centre.

Ecotourism providers or services can easily tell in what categories they are strong in and which categories need work. Instead of regulation, the author proposes a new form of communication. This gives the services or destinations a better understanding about their need to improve.

Certainly, national and local governments will need to regulate the tourism industry for safety as well as or environmental protection. But any attempt to certify the actual providers or guides will only succeed if there is a pre-existing infrastructure and culture that has a more unified understanding of ecotourism.

Specific Recommendations

(1) Certification of ecotourism must be kept on par with more constructive acts such as improving the channels of communication among conservationists and tourism leaders within both regional and international spheres.
(2) People working in ecotourism should respect each other's differences and build the bridge across the chasm separating traditional tourism and conservation.
(3) The cost for ecotourism consulting, workshops and conferences should be in line so that rural groups and students have access.
(4) Development agencies, foundations and environmental groups should make project reports, budgets, and personnel lists freely available on their websites.

Correspondence

Any correspondence should be directed to Ron Mader, Alcala 902-Bis, Centro, 68000 Oaxaca, Mexico (ron@planeta.com).

References

Barkin, D. (1999) Strengthening domestic tourism in Mexico – challenges and opportunities. Unpublished report.
Blake, B. and Becher, A. (1994) *The New Key to Costa Rica*. Berkeley, CA: Ulysses Press.
Blake, B. and A. Becher (2001) *The New Key to Costa Rica*. Berkeley, CA: Ulysses Press.
Ceballos-Lascurain, H. (1996) *Tourism, Ecotourism and Protected Areas*. Gland/Switzerland: IUCN.
Chase, M. (1998) *Tour de Force: Industry Aims for Higher Return in Mexican Tourism*. Business Mexico
Cummings, J. (1998) *Northern Mexico Handbook*. Chico/California: Moon Publications.
Edwards, S, McLauglin, W.J. and Ham, S.H. (1998) Comparative study of ecotourism policy in the Americas. Ongoing research for the Organization of American States.

Inter-Sectoral Unit for Tourism and the Department of Resource Recreation and Tourism, University of Idaho.
Mader, R. (1998) *Mexico: Adventures in Nature.* Santa Fe, NM: John Muir Publications.
Mader, R. (1999) Exploring Ecotourism, work-in-progress and online guide to Latin American ecotourism. On WWW at http://www2.planeta.com/mader/ecotravel/etour.html. Accessed 08.01.99.
Mader, R. (2001) *Exploring Ecotourism, work-in-progress and online guide to ecotourism in the Americas,* http://www.planeta.com/ecotravel/etour.html, (date of access: 08/01/01).
Mader, R. and Gollin, J. (1998) *Honduras: Adventures in Nature.* Santa Fe: John Muir Publications.
Mahler, R. (1997) *Belize: Adventures in Nature.* Santa Fe, NM: John Muir Publications.
McLaren, D. (1997) *Rethinking Tourism and Ecotravel – The Paving of Paradise and How You Can Stop It.* West Hartford, CT: Kumarian Press.
Stevenson, M. (2001) *Megaresorts on Wish List for Mexico.* Associated Press.

Personal communication

Bien, Amos (June 1999) Owner of Rara Avis Lodge, Costa Rica.
International Ecotourism Society (January 1999).
Rhodes, Doug (March 1998) Owner of Hotel Paraiso del Oso in Cerucahui, Chihuahua.

Pastoral Livelihoods in Tanzania: Can the Maasai Benefit from Conservation?

Ric Goodman
36 Henley Street, Oxford OX4 1ES, UK

The Maasai pastoralists of Northern Tanzania live in areas of unique conservation value. There is a widespread belief dating from colonial times that Maasai cattle herding is unproductive and detrimental to the region's wildlife. The increase in the Maasai population has fuelled this belief and has led to their exclusion from their traditional land and a breakdown in their land management strategies. This decreases their capacity to maintain a livelihood, and so they must turn to non-traditional methods. This paper looks at how the Maasai have been excluded from their lands and why this has caused traditional livelihoods to become unsustainable. It then goes on to suggest that community-based tourism offers possible alternative sustainable solutions both to the Maasai and to conservationists.

Background

The Maasai are the largest pastoralist ethnic group in Tanzania, but by no means the only one.[1] Maasai number around 150,000 on the eastern and northern fringes of the Serengeti National Park, the Ngorongoro Conservation Area (NCA) in Tanzania and the Maasai Mara National Reserve in Kenya. They are unique for their cultural prohibition of the use of meat from wild animals. For the Maasai as a whole, cattle are the pivotal livelihoods resource, rather than the wildlife. Their traditional diet comes from the blood and the milk of cows, rather than their meat.

Pastoralists on the semiarid grasslands of East Africa have various mechanisms enabling the community as a whole to survive from generation to generation. The most visible strategy is their mobility. When food sources are scarce, pastoralists move to better grassland and more permanent water sources. As a consequence, their property regime is based on communal ownership of resources and communal access rights. Reciprocal resource rights with neighbouring groups existed, for example between other pastoral groups or neighbouring agriculturists.[2] The ungulate population in the region adopts the same survival strategy. At the onset of the rains, the wildebeest and zebra population moves northeast and emerges beyond the boundaries of the region's protected areas. For many years this seasonal migration pattern, following food and water, has been mistaken as random wandering and has exposed pastoralists to claims on land seemingly unused and unclaimed.

Land Tenure

In Tanzania, land law is still derived from the 1923 Land Act, drawn up by the British colonial administration and which forms the basis of Tanzania's land legislation, granted secure land tenure to economically productive holdings while leaving the majority – the peasants and pastoralists – community lands under customary tenure. One of the forces driving tenure insecurity is the expansion of agricultural farming. If land is shown to be potentially productive, customary land title is often lost to private title. This happened under colonial rule and continues today.

Agricultural Pressure

In the 1930s, much communally held land was privatised for agricultural production (Cheeseman, 1999). Adoption of agricultural production often shifts the burden of work to women just as the main burden for pastoral activities reduces for men. However, women do not control the agricultural produce and the income it fetches. Agriculture also reduces the diversity of wild foods by killing off the 'weeds', including the very wild foods and medicinal plants that are important to the Maasai. Excluding people from traditional access to wild plant sources is denying them nutrition and an important component of their livelihoods, forcing people to resort to other unsustainable means of providing for themselves. This is especially detrimental for the most vulnerable in the society: the poor, women and children. There are also a number of environmental problems associated with conversion from pastoralism to agriculture. Increasing tree loss is serious, not only from clearance for planting crops but also resulting from demand for cooking and construction of permanent dwellings. This has serious implications for the women who have to travel and collect the firewood.

Land Speculation

Evidence suggests that people with money or political connections can influence state decisions on granting of land resources (Oxfam, 1996). The 1992 Land Commission heard evidence from villages of the arbitrary allocation of land including much to outside speculators: this has meant that pastoralists continue to lose both land and the option to move elsewhere if they are forced to do so by drought (Kaijage & Tibaijuka, 1996). Further, opportunists within the pastoral communities are persuaded to sign away land titles to third parties, often by broken promises that are not in the best interests of the community, especially the poorest. Women in pastoral communities lose out disproportionately through land sales by dominant male members of the families. Patrilineal families tend to disinherit female children as they customarily marry men from other clans, by whom it is expected that they will be taken care of. However, this does not happen so often now, and therefore traditional cultural responses are distorted by new patterns of land tenure (Oxfam, 1996).

Conservation

The Serengeti's status was changed in 1959 from Reserve to National Park, evicting the Maasai. The Maasai of the Western Serengeti and Loliondo Districts (on the east side of the Park) lost important grazing land, salt licks and permanent sources of water. These resources were invaluable to them in times of drought. On the eastern fringes, when the Serengeti was split into two, the Maasai were guaranteed land, and priority of interest and development of water points within the Ngorongoro Conservation Area (NCA).[3] However, the water dams and boreholes built within the NCA were insufficient for the needs of the 40,000 Maasai living within the area, who continue to suffer a shortage of water for livestock and themselves. When promised delivery of grain supplies and veterinary support for their livestock failed to live up to expectations, the Maasai had to plant crops to survive (Lane & Swift, 1988). When the Ngorongoro Act was revised in 1975, cultivation was prohibited altogether, seen as a threat to conservation interests, although research had shown controlled cultivation was compatible with conservation. This makes food security a severe problem, as for pastoralists in this area growing food is especially important due to declining cattle numbers.

It is also argued that pastoralists keep too many cattle as a matter of social prestige and that this will lead to a collapse of communal resources owing to a lack of personal responsibility. There is a rational strategy for keeping many cattle. Cattle populations are built up in times of relative abundance so they could survive the considerable shocks of periods of drought and disease, when many cattle, people and wild animals would die. The huge increase in the ungulate population and studies on land degradation which have shown that high populations do not necessarily lead to resource depletion have undermined this argument.

Unsustainable Livelihoods

The exclusion of the Maasai from their lands through insecure land tenure and speculation, agricultural pressures and conservation have led to a cycle of tenure insecurity–community breakdown–overuse–eviction–marginalisation which is difficult to break. Once a community has been denied access to traditionally used areas, traditional land-use practices cannot be carried out; for example extensive grazing and wild-food collection. The claiming of private property title by others leads to further prohibition of resource access. As land is put to economically productive uses, such as agriculture or tourism, collective usufruct rights are broken. This leaves pastoralists at the margins of their former lands and the margins of their former existence. At this point, conservationists' claims that the evicted people would abuse land are probably correct, as there is simply not enough land at their disposal to manage in the traditional way. They are forced to seek out alternative livelihood strategies to survive. Cultivation and trading are two common alternatives for pastoralists. Selling the land title and moving away is common. Employment in private tourist enterprises is another alternative. The opportunities that formal schooling offers is a mixed blessing. Those that do not succeed in entering business and return to their pastoral communities have lost out on vital knowledge normally gained during these years, having been educated in agricultural practices.

Tourism: An Alternative Livelihood Strategy?

There are many reasons why the Maasai are unlikely to be able to practise their traditional livelihoods in the future and it is clear their livelihood options need to be widened. The prescriptive nature of centralised development priorities has stifled and suppressed much of the indigenous knowledge systems on which it might be possible to build. Land has largely disappeared to the Maasai and other pastoralists in the area. Complex land claims and counter claims do not seem likely to resolve themselves in the foreseeable future. One alternative is harnessing the revenues accrued from conservation and tourism to prevent further depletion of livelihoods.

In theory, the tourism industry seems attractive both at national and at local level. Tourism is suited to rural and marginal areas, is labour intensive and can create linkages to the local economy as supply chains for food, construction, employment and so on can be far reaching. Potentially, there are diverse opportunities for employment, for example either as self-employed guides, rangers or through working in and owning accommodation. Regionally too, pursuing tourism promises economic diversity and private sector investment, based on wildlife: an abundant and renewable resource. Economic returns can be greater than other land uses. Tourism is one industry that is not controlled by international protectionist barriers, bringing in valuable hard currency. It is relatively stable, excepting civil strife, war and oil prices (for example witness massive drop in tourism during the Gulf War).

Community Conservation Projects

International conservation non-governmental organisations (NGOs), who realise state resources are insufficient to exclude local people from protected areas and the surrounding land, have concluded that making development aid dependent on conservation results can provide incentives to a community to preserve marketable wildlife and its supporting ecosystems. 'Community conservation' projects have come into fashion. Community conservation and tourism, it is claimed, generates direct benefits for the people living in or around areas of high conservation importance, in return for forgoing certain rights to facilitate the protection of biodiversity. However, a closer look at these types of project show a different reality. An evaluation of alternative income generating schemes which encourage entry into the tourism and wildlife sector, or create alternative non-traditional industry, have shown that the majority fail. The major problems are the lack of secure resource rights, the lack of technical skills and the role of NGOs, the government and other organisations in ensuring participation. The next section will look at these problems and suggest possible ways of overcoming them.

Lack of Secure Resource Rights

Without secure resource rights the community does not benefit from the revenue from these resources such as cash from hunting concessions, bed charges and entrance fees. Tourist revenues often leak out of the local economy, with profits either captured by the external tour operator in the city or originating country. The other major problem is conflict over resources, for example competition for water is important for tourism, wildlife and agricultural uses. Land access is contested in instances where pastoral activities are prohibited from using land because it has been dedicated to tourism. Understanding of resource rights is also important as there are cases of Maasai individuals signing land resource rights away to hunting operators or conservation organisation, who are granted private ownership of land and resource rights.

To ensure that tourism benefits the local economy and that local communities do not lose out in conflict over resources, it is necessary to establish collective resource ownership: land rights. Furthermore the community must understand these rights and be able to use them, which means legislative change to support grassroots and local initiatives. There also needs to be supportive economic policies giving people incentives to value wildlife directly instead of seeing it as an obstacle to their livelihoods. However resource security must be established not only just on the park boundaries, where people congregate to take advantage of the incentives but equally extend far beyond.

Lack of Technical Skills

Many of the community conservation projects attempt to substitute the resources denied to people through the creation of jobs. However, the poorest members of the community often lack the technical skills needed to secure employment that can provide a sustainable livelihood. Although the regular jobs provided by tourism and more informal work such as souvenir selling, cultural performances, sale of charcoal, collection of camping fees, etc. can provide links to the local economy and supplement people's income, many would agree that this type of employment leads to debasement of their dignity and weakening of traditional cultural practice. As the tourist industry is a non-traditional revenue earner which revolves around the entrepreneurial spirit, those with language skills, entrepreneurial experience and education have advantages. Thus the main beneficiaries of tourism tend to be the (mostly urban) national and local elite. For the poorest people, the resulting income disparity (and cultural dilution) can cause conflict within a community by exacerbating differences (Berger, 1993).

Development initiatives should be supported by equitable and communal management responsibility, local skill improvement and training, rather than solely by financial reward or handouts. Any initiative must be negotiated with the whole community using communal mechanisms for resolving disputes that arise. In addition, appropriate incentives are needed to establish fair, negotiated, profits in recompense. For the poorest people, creating a livelihood must include more than an unstable weak link into the cash economy. Attempts to sustain livelihoods for people must build on a range of strategies, not just tourism and job creation. Weaker groups in a society, for example: women, illiterates, elderly and poor people will still be denied this access. These groups of people might rely more on collection of wild resources, social networks, and the traditions of communal access to resources than others.

The Role of NGOs, the Government and Other Organisations

It is not easy to ensure that the whole community participates in these development initiatives. Even when participation mechanisms are said to be in place, it is often of a lesser degree than that in which the community, or the most vulnerable of the community, have any real influence in the outcome of the decision to be made. One inherent flaw in the process is that the instigating agency calls together the stakeholders it identifies, but ironically fails to recognise themselves as one. It therefore retains control over the agenda throughout the process, to the extent of selection or emphasis of local views (Lane, undated). Training in participatory techniques by agency staff and rural extension agents is not sufficient to achieve participation; institutions themselves must change, to reorient their structures and goal-oriented approach, reporting lines, rewards systems and finance management if they are truly able to effect a change. Local institutions must be built on if local livelihoods and natural resources are to survive. In addition to livestock practices, notice must be taken of local institutional mechanisms such as women's groups, credit unions, food crops processing, community forestry, water-source management and watershed protection. All stand a greater chance of continuing after the withdrawal of donor funding if instigated by the community for the community, building on their own knowledge (Cernea, 1993). Local capacity and institutions must be built on if local people are to carry the application forward with their own resources, based on local knowledge and the need to protect people's long-term livelihoods. Encouraging development in and around protected areas based on indigenous knowledge would result in synergy and a mutual combination of interests: both from the point of view of the rural poor and that of conservationists.

Conclusion

The solution lies in secure communal land rights and devolved management responsibility for resources to the people who have the most to benefit from them. These rights need to be supported legally and through macro policies if the local community is really going to gain control. Any new land tenure framework and protected areas network must be negotiated considering the needs of both conservation groups and pastoralists.

Provision must be given for access to skills and training to enable communities to take full advantage of their resource rights and allow the poorest people to benefit from alternatives such as tourism. This would provide the multiple dividend of creating conditions for stable and time honoured grazing practices to support pastoral populations, at the same time preserving optimum conditions for the region's wildlife and continuing to attract revenue opportunities from community-managed tourism. Revenue from tourism would stay closer to the point of attraction, where it is needed the most.

While pastoralists are undoubtedly interested in participating and accessing the revenues that tourism can bring, their ultimate interest is in their herds and access to former lands. Tourism offers an alternative livelihood strategy but must be complemented by alternatives so that people can choose which strategy to adopt.

Correspondence

Any communication should be directed to Ric Goodman, 36 Henley Street, Oxford OX4 1ES, UK (goodman@pobox.com).

Notes

1. Other pastoralists include Ilparakuyo and Datoga, of whom the Barabaig are the significant group.
2. For example, in the Sale division of Ngorongoro, where Maasai traditionally took cattle to irrigated agricultural land of the Sonjo in the dry season. In the wet season

they returned to Maso. Shivji, I. *A Legal Quagmire: Tanzania's Regulation of Land Tenure (Establishment of Villages) Act*, 1992, IIED, London 1994.

3. Governor of Tanganika addressed the Federal Council on 27 August 1959.

References

Berger, D.J. (1993) *Wildlife Extension*. Nairobi: Acts Press.

Cernea, M.M. (1993) Culture and organisation – the social sustainability of induced development. *Sustainable Development* 1 (2), 18–29.

Cheeseman, T. (1999) Policy failure in Kenyan conservation and Maasailands. On WWW at http://www.cheesemands.com/kenya.policy.failure.html

Kaijage, F. and Tibaijuka, A. (1996) *Poverty and Social Exclusion in Tanzania*. Research Series 109. Geneva: UNDP, International Institute for Labour Studies.

Lane, C. (undated) *Ngorongoro Voices. Indigenous Maasai Residents of the Ngorongoro Conservation Area in Tanzania Give their Views on the Proposed General Management Plan*. Forests, Trees, and People Programme, FAO.

Lane, C. and Swift, J. (1988) *East: African Pastoralism – Common Land, Common Problems*. Report on the pastoral land tenure workshop, Arusha, Tanzania, 1–2 December. Drylands Issues Paper No. 8.

Oxfam (1996) Land tenure and claims in Ololosokwan Ngorongoro district in Tanzania. Oxfam UK/I and KIPOC Research Report, unpublished.

Shivji, I. (1994) *A Legal Quagmire: Tanzania's Regulation of Land Tenure (Establishment of Villages)* Act, 1992. London: IIED.

Socio-political Aspects of Establishing Ecotourism in the Qwa-Qwa National Park, South Africa

Thea Schoemann

Department of Geography and Environmental Management, Rand Afrikaans University, South Africa

Large portions of rural South Africa can be considered to belong to the Third World. Tourism has been shown to often be the catalyst for the economic empowerment of such regions. Since 1993, there has been no tourism development in the former Qwa-Qwa homeland, therefore the purpose of this study is to investigate the lack and problems of tourism development in Qwa-Qwa, with emphasis on ecotourism in the Qwa-Qwa National Park (QNP).

Although the QNP has all the necessary resources and features to provide specialised tourist facilities, the following were identified as the major factors affecting ecotourism development in the area:

(1) the dispute over the legal tenureship of the land covered by the QNP;
(2) the almost endless restructuring and re-organisation of departments and reporting structures in Agri-Eco and the Free State Provincial Government;
(3) the inability of the Free State Provincial Government to provide clear policies and direction for ecotourism development in the QNP; and
(4) the inefficiency in the manner in which the Free State Provincial Government conduct its funding operations.

Unless the Provincial Department gets its house in order and starts making constructive decisions regarding the development in the Park, the future of ecotourism development is bleak. There is much at stake: the community in and around the Park cannot share in the benefits associated with ecotourism development, and in addition, South Africa stands to lose the use of one of its important sensitive catchment areas.

Introduction

Large portions of rural South Africa can be considered to belong to the Third World. As is a general trend in Third World and developing countries, the population is frequently impoverished and in great need of economic growth and job creation. Tourism has often been shown to be the catalyst for the economic empowerment of such regions. There is no exception to this in the Free State Province of South Africa and particularly in the area formerly known as the Qwa-Qwa homeland. Qwa-Qwa's tourism potential has not been utilised nearly well enough and the possibilities in terms of jobs and funds are enormous. The issue is simple: the greater the number of tourists, the greater number of people needed to look after them. This means more money for local communities, more jobs and greater funding to continue conservation. Since 1993, there has been no development of tourism in Qwa-Qwa, therefore a study was undertaken to investigate the problems (social and political) that are responsible for the lack of tourism development. Particular emphasis was given to the development of ecotourism in the Qwa-Qwa National Park (QNP).

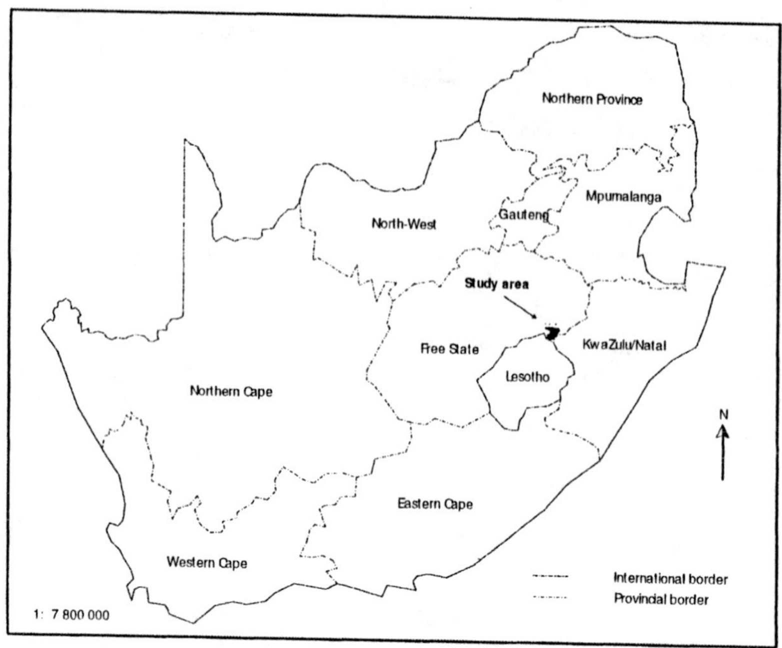

Figure 1 Location of study area in South Africa

The QNP is located in the North-Eastern Free State Province of South Africa as shown in Figure 1. The QNP is about 60 km from the town of Harrismith on the Harrismith/Golden Gate main road (R712) and forms an integral part of the Highlands Treasure Route (for more detailed maps, see Figures 2 and 3).

The Role of Tourism in South Africa

'With a population of approximately 41 million and a land area of 1.27 million km^2, South Africa's resource base for tourism is phenomenal' (Department of Environmental Affairs and Tourism, 1996: 1). The tourism attractiveness lies in South Africa's diversity and includes wildlife, varied scenery, areas of unspoiled wilderness, diverse cultures, a generally hot and sunny climate, hiking, hunting, diving, etc. These resources make South Africa ideally suited for ecotourism. Ecotourists' primary interest relates to the natural environment and traditional cultures – resources South Africa has in abundance.

Current situation

With South Africa having shed its notion of being a pariah state internationally, there are hopes and predictions of an international tourist boom. Already there has been an increase in international tourism, especially in provinces such as the Western Cape and Mpumalanga. South Africa's competitiveness in tourism is not only 'judged' by the stock of natural resources, but also by how these resources are managed and to what extent they are complemented with man-made innovations.

According to the White Paper for Tourism (Department of Environmental

Affairs and Tourism, 1996), South Africa scores well in three important areas. First, there is already a well-established network of national parks, together with private reserves. Thus South Africa is very much on track with the demands of the increasingly environmentally sensitive tourist. Second, some companies are already global leaders in ecotourism, while others have created Disneyland-like attractions, boosting the country's name internationally. Third, the recent developments in South African politics have opened the country's tourism potential to the rest of the world.

Despite these advantages, South Africa has not been able to realise its full potential in tourism. As will be discussed later in the third section, the political transformation has definitely also had negative effects on ecotourism development in the QNP. The contribution of tourism to small business development, employment, income and foreign exchange earnings remains limited and largely unrealised.

Ecotourism and the Reconstruction and Development Programme

The South African Government policy of Reconstruction and Development (RDP) is the primary strategy for the fundamental transformation of the country in the post-Apartheid era. It is based on the notion that reconstruction and development are parts of an integrated process and was specifically developed to integrate growth, reconstruction, development, redistribution of wealth and reconciliation into a unified programme.

Although the delivery of some programmes of the RDP are slower than communities would like, some progress is being made. Some of the objectives of the RDP are job creation, building the economy, the acceptance of democratic institutions and practices, protection of the environment, the provision of transport, etc. In short, the population needs to be provided with employment and entrepreneurial opportunities so as to be able to meet the costs of basic needs such as housing, water and sanitation, and electricity. The growth potential of ecotourism in South Africa is phenomenal. Ecotourism can therefore provide the necessary opportunities for the people and Government of South Africa to make the RDP work for them.

Tourism in the Free State Province

The tourist industry in the Free State currently does not have any real impact on the economy of the province. According to a paper by Strydom and Van der Merwe (1996), the reason for this is the lack of a strategic plan to serve as a guideline for marketers, developers and other role players. The Free State possesses sufficient tourist attractions and thus has the potential to stimulate the regional economy.

Ecotourism has been practised in the Free State for many years, although not under the name of ecotourism. There are a variety of hiking and pony trails, angling, etc. Most of these activities have been regulated to some extent by the Directorate of Nature and Environmental Conservation, local governments and private landowners.

Tourism in Qwa-Qwa

In studying the status of tourism in Qwa-Qwa, two important documents

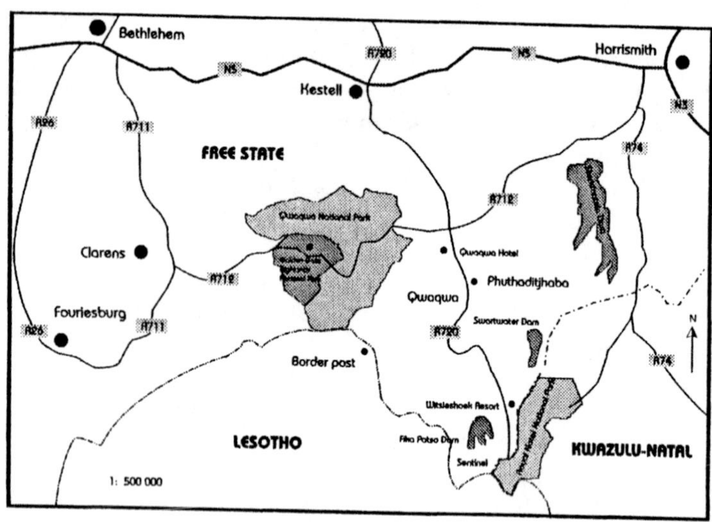

Figure 2 North-eastern free state

were considered. The first of these is a study entitled 'Qwa-Qwa Maluti Bewaringsgebied – Beplaningsvoorstelle' which translates as 'Qwa-Qwa Maluti Conservation Area – Suggestions for Planning'. The report was compiled by Gouws, Jordaan, Uys and White, a Pretoria-based firm specialising in landscaping architecture. The report was completed in 1988 and was commissioned by the South African Development Trust Corporation.

The second document of significance is a five-year development plan for tourism in Qwa-Qwa which was produced by Landplan and Associates, a consultancy firm based in the town of Aliwal North. This was completed in September 1991 and was commissioned by the Qwa-Qwa Tourism and Nature Conservation Corporation.

In their report, Landplan and Associates discussed tourism development in Qwa-Qwa on the basis of three zones. The first of these is known as the Elandsriver catchment zone and is located at the easternmost extent of the former Qwa-Qwa homeland. The second and third zones are known as the Liebenbergsvlei and Klerkspruit catchment areas respectively, the former being located in the westernmost and the latter in the central area of the former Qwa-Qwa homeland.

The Elandsriver catchment zone (eastern zone)

This zone is classified by Gouws *et al.* (1988) as the most scenic area within Qwa-Qwa. The zone features breathtaking mountain views, is home to the Swartwater, Fika Patso and Sterkfontein dams and is easily accessible via relatively major roads (Figure 2). As such, it has obvious tourist potential. It is, however, also in this zone that the potential is most at risk, due to several perturbing issues. Certainly the most serious of these is the high population density of Phuthaditjhaba, the former capital of the Qwa-Qwa homeland which is situated in this zone. In addition, the overstocking of the mountain area surrounding the residential areas poses a threat to the tourism potential in that the destruction of the natural vegetation is leading to excessive erosion and the loss of the area as a productive zone.

The existing tourism attractions in this area are the Witsieshoek Mountain Resort, the Sentinel Car Park and Cable Car, the resort development on the slopes above the Fika Patso dam, the Qwa-Qwa Hotel, an overnight hut at the Swartwater dam and the Tseki Youth Centre.

The Liebenbergsvlei catchment zone (western zone)

The Liebenbergsvlei catchment area has the lowest tourism potential rating of the three zones. It does not share the spectacular scenery of the easternmost zone, nor is its use as a tourism development area recommended by either Gouws or Landplan. The reason for this is more than its inferiority in scenic beauty – the steep mountain slopes within this zone are considered to be a sensitive environmental area to which strict conservation principles should be applied.

The Klerksvlei catchment zone (central zone)

The Klerksvlei catchment area is located in the central part of the former Qwa-Qwa homeland. Although it is not as spectacular as the easternmost zone, it still features scenery that is highly rated by SATI (the South African Tourist Industry). At present, it is wholly contained within the QNP.

The Landplan Report identified this area as the most suitable for the development of tourism. It recommended that such development should focus solely on offering activities and facilities not offered elsewhere in the area. It discouraged the development of mass tourism icons such as hotels, casinos and the like, not only because these were already available in surrounding areas, but also due the large capital requirements involved. In particular, projects such as hiking, trout fishing and gamebird hunting, all of which attract specialised groups, were suggested.

It should be noted that the QNP had not been established at the time of the Landplan & Associates Report. However, it is obvious that the subsequent Park Management had heeded the recommendations of the report. As a result, it is being promoted as an ecotourism destination. Tourist accommodation is available at Eerstegeluk Farmhouse, which is fully equipped, while rustic accommodation is available at four overnight dwellings named Avondsrust, Spelonken, Welgedacht and Kliprivier (Figure 3).

As suggested by the Landplan report, tourism activities offered include game-viewing, bird-watching, night drives, horse-riding, hiking and bird-hunting. In addition, provision is also made for trophy-hunting during the hunting season, while adventure trails specifically designed to be navigated by four-wheel-drive vehicles (commonly known as 4 × 4 routes) are proving to be popular.

A must-see attraction is the Basotho Cultural Village which is situated within the boundaries of the park. The village is a reconstructed traditional village illustrating the South Sotho's culture and history. It features several specimen of the building methodologies of this tribe at various points in time, cleverly arranged to show both the lifestyles and the influence of the tribe's interaction with other tribes in the area and the early European settlers. The village prides itself in accurately reproducing the exact styles of each period in its depicted history. As such,

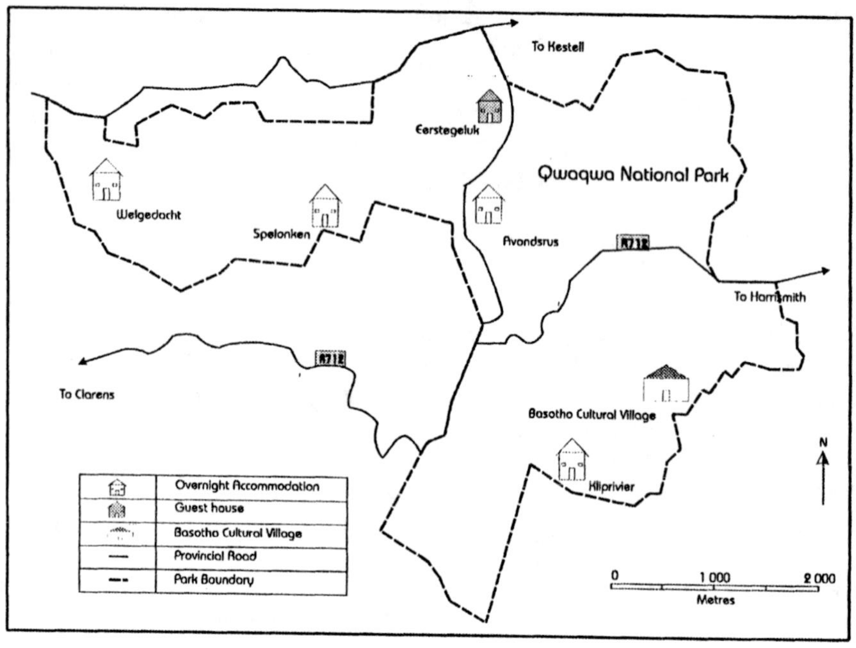

Figure 3 Qwa-Qwa National Park

the village offers the visitor an unsurpassed experience of South Sotho culture and history.

Summary

Qwa-Qwa has all the necessary resources and features to provide specialised tourist facilities as recommended by Landplan & Associates. It certainly has the potential to draw tourists since it fulfils many of the requirements set by holiday-makers when choosing a destination. Primarily these are the relatively short distance from the populous area of Gauteng which Gouws has identified as the largest source of tourists to the area, the already mentioned beautiful scenery, the friendly attitude of locals and the unique nature of facilities offered.

The efforts of the QNP in applying and expanding on the recommendations of the Landplan & Associates report are commendable. A programme consisting of three phases towards the full implementation of ecotourism is being followed. Phase 1 and 2, dealing with the establishment of administrative and service components as well as the fencing off and introduction of game into the park, have been completed. Phase 3, dealing with the further development of already existing and new ecotourism facilities, has come to a standstill due to various problems.

The QNP can truly be said to be one of the few organisations committed to the concept of ecotourism. It is, however, also facing severe problems in continuing this leading role as will become apparent in the discussion of the problems and the various role-players in the following section.

Role-players in the QNP

As discussed in the previous section, the QNP is well suited to and actively promoting the concept of ecotourism. It is, however, experiencing some difficulties in the further implementation and development of this. The primary factors affecting the development of ecotourism can largely be attributed to socio-political issues in the area. Three role players are involved: the community resident in the park, Agri-Eco (a parastatal of the Department of Environmental Affairs and Tourism, established to administer the Park on its behalf) and the provincial government. These role players and their associated problems are outlined in the following sections.

The community

The community as discussed here is defined as the people resident within the boundaries of the park. At the time of writing, it consisted of 35 indigenous families. The definition excludes formal employees of the parastatal Agri-Eco who are also accommodated in the park.

Background

QNP was formerly owned by white commercial farmers. In 1984, the National Government acquired this land through the South African Development Trust with the objective of extending the Qwa-Qwa homeland. The commercial farmers vacated their farms later in the same year, leaving their farmworkers behind. In the ensuing uncertainty of land allocation, these former farmworkers and their families made the land their home and used the land for subsistence farming. No restrictions on the cultivation or the keeping of livestock were introduced, since there was not yet a firm policy on how to allocate the newly acquired land. Eventually, the Qwa-Qwa Government did lease part of the land to new outside farmers. The introduction of this leasing arrangement was also supposed to be applicable to the population already living on the land, although it does not appear as if this was formally stated or rigidly applied.

It emerged from a study by Conchuir (1996) that very few residents of the Park knew exactly how they came to be on the land, just that they were born there and thus were exercising their birthright to the land. When further questioned, it usually emerged that they were largely part of the original commercial farming workforce or their descendants.

In 1991, the land was proclaimed as a National Park for the purpose of tourism and nature conservation. Rules and regulations emerged to control the residents concerning their livestock, usage of land, resources and tenureship in 1992. In April 1994, Qwa-Qwa was reincorporated back into South Africa and Agri-Eco became the official administrator of the Park.

The aforementioned park population has increased to approximately 300 rural dwellers residing in 11 villages within the boundaries of the Park. Legislation, introduced in 1995, makes it clear that residents in the Park have no right to claim ownership or grazing rights. There is now a move to reduce the number of livestock, and permanent employees of the Park are not permitted to keep livestock.

This situation is causing conflict and tension between the residents of the Park, Park Management and the neighbouring communities. Park Management is bound by their mandate to develop the Park for the purposes of ecotourism and conservation. In this respect they have recourse to the 1995 legislation when effecting these two goals. The Park residents feel that they are being denied full utilisation of land which they consider to be their own. Neighbouring communities feel that the residents of the Park are enjoying unfair commercial and residential advantages due to their being accommodated in the Park. Continual discussions to raise and possibly resolve the tensions are taking place. The nature and effects of these are discussed later.

Despite the conflict and tensions mentioned here, some positive interactions between the three role players do take place. These interactions have beneficial results for all the players involved, and are discussed in more detail in the following two sections.

Benefits to Park Management

Park Management has in the past indicated that they do not only have problems with the residents in the Park, but that the Park also benefits from their presence. In particular, some of these benefits include:

- Residents form 50% of the workforce in the Park,
- In a spirit of cooperation, farm labourers often inform Park Management of animals that have strayed from the Park area. In many cases this has even been done when the Park Offices are several hours' walking distance from the person's residence.
- During informal talks with residents (usually when residents are offered a lift by an Agri-Eco employee), information is obtained about the movement of animals as well as outsiders in the Park. This is an invaluable source of information in the battle against poaching.

Benefits to the community

The residents in the Park share in the following benefits:

Employment. About 90% of the park residents are involved in some form of employment generated by the park. This takes the form of permanent work, contract work, temporary work or project work. Residents from QNP make up 50% of the permanent workforce. The removal of the old farming infrastructure is handed out on a contract basis. Work assignments of a temporary nature include the cutting of thatch-quality grass during the winter months. Project work provides an array of casual employment opportunities. An example of the latter is the provision of employment for the filling of gullies as part of a soil conservation project, funded by a grant from the National Economic Forum.

A substantial amount of secondary employment is also generated directly from Park/community interaction. This benefits not only residents of the Park, but also the neighbouring communities. At regular intervals, neighbouring farmers are given the opportunity to cut natural and cultivated grasslands for fodder on a share basis with the Park, which is in turn sold to consumers in the area.

In addition, Park Management has started a broader community development programme. This programme specifically addresses the need to develop local business by more than just the provision of casual labour. Key elements of this plan involve the provision of park-generated opportunities to local entrepreneurs. The Park, where possible, assists with small loans to provide the entrepreneurs with the necessary tools and infrastructure and supports the new small enterprises by purchasing their product. Purchase of the product goes hand in hand with the repayment of the loan.

An instance of this plan that has worked exceptionally well is the Park's exotic plant control project. This project involved the cutting of black wattle trees. Each of ten local entrepreneurs obtained a loan from a revolving fund managed by the Park in order to buy a power saw. The Park purchased all the wood and sold it to the neighbouring communities. The Park only purchased wood until the loan was amortised. On completion of the repayment term, the entrepreneurs retained the opportunity to cut down the unwanted trees, but gained control of the sales as well. This in turn created further employment, as two tractor drivers were employed to transport the wood. Residents from neighbouring communities have also benefited from the community development programme by buying the wood from the Park, and selling it in their local communities.

Use of natural resources. Residents get to use the natural resources of the Park, without paying for it. Natural resources are mainly used for cattle farming. Therefore, grasslands for grazing are the natural resource with the highest utilisation by residents. Residents do not pay for any services, including water. The free use of natural resources is the major point of conflict with residents of neighbouring communities.

Other benefits. Park residents benefit directly from the presence of Park Management in the Park. Residents often contact Park Management when there is a need for water to be transported or when a family member needs to be taken to hospital. Often residents are offered a lift within the Park or to one of the urban areas like Kestell or Phuthadithjaba.

Problems

As a result of the Park's alternative income generation projects, there has been an influx of family members from other areas. Family members move back to the Park to make use of the job opportunities generated by these projects. This, in turn, is leading to the problem of the Park not being in a position to accommodate them. The resulting uncontrolled movement of people in and out of the Park is a significant matter of concern expressed by Park Management.

At present, Park Management allows Park residents free use of land for grazing. The use of this concession is, however, becoming a problem to management due to a substantial increase in livestock under residents' control. Table 1 shows current resident ownership of livestock in the Park. It illustrates the percentage of Park families that have a certain size herd of a specific livestock type. As it can been seen from Table 1, all families owned cattle, while 46% owned horses, 26% owned goats and only 25% owned sheep.

Although very few residents own large cattle herds, Park Management pointed out that a few can be classified as commercial farmers. Livestock farmers with herds exceeding 150 animals are considered to be commercial. Furthermore, some of the residents hire out grazing inside the Park to people outside the Park. These animals do not belong to the Park residents and they are operating

Table 1 Residents´ownership of livestock (modified from Conchuir [1996: 13])

Livestock type	*Cattle*	*Horses*	*Goats*	*Sheep*
Herd size	(%)	(%)	(%)	(%)
1–4	26	32	03	07
5–10	18	14	14	07
11–20	39	–	03	11
21–35	11	–	03	–
36–60	03	–	–	–
Over 60	03	–	03	–
Total	100	46	26	25

their Park concession as a profitable scheme. Although the Park encourages entrepreneurship, this practice is detrimental to the Park in terms of overgrazing and the resultant erosion, and actually violates the basic Park mandate of conservation.

Other problems experienced by Park Management due to the presence of residents in the Park include fire hazards, dogs and the cutting of fences. During the bitterly cold winter months, it is not uncommon for residents moving through the Park to start a fire for warming. This has led to devastating veld fires on more than one occasion. Dogs owned by Park residents have been known to hunt and kill some of the game in the Park, and may also pose a security threat to visiting tourists and hikers. People moving in and out of the Park have been known to cut fences, which results in game and cattle straying from the Park.

Summary and discussion – community

As seen from the previous discussions, the community resident in the QNP has a definite effect on the operation of the Park and hence also on its ecotourism development efforts. It is true that the Park benefits from the community resident within its borders and *vice versa*. Yet, the problems (and benefits) are an issue purely because the community is actually resident in the Park. From the Park's perspective, if the community were not present, the majority of the problems would not be there. Without Park residents, the Park could concentrate on its mandated tasks of conservation and the development of ecotourism supporting it. In addition, all the benefits from the community could actually be obtained through employment.

From the community's perspective, the situation is almost identical. If the Park were non-existent, the community would be able to utilise the land as they pleased. They would not have access to any of the benefits that they are enjoying as a result of the existence of the Park, but this would also nullify the socio-political argument that residents are enjoying unfair advantages when compared to neighbouring communities.

The real issue is actually a dispute over the legal tenureship of the land covered by the QNP, an issue which is of course faced by all national parks in South Africa. One cannot dismiss the expectations of the population in the light of the new political dispensation. In addition, there are favourable arguments in support of the community's claim to the land. In the same breath, one cannot ignore previous legal acquisitions of the land or the mandate of conservation given to the Park by previous governments.

Agri-Eco

The second role-player in the development of ecotourism in the QNP is Agri-Eco. Agri-Eco, properly known as Free State Agriculture and Ecotourism Development (Proprietary) Limited, was formed on 11 May 1994. The background, structure, functions and problems of this parastatal is discussed in the next sections.

Background

In 1990, the Qwa-Qwa Tourism and Nature Conservation Corporation was founded with the Qwa-Qwa Government as the sole shareholder. From 1990–93, ecotourism in Qwa-Qwa was managed and developed under the auspices of this corporation. At the end of 1993, just before the general elections of April 1994, the Qwa-Qwa Government rationalised all state-controlled corporations. A new corporation, Highlands Development Corporation, took over the management and development of ecotourism in Qwa-Qwa.

The establishment of new provincial governments after the 1994 elections, had an immediate and urgent impact on the Department of Agriculture and Environmental Affairs of the former Free State Province. In essence, the Department was charged with the incorporation, restructuring and where necessary, dismantling of the fragmented agricultural parastatals belonging to the Qwa-Qwa and Bophuthatswana homelands, and the 'old' Free State governments.

The initial view taken during the incorporation process was that the previous parastatals had been designed to support the master plan of Apartheid. They were therefore deemed to have no legitimate role in a future vision for development in the Free State. A major exercise was undertaken and an in-depth study conducted to redefine the role of these former parastatals. The study and consultation on a wide front revealed that, with restructuring and re-orientation, the resources of the former parastatals had the potential to become a major delivery agent for the reconstruction of agriculture and ecotourism within the Province.

As a result, parastatals such as the Highlands Development Corporation were unbundled and put under the direct control of the MEC (Member of the Executive Committee of the Provincial Government). This control was (and still is) exercised through Agri-Eco, a private company funded by the Free State Government with the MEC for Agriculture and Environmental Affairs as the sole shareholder.

Agri-Eco's board of directors, with guidance from the Rural Strategy Unit (RSU) recognised that the rural communities would require a range of services which would take them from poverty, beyond subsistence, to become full participating members of the broader South African economy. The company's new focus is specifically geared towards the development of entrepreneurs in agriculture and ecotourism. It is interesting to note that this entrepreneurial development beyond subsistence is considered so crucial, that even Agri-Eco is expected to become self-sufficient within four years of its inception.

Structure and functions

Agri-Eco is divided into three departments. These are Rural Entrepreneurship Development, Support Services and Entrepreneurship Development Ecotourism. Each Head of Department reports to the Chief Executive Officer, which in turn reports to the Board on a monthly basis during management meetings. The Board reports to the responsible MEC once a year, but also on an *ad hoc* basis if needed.

As this study focuses on the spatial aspects of political and social problems involved in establishing ecotourism in the QNP, only Entrepreneurship Development Ecotourism and the role of the QNP is discussed. The mission and functions of this Department, as outlined in Agric-Eco's public marketing literature, is as follows :

> The company will strive for substantive opportunities in ecotourism through entrepreneurial development, to involve rural communities in the Free State to reap social returns through long-term investments and to promote sustainable living. The company will be responsible for the creation and promotion of entrepreneurship opportunities within ecotourism. The focus will be on development operation in rural areas, where communities and other role players work together for mutual benefit and support.
>
> Furthermore, recognizing the link between rural poverty and environmental degradation, the company will support and encourage environmentally appropriate socio-economic development. Where, to the benefit of the company, its staff, local communities and the environment, the private sector will be encouraged to become involved in the entrepreneurial activities, whether as operators, suppliers of services, developers of financiers. This involvement will be subject to a code of conduct (Free State Agriculture and Eco-tourism Development (Proprietary) Limited: Ecotourism Division, 1995).

One of Agri-Eco's ultimate goals is to contribute to the improvement of the quality of life of the Free State's people. At the same time it is to ensure that entrepreneurial development has a direct and positive impact on the well-being of its host communities. Due to the political climate at the end of 1993, beginning of 1994, not much was done to solve the problems concerning the development of ecotourism in QNP. Agri-Eco inherited all of the socio-political issues mentioned earlier. In addition, further stumbling blocks in Agri-Eco's path to achieving its goals became apparent. These are detailed in the following subsection.

Problems experienced by Agri-Eco and its QNP staff

Within four years, the corporation or company responsible for ecotourism development in QNP has changed three times. This, together with the wide range of socio-political and other problems negatively influence the development of ecotourism in the QNP. The problems as experienced specifically by the QNP contingent of Agri-Eco staff are discussed in the following subsections:

Problems in developing ecotourism infrastructure. Current ecotourism activities are distributed disproportionally through the Park and include overnight accommodation, hiking trails, pony trekking, 4 × 4 trails, game-viewing, bird-watching and hunting, the Basotho Cultural Village, as well as trophy-hunting.

Ecotourism in the QNP was supposed to take place in three phases. The first phase was the development of the administration and service components, as well as putting the necessary systems in place. The second phase was the fencing off and introduction of game into the Park. These two phases were completed but the third phase, the development of ecotourism in the Park, is being affected by severe funding cuts by the Provincial Government. The only ecotourism development that has fully materialised is the Basotho Cultural Village.

The provincial road running through the Park has not yet been deproclamated by the Provincial Government. This means that the road is considered to be public as opposed to being under control of the Park. As a result, access to the Park cannot be controlled, and the general public can move freely through the park. Park Management views this uncontrolled movement of both tourists and passers-by through the Park as a problem. In the first instance, revenue is lost by not being able to charge admission fees. In addition, vehicles driving through the Park, seldom observe the speed limit of 80 km/h, thereby posing a safety risk to both visitors and game. Further, the ability of commercial trucking to pass through the Park at all hours hardly reinforces the desirable image of a quiet ecotourism-driven nature reserve.

The large herds of livestock in the Park result in two problems. The first problem is that of overgrazing. In particular, grazing by the 500–600 cattle in the Park is currently at a level where the carrying capacity of the veld is being exceeded. This affects grazing availability for game and accelerates soil erosion. In addition, the large cattle population and its resultant demand on grazing is impeding the introduction of more game into the Park. The presence of livestock and cultivated fields also reduce the aesthetic value of the Park. Tourists are invited to 'get away from it all' and enjoy the unspoilt beauty of the area. This marketing approach is being nullified when tourists discover livestock and farmlands in the game reserve. The cultivation issue also affects investment by private companies in that a large proportion of these have been known not to invest in game reserves where conservation is run in parallel to farming.

The development of ecotourism is further hampered by the fact that no comprehensive Environmental Impact Assessment (EIA) has ever been completed in the Park. The issue is of serious consequence since the QNP forms part of the sensitive catchment area that provides water to the interior of South Africa. Current legislation requires that the development of such areas be subject to the findings of a comprehensive EIA. The lack of such an assessment is casting doubt over the legality of the development plans. It is ironic that this legislation is affecting the development process, but not the greater problem of environmentally damaging farming practices. EIAs for some parts of the Park have been hinted at in the studies by Landplan & Associates (1991) and Gouws *et al.* (1988). The studies themselves can however hardly be considered as EIAs, as they did not cover all environmental aspects that need to be taken into account when developing tourism facilities in the area.

Although not a tourism activity as such, the Environmental Education Centre, which catered mainly for pupils from disadvantaged communities, had to close at the end of July 1997. The failure of the centre to obtain the necessary funding and state subsidies led to the closure. With the centre closed, QNP has lost yet another conservation-oriented facility, thereby weakening its position as a player in nature conservation.

Problems experienced with the Community. In addition to the previously discussed issues, Agric-Eco's QNP management has identified a shortage of conservational manpower in the Park. The ratio of worker per hectare is of the lowest in South Africa when compared with other game reserves (Hugo, 1996/97). This in itself is an indication that time is a limited resource for Park employees.

Very often Park Management is called to assist in transporting sick residents to hospital or to transport water to a village inside the Park. Concerns were expressed by Park Management about this and whether it forms part of their mandate. It takes up a lot time and also incurs costs and the feeling was that somewhere 'a line should be drawn'.

The various community and entrepreneural projects running in the Park also demand time from Agri-Eco employees. It is estimated that the services of two park employees are effectively lost due to project coordination undertaken by them. Park Management tries to carry the project workers beyond subsistence as one of the Agri-Eco founding goals, but as this entitles a full-time job, it cannot always be performed to the extent envisaged.

Problems pertaining to law enforcement. Law enforcement in National Parks has always been an issue. The QNP is no exception in this regard, as it needs to deal with poaching, wilful destruction of endangered species and other abuses of the land under its control. In the case of the QNP, the issues of law enforcement are complicated by the recent developments in the area.

After the 1994 general elections, the former homelands of Qwa-Qwa and Bophuthatswana (Thaba Nchu) were incorporated into the 'old' Free State Province. Each of the former homelands had its own laws pertaining to nature conservation. To solve this problem, the provincial government gazetted a ruling that the laws of all three former territories were binding. Attempting to enforce law subject to three different statutes in the QNP is proving to be most challenging. It is extremely difficult to assess the applicability of the three sets of laws in any one specific case, especially since the enforcers of these laws are normally not experts in the finer interpretation of three sets of different laws, a daunting task even to trained legal practitioners. At present, it is attempted to prosecute transgressors in the Park under criminal law rather than the nature conservation statutes.

Problems resulting from internal restructuring within Agri-Eco. At the moment Agri-Eco is restructuring the company. This is leading to changes in management staff, their management spheres and the allocation of responsibilities. The restructuring process has also cut staff numbers by up to 50%, resulting in a capacity problem. Since many experienced members of staff have accepted severance packages, the required skills and knowledge are largely absent in the newly appointed management, a situation that a large number of interviewed Agri-Eco employees confirmed.

Problems related to the Agri-Eco Board of Directors. The initial Agri-Eco Board of Directors consisted of five members appointed by the Provincial Government in 1994. The individual members were:

the chairperson of the Rural Strategy Unit, a Free State based organisation active in the development of rural communities,
a lecturer in the Department of Geography (Free State University),
a farmer/businessman from Qwa-Qwa,
the chairperson of the Free State Development Corporation and
a community representative with political affiliation.

At the start of 1997, two additional members were appointed by the Provincial Government, increasing the board from five to seven members. These two new members originated from the government's Department of Nature Conservation and Tourism, where they were employed in a temporary capacity. After just seven months of service, the two board members were replaced by another duo of government officials. As with the previous two board members, the appointments were temporary since their employment has not yet been sanctioned by the Free State legislature. In addition, one of the original five board members (the community representative) had passed away and at the time of writing, this post is still vacant.

The reshuffling and high turnover of board members has had a profound effect on the capability of the board to perform its functions. Since new board members have not been fully familiar with the prevailing state of affairs or the issues affecting the QNP, large portions of the liaison time between the Board and Park Management is being spent on orientating the new members and explaining the issues to them. Understandably, each new Board member tries to make his/her own contribution in these discussions, which often results in the re-negotiation of the vision for ecotourism development, the consultation process, how to solve the problems, etc.

Compounding the problems caused by the large turnover in Board membership was the uncovering of irregularities within the establishment and running of Agri-Eco itself. The subsequent Commission of Enquiry, which is discussed later, resulted in the suspension of new appointments to the Board, as well as a feeling of uncertainty as to the future existence and role of the Board.

The change for the QNP in its upper management structure from a localised corporation to part of the province-wide Agri-Eco was accepted with mixed attitudes. Used to being left to 'get on with the job', the QNP was now exposed not only to the Agri-Eco Board's directives and policy formulation, but also to direct management approaches from the Board.

Conflicting views were expressed by Agri-Eco employees about the Board getting directly involved in management. Some felt that the entities of Provincial Government, the Board and Agri-Eco employees were brought closer together in the 'new order' and that within the dynamic relationship, they have no problem with the Board managing as well. Others felt that the Board was interfering with their jobs. Another view expressed was that the Board was incompetent. Very few Board members actually lived in the vicinity of the QNP. It was felt by the proponents of the latter view that this lack of participation in the community largely marginalised the role that the Board can play in the Qwa-Qwa area.

Problems resulting from government interaction with Agri-Eco. From April up to September 1995, the Ecotourism Division of Agri-Eco functioned under the Free State Government Department of Economic Affairs and Tourism. A moratorium was placed on all new projects, blocking their continuation until such time as they had been fully investigated by the Department. Good cooperation with the MEC resulted in the abolition of the moratorium with the understanding that any ecotourism projects should be resubmitted to the Board for approval. As a result, Agri-Eco could continue operating efficiently with regards to its plans for ecotourism.

Shortly afterwards, a dispute developed concerning the placement of Agri-Eco's Ecotourism Division within the structure of government departments. Since ecotourism is closely linked to nature conservation, it was felt that the two should both be facilitated by the same government department. Nature conservation formed part of the portfolio of the Member of Executive Council (MEC) for Agriculture and Environmental Affairs. After consultations between the MEC for Agriculture and Environmental Affairs and the MEC for Economic Affairs and Tourism, it was decided to place the Ecotourism Division of Agri-Eco under the control of the MEC for Agriculture and Environmental Affairs. The change involved the re-allocation of reporting structures and revision of former policies.

During June/July 1996 the ruling ANC (African National Congress) government in the Free State experienced severe friction amongst its own ranks. This friction was covered extensively in the media which amongst others reported allegations of widespread mismanagement and nepotism. The causes and validity of these allegations are not of relevance to this study – what is, however, relevant is that this event led to intervention from the National Government and that an extensive reshuffling of the entire Free State Government and its departments resulted.

The reshuffling directly affected the departments that had until then exercised control over Agri-Eco and, in particular, its ecotourism division. The most serious effect on Agri-Eco was that the controlling body was changed once again (from the Department of Agriculture and Environmental Affairs back to the Department of Economic Affairs and Tourism). This largely 'back to square one' issue once again caused the changing of reporting structures and the inevitable re-scrutiny of policy.

As can be expected after three changes of responsible government structures in two years and another three changes within four years of the company or corporation responsible for developing ecotourism, Agri-Eco employees and specifically QNP staff were negatively affected. There was much uncertainty about their job security, whether the 'new' MEC would still favour the continuation of the Park or whether the country-wide National Parks Administration would be called in to take control of the QNP. The lack of any clear direction from government resulted in the situation where the development of ecotourism stagnated and the associated projects ground to a halt.

The seeming lack of any one body empowered to approve or cancel any of the developing ecotourism projects effectively dismisses any work done on ecotourism projects as of little consequence. A good example of this issue is the response Park Management encountered on attempting to obtain permission to build a new guest house. Different government officials provided different responses, one being affirmative, the other negative. Neither of the two officials was prepared to put his directive in writing. Effectively, Park Management's administrative powers have been entirely nullified.

Problems with government funding. At the time of writing, the three divisions of Agri-Eco were being funded by two different government departments. The divisions of Rural Entrepreneurship Development and Support Services were funded by the Department of Agriculture, while the remaining division of Entrepreneurship, Development and Ecotourism was funded by the Department of Environmental Affairs and Tourism. This created management problems within Agri-Eco, as the two government departments have different policies and methods of operations.

The 'commuting' of Agri-Eco's divisions between various government departments, as mentioned earlier, has also been a factor in the procurement of funding for Agri-Eco. In the case of the Entrepreneurship, Development and Ecotourism division's case, the change in overseeing government department from the Department of Agriculture back to the Department of Environmental Affairs and Tourism in July 1996 caused a serious dilemma. At the time of the reinstatement of the Department of Environmental Affairs and Tourism as the department responsible for the division, the latter had already received its funding from its former department (the Department of Agriculture). This funding had to be returned but, since this change could probably not have been foreseen at the time of budget allocation, no replacement funding was forthcoming. It is interesting to note that at no time the required funding was officially refused or any notification of cuts provided. The expected funding from the Department of Environmental Affairs and Tourism simply did not materialise. At the time that research for this study was completed (October 1997), no trace of the 'missing' funding has come to light. The 'disowned' division has been using funds from its reserves as well as funds from its sister divisions within Agri-Eco to survive. Needless to say, this survival has been achieved by particularly frugal spending.

In similar style, the subsidy for the Agri-Eco division of Entrepreneurship Development and Ecotourism has not increased in the last three years. In fact, a general directive given by Provincial Government has demanded a cut in expenditures by 15%. When considering the presiding rate of inflation in South Africa, the current budget deficit is approaching 30%. This is, of course, somewhat inconsequential since the funding itself, whether cut by 15% or not, was at the time of writing simply not forthcoming.

The effects of this lack of funding have been predictable. Park Management has scaled down operations and cut back on normal expenditures. The Environmental Training Centre was closed at the end of July 1997, uniforms for personnel were not replaced and necessary maintenance on buildings shelved. Although the day-to-day running of the Park continues, funding for ecotourism and infrastructure development has effectively been terminated. With ecotourism having been considered a valuable source of income in the future, this having been proven by the success of the Basotho Cultural Village and the QNP guest houses, the original Agri-Eco goal of self-reliance within four years now seems unlikely to materialise.

The only hope of resuscitating ecotourism development appears to be development on a joint venture basis with the private sector. This seems to be backed by the Free State Government, although no clear directive to this effect appears to exist. It is certainly not apparent in the government's actions with regards to the privatisation of other projects such as the Qwa-Qwa Hotel, Witsieshoek Berg Resort and Fiko Patso Resort which were put on hold by the 'new' MEC. Despite this, initial investigations into the feasibility of private-sector involvement has provided promising results. Several parties, amongst them a large corporation, have expressed interest in such ventures and have conditionally committed themselves to investments

There remains one major obstacle though – the private sector indicated that it is not prepared to invest in the development of ecotourism unless the land for the proposed projects is owned by Agri-Eco. When the QNP became the responsibility of the then MEC for Agriculture and Environmental Affairs through the parastatal Agri-Eco, the idea was that Agri-Eco would eventually become the owner of the Park. Although the possible future ownership of the QNP by Agri-Eco appears to have been assured, it is not at present the case and its realisation cannot be taken for granted. A major obstacle in the way is the issue of land claims as discussed in the following section.

Problems related to land claims. Land claims are at the centre of a heated debate throughout South Africa as well as countries which were formerly subjected to European colonisation. It is beyond the scope of this study to address the history of and reasons behind the issue of land claims. It will suffice to say that land claims by the previously disadvantaged communities of South Africa is proving to be a major factor in the QNP.

Both individuals from inside and outside the Park have lodged claims to parts of the land currently constituting the QNP. The National Department of Land Affairs has appointed a person to investigate these claims and to make recommendations. This report is expected to be concluded in the second quarter of 1998. Since the report is not likely to be released before the conclusion of this study, its recommendation cannot be included here.

Summary and discussion – Agri-Eco

The establishment of Agri-Eco to develop and manage tourism in the Free State must be commended as a good idea. Not only was the idea to provide a means of helping previously disadvantaged communities establish entrepreneurial businesses in line with the National Government's policy of economically empowering the nation, but its focus on protecting the environment through the development of ecotourism as opposed to mass tourism, visionary. To further accomplish these goals with a strong possibility of eventual self-sufficiency, and hence no burden on the tax-payer, has the characteristics of a winning combination.

What followed is a prime example of how things should not be done. Of all the Agri-Eco problems discussed, there are essentially just two major issues. The first of these concerns government. It is simply impossible for any person or corporation to perform a task if one is not given the authority to make decisions. The almost endless restructuring and re-organisation of departments and reporting structures is simply not conducive to getting the job done. It is true that consideration should be given to the difficulties that the new Free State Government faces, it is after all the very first time that it has had the opportunity to govern and it is far-fetched to assume that it has all the experience to perform this task faultlessly. It also faces the tremendous expectations of the population that voted it into power. Nevertheless, its inability to provide clear policies and direction, the appalling inefficiency in the manner that it has been perceived to conduct its funding operations and its inability to make firm decisions, may have destroyed the opportunities that ecotourism development can offer.

The second major factor once again deals with the land issue. Ecotourism can only be conducted in areas where the environment is of an attractive and unique nature. It is largely pointless to attempt ecotourism development in the featureless flats of the western Free State for example. This means that the scenic areas as exemplified by the QNP are scarce resources. For ecotourism development to still have a chance, land claims in this area should be settled in another manner, whether it be by cash settlement, eviction or the granting of alternative land.

The Provincial Government

The Free State Provincial Government is the third role-player involved in ecotourism development in the QNP. No information had been forthcoming from the MEC's offices or government officials. The lack of cooperation from the Free State Provincial Government, was a major problem during data collection. The responsible MEC (Member of Executive Council) for Ecotourism in the Free State changed three times within two years. Numerous phone calls were made to the different MEC's offices and the department heads, to no avail. Faxes were also sent to the MEC's offices as well as the Director for Tourism, but to date, no response has been received.

Although information about the Provincial Government and the problems experienced in the Department of Environmental Affairs and Tourism had been received from other role-players, it would be presumptuous of the author to use this information. Therefore, not much can be said about the third role-player and the problems experienced by the Provincial Government with regard to ecotourism development.

It is a great pity that the Provincial Government was not prepared to discuss its point of view on ecotourism with the author. It is felt that participation would not only have highlighted issues that they may not be aware of, but also illustrate the danger they face in sidelining a potential industry that could offer them achievement of some of their primary goals.

Solutions

Up to this point, this study has concentrated on highlighting all the factors surrounding the development of ecotourism in the QNP. Even though opinions were provided in the summary paragraphs, it would be incomplete without presenting some recommendations for solving the problems pertaining to ecotourism development in the area of the QNP. It is attempted to provide three possible solutions here.

Solution 1 – Abandonment of ecotourism (not suggested)

This cannot truly be labelled as a real solution from the point of view of the author. Nevertheless, it is an option that needs to be considered as a solution to the issues facing the development of ecotourism. It effectively calls for the disbandment of the QNP, the abandonment of its ecotourism initiatives and the allocation of the land to a committee for the handling of land claims. The disbandment of the Park does settle the land claims, but it does nothing to empower the community economically. In fact, it actually deprives the community of an invaluable resource towards obtaining economic empowerment and is likely to cause discontent in the community as to the exact land allocation granted. It is further likely to destroy the sensitive catchment area that the QNP currently constitutes.

Solution 2 – Full conservation and eviction of Park residents

In this solution, the QNP is declared to be an important catchment area and accordingly placed under full conservation. Park residents are evicted, perhaps with some form of compensation. The Park is put under direct state control which may or may not opt to allow low environmental impact visits such as ecotourism.

Although this is probably the best solution from a purely conservational point of view, the human impact needs to be considered. Enforced relocation is rather reminiscent of the previous government's eviction under the Apartheid Group Areas Act. In addition, the solution is not likely to provide the full economic benefits that intense ecotourism development are expected to yield.

Solution 3 – Controlled accommodation of Park residents and full ecotourism development

In this possible solution, each Park resident family gets a subsidy from the Government to buy their own land, either in the Park where it is fenced off with communal grazing within this fenced-off area or with grazing situated completely outside the boundaries of the Park. Alternatively, the government grants Park residents sections of the Park and separates the Park from the current Park residents by means of fencing. The Park, or what remains of it, becomes Agri-Eco property to be developed as an ecotourism destination in combination with the private sector.

This solution offers the best of both worlds. Park residents can remain in the area and are likely to continue enjoying most of their Park benefits. The QNP continues to preserve the sensitive catchment areas. Ecotourism development is possible due to private-sector funding which generates income and provides entrepreneurial opportunities to the surrounding communities.

Final Observations

The three solutions outlined are highly simplistic. Combinations and permutations are possible and the amount of detail required to implement any of these is envisaged to be substantial. Nevertheless, they do capture the essence of the two extremes and the benefit of a compromise solution somewhere in between.

Conclusion

QNP has tremendous potential for ecotourism development. This type of development can provide the much needed employment and economic growth in the area. The advent of the new Free State Provincial Government and, in particular, the establishment of Agri-Eco has provided an ideal vehicle for unlocking the wealth promised by ecotourism development. Ecotourism should be prioritised because of the rapidity with which economic growth can be generated – even in previously uncommercialised regions such as Qwa-Qwa.

At present, the development of ecotourism and its resultant benefits are under severe threat. Exploitation of the area is steadily eroding the suitability of the Park as an ideal location for ecotourism development. The pronounced absence of funding has resulted in existing development grinding to an abrupt halt. Disputes over the ownership of the QNP land are not only threatening the destruction of the Park as a nature reserve, but also the financial investment desperately needed from the private sector. Changes in the structure of the Provincial Department and frequent replacement of the responsible MEC for Ecotourism result in the lack of directive policy. Aggravating the situation is the Free State Government's apparent ignorance, lack of interest and appreciation of the opportunity being expended.

Unless the Provincial Department gets its house in order and starts making constructive decisions regarding the development in the Park, the future of ecotourism development is bleak. There is much at stake: the community in and around the Park cannot share the benefits associated with ecotourism development, Agri-Eco employees face the real possibility of losing their jobs. In addition, South Africa stands to lose the use of one of its important sensitive catchment areas.

Correspondence

Any correspondence should be directed to Thea Schoemann, PO Box 601, Randpark Ridge, 2156, South Africa (thea@internext.co.za).

References

Conchuir, R. (1996) People and parks: Qwa Qwa national park. Unpublished research report (pp. 1–22). Bloemfontein: Free State Rural Committee.

Department of Environmental Affairs and Tourism (1996) *White Paper. Development and Promotion of Tourism in South Africa* (pp. 1–25). Pretoria: Government Printer.

Explore South Africa (1996) *Ecotourism: Principles and Practice.* Pretoria: s.n.

Free State Agriculture and Eco-tourism Development (Proprietary) Limited (1995a) Eco-tourism division strategic plan – Phase I – Jan 1996 to July 1997 (pp. 2–5, 7–11). Unpublished planning report. Bloemfontein.

Free State Agriculture and Eco-tourism Development (Proprietary) Limited (1995b) Financial statements for the year ended 31 March 1995 (pp. 2–3, 7–10). Bloemfontein: s.n.

Free State Agriculture and Eco-tourism Development (Proprietary) Limited (1995c) Division: Eco-tourism. Management plan eco-tourism and conservation policy (pp. 2–3, 11–12, 41–43). Unpublished planning report. Bloemfontein.

Gouws, E.V., Jordaan, P.F., Uys, L.W.R. and White, N.G. (1988) Qwa-Qwa Maluti bewaringsgebied beplanningsvoorstelle (pp. 1–60). Unpublished planning report. Pretoria.

Landplan & Associates (1991) Five year plan for conservation and tourism facilities in Qwa-Qwa – 1991 to 1996 (pp. 1–27). Unpublished planning report. Aliwal North.

Personal communication

Botha, A. (1996) Nature Conservationist, Agri-Eco.
Chauke, R. (1996) Administrator, Curio Shop: Basotho Cultural Village.
Gernetzky, P. (1996) Nature Conservationist, Agri-Eco.
Hugo, T. (1996/97) Qwa-Qwa National Park Manager, Agri-Eco.
Joubert, G. (1996/97) Accountant, Agri-Eco.
Krause, P. (1996/97) Manager Reconstruction, Agri-Eco.
Moloi, E. (1996) Acting Manager, Witsieshoek Berg Resort.
Nel, J. (1996) Property Manager, Agri-Eco.
Roberts, L. (1996) Project Development Manager, Agri-Eco.
Thabana, N. (1996) Tour Guide, Basotho Cultural Village.
Van Zyl, W. (1996) Head of Geography Department, Qwa-Qwa University.

How Ecotourism can go Wrong: The Cases of SeaCanoe and Siam Safari, Thailand

Noah Shepherd
Environmental Tourism Consultants, PO Box 1, Phuket, Thailand

In 1989, two ecotourism operators started business in South Thailand – SeaCanoe, running kayaking trips in Phang Nga Bay, and Siam Safari, running nature tours in Phuket and South Thailand. Both companies have received international awards and recognition for their work in promoting environmentally sensitive tours yet their efforts seem to have been thwarted by the growth in mass tourism within South Thailand. Throughout the 1990s, Phuket received a three-fold increase in arrivals, and with it the establishment of many imitators of the original pioneers. This paper looks at the relationship between mass tourism and ecotourism and questions whether the two are compatible or mutually exclusive.

Background

In 1989, two ecotourism operators started business in South Thailand. SeaCanoe, running kayaking trips in Phang Nga Bay, and Siam Safari, running nature tours in Phuket and South Thailand. Both companies have received international awards and recognition for their work in promoting environmentally sensitive tours yet their efforts seem to have been thwarted by the growth in mass tourism within South Thailand. This chapter looks at the relationship between mass tourism and ecotourism and questions whether the two are compatible or mutually exclusive.

Phuket – a Growing Tourism Destination

Phuket, Thailand's largest island, is promoted by the tourist industry as the 'Pearl of the South'. Throughout the 1980s and 1990s, Phuket has developed into Asia's top tourist resort. Phuket lies 7 degrees north of the equator and has a varied terrain with sandy beaches and limestone cliffs. Inland are found forested hills and rubber plantations plus a huge variety of tropical vegetation. The island is one of South East Asia's main yachting destinations with full marina facilities and a deep sea port that is used by cruise ships.

Phuket was a destination for Thai tourists and backpackers until the start of mainstream tourism in the mid-1980s with the development of major hotels including Holiday Inn, Le Meridien and Club Med. Phuket International Airport receives hourly flights from the capital Bangkok, and daily scheduled international flights from around the region. With the advent of charter flights in the mid-1990s, the airport now handles 20,000 arrivals and departures a year. The island is connected to the mainland by two bridges, with bus services from Bangkok and Southern Thailand. There are 20,600 licensed hotel rooms on the island ranging from five star international resorts to small bungalows plus a large number of unlicensed guesthouses. Tourism has achieved a meteoric growth in the 1990s. Official arrival figures have doubled over a 10 year period to 2.6 million in 1998 (Tourism Authority of Thailand, undated). More recently, Thailand's tourism arrival figures have been boosted by three factors – the Tourism Authority of Thailand's (TAT) *Amazing Thailand 1998–1999* campaign, the Asian financial crisis and political instability in Indonesia (Bangkok Post, 1998; Bailey, 1998).

The area surrounding Phuket is a nature lover's paradise. The dramatic Phang Nga Bay, a proposed UNESCO World Heritage site, is situated to the north east of the island and contains over 150 limestone islands, with stunning cliffs, pock-marked with caves that are home to swiftlets, bats and other tropical wildlife. Mazes of mangrove forest line the estuarine bay. Once in the bay, whilst only an hour or so from the mainland, the experience is like being in the wilderness. Caves link the outside of limestone sea stacks to internal rooms, open to the sky known in Thai as 'hongs'.

Within the caves and caverns, swiftlets make nests that are harvested by the Birds Nests Monopoly. The nests are sold for prices up to $US1000 a kilogram and used in such delicacies as bird's nest soup. Traditional methods are used whereby bamboo scaffolding is erected in the caves and workers scale the poles precariously to hand pick the nests from the walls of the caverns. The rights to harvest the birds' nests lie with the Birds Nests Monopoly. Until commercial tour operators started operating in Phang Nga Bay, the monopoly had no interest in the caves other than harvesting nests.

Kayaking – the Perfect Ecotourism Product?

John Gray founded SeaCanoe, initially as an extension of his kayaking operation based in Hawaii. Gray had specialised in multi day kayaking tours in the South Pacific Islands with a customer base almost exclusively of US tourists. Gray had planned to expand his operating territory to the South East Asian region and in 1988 ran his first survey trip to South Thailand.

In exploring Phang Nga Bay, Gray found that it was possible to take inflatable kayaks through the caves to the inner rooms or 'hongs' within the islands. Whilst these caves were known by local fishermen, their exploitation for commercial tourism had never been considered.

The tourist market at that time whilst growing, was at a transition stage. Wealthy tourists, staying at luxury resorts, were beginning to force out the backpacker market that had moved on to other destinations such as Ko Samui in the Gulf of Thailand. Phuket was growing as an up-market destination, with some rooms in luxury resorts rented out for several hundred dollars a night. There was certainly no real charter or package tourism market at that time, most of the tourists in hotels being FIT travellers, purchasing mix and match packages from specialist Asian destination travel brochures.

Gray found several local partners and the fledgling company started day trips to visit Phang Nga Bay. Gray's plan was to establish Thailand as a destination for multi day trips sold abroad, but cashflow was essential and he decided to run day trips into the bay to build up the business.

Initially, SeaCanoe sold tours from the Diethelm Travel hotel tour desk at Le Meridien Hotel, near the resort town of Patong Beach. The tour was in stark contrast to others offered to tourists in Phuket. Phang Nga Bay's 'James Bond Island' made famous by the film 'The Man with the Golden Gun' was visited by many other tour operators. These tours sold for less than 1000 Thai baht (then

$US40) and included a boat trip to the island, with a stop for lunch at the stilted Muslim village of Ko Panyii in the north of the bay. The trip Gray offered was initially viewed by many as bizarre and expensive. Starting with a local 'long tail' boat, the vessel traditionally used by local fishermen, Gray and his colleagues took four people at a time into the bay. The boat was loaded with inflatable kayaks and a cook who would prepare lunch for the guests. In the bay, the guests would board the kayaks, and be taken, when the tide was just right, through the caves, to the hongs in the middle of the islands where wildlife could be stared in the eye. The hongs were like stepping back in time and remain to this day a marvel to tourists. The tour was very popular with guests, and sold for double that of any other tour offered around Phuket.

Quality, safety and environmental issues

One of the key points to SeaCanoe's day trip tours was that the caves and hongs could only take a limited number of kayaks at any one time. Furthermore, the time factor was crucial, because the caves could only be entered at certain tide levels. Too many kayaks would mean congestion with subsequent burdens being put on the environment itself (something that SeaCanoe felt very strongly about). Safety was also a major issue – too many kayaks with untrained guides could (and would) result in dangerous situations. For these reasons, SeaCanoe decided to limit the number of tourists that it would handle in one day – enforcing a no drinking, smoking, eating, talking or taking of souvenirs policy for its customers. Guide staff amazed customers by paddling off to collect floating garbage and taking it back to the escort boat for proper disposal. The company had developed a statement of purpose, which claims that:

> SeaCanoe develops sustainable business opportunities with local people that promote environmental conservation by providing high quality recreational adventures specialising in natural history and cross-cultural education. (SeaCanoe, 1997/98, 1998)

SeaCanoe's business ethics, training and approach to the environment are not in question; on the contrary, there are very few businesses within the tourism industry in Thailand that are as passionate about environmental protection and rural development as SeaCanoe. Moreover the company had involved locals in its share structure, thus embodying the principles that were widely becoming accepted by the fledgling ecotourism movement.

In 1992, SeaCanoe experienced its first taste of competition, started by an ex partner. The tours offered the same destinations as SeaCanoe and used a network of the now extensive tour counters on the resort beaches of Phuket to sell their trips. At the time, it was widely recognised by the travel business that SeaCanoe was by far the better operator in terms of trip quality, staff training, equipment used and responsibility to the environment. However, bigger commissions to tour counters and a cheaper selling price helped to promote the growth of the fledgling competitor.

In many ways, SeaCanoe has been more successful in its overseas marketing than locally. By 1998, the company had received five tourism accolades, the first, in 1995 was a regional winner in the British Airways Tourism for Tomorrow

Awards. This was followed by a commendation by Green Globe (1996); a Gold Award for ecotourism by the Pacific Asia Travel Association (1996); an environmental/ecotourism award from the American Society of Travel Agents/Smithsonian Magazine (1997) and Best Inbound Tour by the Tourism Authority of Thailand (1998). The SeaCanoe management was experienced in marketing and promotion of its activities and over the years has been written about in dozens of newspapers and travel magazines as well as receiving extensive television coverage.

Competitive threats

By 1996, the term *SeaCanoe* had more or less come to mean 'sea kayaking tours in Phang Nga Bay'. The number of competitors had grown, and tour counters, respectable travel agents, tour operators and representatives were selling any of the now three other companies' products as 'SeaCanoe'. In many cases, a SeaCanoe logo and sales brochure was shown on display, but the actual product sold was a cheaper imitator. Over the years, SeaCanoe hosted overseas tourism students for internships. The students were routinely sent to Patong Beach, the main resort town in Phuket to pose as potential customers. In nearly every case, when contacting tour desks to buy an original SeaCanoe trip, they were presented with other operators as better options, or indeed as 'the original' company. Names like 'Sea Cave Canoe' and 'Sea Safari' confused tourists, many of whom thought they were taking a trip with the company that they had seen on television (Faculty of Hotel and Tourism Management, 1998).

Nick Kontogeorgeopolous' unpublished PhD thesis (Kontogeorgeopolous, 1998) is probably the most thorough documented study of SeaCanoe's business activities. In 1996, Nick made a survey of other kayaking operators and his field notes were published on the SeaCanoe web site to the annoyance of the other companies. In this report, Nick referred to other companies' *unappealing* and sometimes *disgusting food, decrepit escort boats*, and noted that some companies *ignored safety and natural history information*. He also reported that some companies had *minimal English language skills* (Kontogeorgeopolous, 1996).

Perhaps the most poignant statement made in Nick's unedited field notes is:

> It basically seems to me that the passengers are all the exact same thing on all 4 companies. They all think the Thai guides are wonderful, friendly, etc., they all believe the food is good (whether it actually is or not), they all say how wonderful and fun and adventurous the trip is, etc. etc. The only difference where the tourists are concerned is that some are FITs and some are not. The actual differences come 100% from the actual companies (supply side). (Kontogeorgeopolous, 1996)

This final comment, in referring to the type of customer was key to the major problems that SeaCanoe were to experience in the late 1990s.

Commercial Pressure on Locally Owned Operations

There are several sales channels that can be, and were exploited that led to the increase in SeaCanoe's problems in the latter part of the 1990s. Within the tourism industry, at a resort level, the overseas holiday company representative is a key figure. Many of the larger operators employ their own staff, smaller operators often use the services of ground handlers. The travelling customer's point of contact with the overseas operator is the representative who can be a mine of information for their clients as well as a sales point for tours. In most cases, the operator such as SeaCanoe will make a contract with the holiday operator or their wholesaler and will pay a commission for all sales made. In many cases, the representative will be salaried, and their company will pay a commission to them for all sales that they make. However, quite often, the representative will.contract directly with a tour supplier, who will pay a full commission directly to him 'under the table'. That representative is then free to sell whatever he pleases to his customers, much like a tour counter, with his own captive market.

As the number of charter and package tours increased in the late 1990s, so did the number of sea kayaking companies. Holiday companies, under continual pressure to increase bottom line profits, found themselves in a position where they could contract with other companies for higher rates of commission. The charter companies' customers were generally less selective about the quality of the tour chosen – price became the deciding factor, rather than quality of experience.

Travel industry margins threaten quality operations

At about the same time, the Asian market started to take an interest in sea kayaking. In 1997, the contract price to agents for a SeaCanoe day tour was 2,000 baht plus sales tax. Some contractors demanded a net rate of 1,000 baht (or less) per customer which was something that SeaCanoe could not, and did not want to offer despite the promised number of tourists. The Asian travel business, with tourists especially from Korea and Taiwan, moves people around in caravans of 54 seat coaches, from tours, to restaurants, to commission paying souvenir shops. The smaller kayaking companies, with their lower standards, were happy to take up the offer of large numbers of low paying customers. Shuttle services into the caves became the norm, with escort boats that were licensed for 20 people (including crew) being loaded with sometimes double that number of people on board. In 1997, the first death at sea occurred, when a boat captain of a 'Sea Safari' vessel outside a cave reversed over one of their own guides who was sitting in a kayak and he was mashed by the boat's propellers.

During the high seasons (December–March) of 1997/8/9 the situation in the bay, in and around the caves and hongs became nothing short of a disgrace. Quite literally, dozens of kayaks form traffic jams and queues which give the impression of Bangkok's 'floating market' rather than a back to nature experience. Many of the kayak operators with no conservation policy and guests and guides were often seen getting out of their kayaks in the hongs, climbing mangrove trees, collecting coral, playing water fights and scaring off the wildlife such as monkeys which are rarely seen in the hongs nowadays. Despite much lobbying to the TAT and the Forestry Department, nothing was done by the authorities to improve the situation in the bay. What was once an exclusive nature experience had become a nightmare. The onus of responsibility was thrown back to the kayaking companies themselves by the authorities to sort out their own problems.

Pressures from outside the tourism industry

By 1998, there were some 11 sea kayaking companies operating in Phang Nga Bay, who formed a cartel known as the 'The Paddle Club for the Protection of the Environment'. Within Thailand, trade associations are quite powerful and are looked to by the authorities to provide the lead in many aspects of business. Several years earlier, at the suggestion of SeaCanoe and the TAT, an attempt was made to form a club to try and regulate the number of kayaks in the bay, but this was unsuccessful. SeaCanoe had advocated a system whereby time slots would be allocated to operators to reduce the number of kayaks in the caves at any one time. The agreement fell apart, and the fledgling association never got off the ground. The role of the new Paddle Club however was far more sinister. A partnership was made with the Birds Nest Monopoly who, under an old Thai law, had the right to harvest the swiflets' nests found in the caves. The agreement was simple – kayak operators had to pay the club 100 baht per guest for the right to enter the caves, this money would be passed to the Monopoly who would restrict the overall numbers of kayaks in the caves. This position was, and is still in question legally and the right of the Monopoly to impose a charge has gone as high as the Prime Minister's office. SeaCanoe refused to pay the charge, arguing that the bay was a National Park and that the Monopoly only had the right to collect nests, not to derive income from tourism. In not paying, they were denied access to the caves by the Monopoly. SeaCanoe attempted to enter the caves, to the displeasure of the Monopoly's armed guards and the dispute allegedly led to one of SeaCanoe's managers being shot and injured outside the company's office in Phuket Town in October 1998 (Rome, 1999).

As a result of SeaCanoe not being able to enter the caves, bookings dropped off dramatically and the company suffered considerably by a lack of sales in the 1998/99 high season.

Financial implications

It has been argued by some operators that *farang* (western) managed companies are not beneficial to Thailand. These arguments are usually based on xenophobia rather than economics. Much of the actual revenues, especially where Asian tourists are involved, end up overseas, not in Thailand. SeaCanoe retains 90% of revenues within Thailand (Lindberg, 1998), but a survey comparison of trip revenues by cheaper operators shows a far different picture. In 1998, SeaCanoe charged 2970 baht for a one day tour. Almost all of their sales were made to local agents, which meant that effectively, all of the revenue remained in the country. One of their competitors, however, sold its trip for 500 baht net rate. This trip was then resold to a Taiwanese operator for 1000 baht which was then offered as an optional tour for 4000 baht equivalent – only 25% of the actual trip selling price found its way into Thailand (Shepherd, 1998).

Elephants, Jeeps and Ecotourism

Robert Greifenberg moved to Thailand in 1989 after an agricultural background in Britain and Saudi Arabia. Greifenberg's approach to starting the business was different to Gray's. Whilst Gray had experience of the travel market from his time in Honolulu, Greifenberg had none. Starting with a small plot of land, together with his wife Srivilai, he ran a small bungalow complex catering to backpackers and FIT clients. Greifenberg offered his *Siam Safari* nature tours to his guests in the form of trekking and jeep safaris around Phuket as well as off the island to places such as Khao Sok National Park. Greifenberg also took interest in showing tourists southern Thai lifestyle, by visiting rubber and other plantations and showing tourists a slice of village life. At that time, Phuket's infrastructure was not as developed as it is today and Greifenberg used his four-wheel drive jeep to take tourists to hidden parts of the island. It was not, however, until 1992 that tour agents began to take interest in his products and Siam Safari took off (Siam Safari, 1999a, b).

Local infrastructure and development

It is often suggested that tourism is responsible for over-development, and in many cases this is true. However in Thailand, whilst tourism development is now a major contributor to the country's GDP, much of Thailand's post-war growth has mainly been fuelled by agricultural exports. As a result of Thailand's increased wealth as a developing nation an infrastructure has been put into place that accommodates tourism well (Phongpaichit & Baker, 1996). One of the benefits to farming and rural development, in Phuket especially, has been the road infrastructure on the island. Previous dirt tracks and paths have given way to paved roads as part of Thailand's accelerated rural development project, which meant that safari tours became less exciting as the island became scarred with asphalt trails.

In 1989, commercial logging was banned in Thailand. Elephants, previously used for logging purposes had in effect destroyed their own natural habitats as Thailand's forests had reduced from 95% of the land area 150 years ago to about 15–20% today. Their mahouts, now out of work, took the elephants into cities such as Bangkok where they were used for begging. Baby elephants were also found in major hotels where they were shown off as tourist attractions (Greifenberg *et al.*, 1998).

At the end of 1994, Siam Safari was the first company to introduce elephants in Phuket providing trekking tours for tourists. Elephants are expensive to keep, eating 250 kg of food and drinking 200 litres of water a day. As with the case of SeaCanoe, imitators sprung up all over the island. Many elephant camps were set up along the picturesque mountain roads in Phuket, which relied on passing trade as well as paying commissions to tour guides. At times of drought, it was been reported that many of the elephants were not given enough water to drink or bathe and many incidents of abuse have been reported. In 1998, Siam Safari, together with the Dusit Laguna Resort Hotel, founded Elephant Help – the Thai Elephant Welfare and Conservation Project. Despite the efforts of Greifenberg and Elephant Help to support elephant welfare in Phuket, the introduction of treks brought many problems.

Siam Safari set up a camp on Phuket from which they run elephant treks and multi experience one day and half day trips. Trip options are numerous with opportunities to also see working monkeys picking coconuts, visit rubber plantations, see traditional Thai food being prepared in the jungle, short kayak trips in mangrove estuaries and trekking in the jungle.

More imitation and unfair competition

As with SeaCanoe, imitators, using similar logos, itineraries and generally passing off as Siam Safari have set up in business. Mass tourism has driven prices down and Siam Safari have experienced similar problems to SeaCanoe with unscrupulous tour operators and competitors. By 1999, there were 17 elephant trekking companies in Phuket with a total of 170 elephants of which Siam Safari had 23.

A different problem in the field of Jeep Safaris took place in Phuket with the advent of illegal operators. One company – and there are no doubt more – operates exclusively during the high season using all foreign guides (which is forbidden under Thai law) using rented Suzuki Jeeps. Package tour representatives sell the tours directly to German tourists. Such activity, apart from being completely clandestine and illegal, does incredible damage to potential tourism income. All of the revenues are taken without paying any tax, no locals are employed and much of the money leaves the country.

Siam Safari was honoured by the TAT as the Best Tour Programme in 1996; in 1997, the company received the British Airways Regional Tourism for Tomorrow Award and in 1999, PATA awarded Siam Safari a Grand Award for Ecotourism and Thai Elephant Conservation.

Greifenberg tries not to use the word 'ecotourism' in his marketing, not because he does not apply those principles to his business, but because he feels that the word is far too abused. Recently, he has been at pains to ensure that his jeep safaris, treks and other activities have no impact whatsoever on the environment by completely avoiding sensitive areas.

Mass tourism versus ecotourism

The problems that Siam Safari has experienced in Phuket are less complicated than those experienced by SeaCanoe, but nevertheless the problems are real. With a fleet of 25 Land Rovers, over 20 elephants and the capacity to handle 150 people on a one-day trip, Greifenberg is not happy with the way his company has grown. He feels that he has been forced into catering to mass tourism as the only means to survive. He claims that competition has forced the product into the mass market from its humble beginnings, which was never his intention. He sells at prices that are similar to those charged 10 years ago, despite considerable inflation, especially as a result of the Asian currency collapse in 1997.

Conclusion

What then is the future for ecotourism operators faced with a market of mass tourism? It is clear that the principles of ecotourism embodied in the two companies discussed are diametrically opposed to large numbers of tourists, bottom line profits of international tour operators and unscrupulous business practices. But what are the options? In both cases, the authorities are rather powerless to help. The Thai government has a somewhat *laissez-faire* attitude to business and the government's agencies and departments are also powerless to help. The Tourism Authority of Thailand has a role of promoting tourism in the Kingdom, regulation is more a matter of registration of a business as a tour operator and there are no real laws to control what could be seen as esoteric principles of tourism activity. Whilst the overall control of the National Parks falls under the Forestry Department, the rules and regulations do not relate to overcrowding. As long as trees are not being felled, and wildlife is not being damaged, there is little that the authorities can do.

It is easy in the West to talk about rules and regulations within the tourism industry. Despite central government rhetoric, in developing nations, understanding and principles of environmentally sensitive tourism at a local level is very hard to get across, especially in the light of potential business opportunities. Industrial development, particularly in the Gulf of Thailand and dam construction for the country's electricity demand, imposes far more environmental damage than dozens of kayaks, jeep safaris or elephants in a discrete area. The new Thai constitution of 1997 includes such provisions, as 'a person's ultimate right to work to provide support for the family'. Ultimately, Thailand is a sovereign nation, and the authorities have the right to govern the Kingdom in whatever way they think is right, as long as international laws and human rights are not abused. Taking this into consideration, whilst ecotourism professionals and environmentalists may lament at such a tragic situation, maybe our efforts should be directed more to the mainstream tourism industry itself. The West is beginning to take the problems of child prostitution in Asia on board in an interesting way – offending nationals involved in sex with minors overseas can now be prosecuted back home in some countries. European Union laws make tourism operators responsible for the welfare of their customers whilst overseas. Maybe the West should be doing more to influence its own tour operators to be more responsible with what they offer to tourists.

Correspondence

Any correspondence should be directed to Noah Shepherd, Environmental Tourism Consultants, PO Box 1, Phuket, Thailand (noah@shepherd.com).

References

Bangkok Post (1998) Economic Review. *Bangkok Post* (31 December).

Bailey, M. (1998) *Asia's Tourism Market – The Ups and Downs, Issues and Trends*. Bangkok: Pacific Asia Travel Association.

Faculty of Hotel and Tourism Management (1998) Survey of Phuket tourists. Unpublished research, Prince of Songkla University, Phuket, Thailand.

Greifenberg, R. *et al.* (1998) *Nature Guide – Thai Elephants*. Phuket, Thailand: Siam Safari.

Kontogeorgopoulos, N. (1998) Roughing it in Phuket, but the Jones' haven't been there (yet). Reconceptualizing tourism and community development in southern Thailand. Unpublished PhD dissertation, Department of Geography, University of British Columbia, Vancouver, BC, Canada.

Kontogeorgopoulos, N. (1996) Unedited field notes.

Lindberg, K, (1998) *Economic Aspects of Ecotourism. Ecotourism – A Guide for Planners and Managers,* (vol. 2). Bennington, VT: Ecotourism Society.

Phongpaichit, P. and Baker, C. (1996) *Thailand's Boom*. Chiang Mai, Thailand: Silkworm Books.

Rome, M. (1999) Shooting to kill. *Action Asia* (February/March). Hong Kong.

SeaCanoe (1997/98) *SeaCanoe Brochure*. Phuket, Thailand: SeaCanoe Thailand.

SeaCanoe (1998) Website at http://seacanoe.com.

Shepherd, N. (1998) Ecotourism in Thailand – where does the money go? Tourism revenues in the light of the Southeast Asian economic crisis. *Third International Conference –*

'Community Based Ecotourism'. Bangkok: Institute of Ecotourism, Srinakarinwiroj University.

Siam Safari (1999a) *Sales Brochures*. Thailand: Siam Safari.

Siam Safari (1999b) Website at http://www.siamsafari.com

Tourism Authority of Thailand (undated) *Visitor Statistics*. Bangkok: Statistics Department.

Sustainability of Small-Scale Ecotourism: The Case of Niue, South Pacific

Heidi C. de Haas
Department of Geography, University of Waikato, Private Bag 3105, Hamilton, New Zealand

This paper examines whether small-scale ecotourism is sustainable. For the purpose of the paper the term 'ecotourism' has been refined, and evaluation criteria compiled for small-scale community ecotourism comprising of three concepts: environmental sensitivity, socio-cultural appropriateness, and economic viability. The case study of Niue was chosen because it met the initial evaluation criteria, and was used to determine whether small-scale community ecotourism was sustainable. Niue's tourism industry was assessed in the areas of environmental, socio-cultural and economic viability and all three must exist in symbiosis to achieve sustainability. The results of the research show that Niue's tourism industry is sustainable only in environmental and socio-cultural aspects, however, due to insufficient visitor arrivals it is not economically viable. Niue is isolated, reliant on aid and is the most expensive destination in the South Pacific due primarily to the cost and frequency of the air service. Niue can increase its visitor numbers to achieve economic viability, or attract higher spending visitors to the island. Care must be taken not to exceed the island's carrying capacity, which would cause negative environmental and socio-cultural impacts. A balance needs to be made between the three concepts to achieve sustainability, with careful planning and monitoring.

Introduction

The development of ecotourism accompanied a growing interest in the natural environment and a reaction to negative effects resulting from mass tourism. Tourism in natural areas has increased in popularity, particularly with the ever-increasing global focus on environmental awareness. Ecotourism has developed in response to mass tourism, as mass tourism destinations were beginning to show signs of degradation resulting from over-use. Therefore, ecotourism was seen as a sustainable alternative, and also a means of interest to all tourists wishing to see natural areas that were remote and exotic. However, the problem has arisen that these ecotourism operations are not as sustainable as once thought. The purpose of this paper is to assess the sustainability of small-scale community ecotourism using academic literature and the specific case study of Niue, in the South Pacific, drawn from six weeks of social science research in Niue during mid-1998.

The potential impacts, both positive and negative, of tourism reviewed in the literature, have been compiled to create the evaluation criteria used to determine whether an ecotourism site is sustainable. A holistic approach has been incorporated to assess whether small-scale ecotourism was indeed sustainable in terms of environmental, socio-cultural and economic aspects. The tourism industry in Niue will be briefly discussed, then assessed in relation to the evaluation criteria.

Tourism in Developing Countries

Ecotourism reaches the most remote areas of the earth, located 'off the beaten path' (Mandziuk, 1995). As many tourists visit fragile environments, however, it is important that these environments remain unspoilt. Many ecotourism destinations are located in developing countries that have a reasonable number of natural areas still intact. Most tropical islands are found in developing regions of the world and have become increasingly popular since air travel has become available. The attraction of travel to developing countries has been led by the influence of 'palm-fringed islands, adventure, intriguingly different cultures and strong northern currencies' (Wheat, 1994: 16). Developing countries often welcome ecotourism developments as they foresee economic profits from the tourists, and will consciously choose economic benefits over environmental sustainability in their struggle to survive (Cater, 1994). As a result there is more concern with short-term gains than consideration for the possible long-term effects or losses (Cater, 1994; Wall, 1997). Tropical island environments, such as the Pacific Islands, have unique natural environments and unique cultures that are very fragile and sensitive to impacts resulting from increased visitor numbers to the islands. These tropical island environments attract ecotourists and as a result the probability of negative impacts resulting from ecotourism increases (Wilkinson, 1989).

Ecotourism over-development

The number of ecotourism destinations and operations has increased rapidly, to the point where some destinations have a larger number of ecotourism operations, resulting in over-use of the natural resources. Ecotourism started with good intentions: to have small-scale, locally owned operations, but over-development has occurred resulting in a form of tourism that closely resembles mass tourism. The concept of ecotourism was developed in response to the negative effects of mass tourism. As Liew (1990: 86) stated, 'people are the cause of environmental degradation and the beneficiaries of development', leading to a cycle of trade-offs between the environment and economic benefits.

Tourism creates a dilemma for developing nations in respect to economic benefits or environmental or social problems. Lanfant and Graburn (1992: 103) state, 'for a developing nation not to choose tourism amounts to eventual death according to economists, but to choose tourism is also death according to anthropologists'. As ecotourism utilises a natural resource as an attraction, over-use may result in resource degradation thus destroying the resource base for the tourism operation. This is a dilemma that tourism operations must consider carefully. It has been implied that small-scale, locally controlled and ecologically sensitive tourism industries can neither sustain many visitors, nor be a big money maker (Higinio & Munt, 1993).

Evaluation Criteria for Ecotourism

The creation of multiple definitions and the wide use of the term ecotourism has resulted in the increasing difficulty in understanding the meaning of the term. Esau (1996 cited in Burton, 1998: 756) wrote, 'ecotourism is an anomaly used to describe anything from operators who demonstrate an awareness of environmental issues and manage their operations accordingly, to operators who base their operations in a natural environment'. Lindberg and McKercher (1997: 66), highlight growing concern in their statement, 'the term ecotourism has been hijacked and by the early 1990's had become a positioning statement and a politically correct form of mass tourism'. This has also contributed to the growing lack of clarity and understanding of the term ecotourism.

Due to the present problems with defining ecotourism, criteria have been created with the understanding that the criteria are flexible to other ideas and approaches. The evaluation criteria were grouped under four concepts. These were consistent with Wall's (1997) concepts of economic viability, environmental appropriateness and socio-cultural acceptability, with the addition of small-scale development. These criteria reflect a way of thinking, a concept that requires full commitment from all those that use the term ecotourism. Tourism ventures that meet these criteria will be referred to in this chapter as small-scale community ecotourism.

Small-scale community tourism should involve limited tourist numbers, limited infrastructure and superstructure specifically for tourist use (Lindberg & McKercher, 1997), and should instead rely as much as possible on facilities already available for local use (Cater, 1994). Development should also be small-scale and locally owned (Weaver, 1991), as well as being environmentally sensitive. In order to realise this, efficient use of resources for tourism development is necessary. This can be achieved through the existing natural features being utilised as tourist attractions (Chalker, 1994; Orams, 1995). Provisions should be made to protect and conserve the natural features, in particular those located on fragile land and threatened areas (Budowski, 1977; Chalker, 1994; Lindberg *et al.*, 1996; Orams, 1995; Weaver, 1998).

Environmental sensitivity

Development restrictions need to be placed on the environment and natural resources as gradual degradation resulting from ecotourism could result in irreversible damage. According to Hjalager (1997), those within the tourism industry attributed environmental problems with the volume and number of tourists. It is common knowledge that tourism can contribute to environmental degradation and be self-destructive, but if tourism is planned and structured properly it can promote significant enhancement of the environment (Pigram, 1992). Money raised from tourism should be re-circulated back into conserving the attraction, although this is not always possible when the profits are required for other necessities such as living expenses or paying off debt. For less developed countries as de Kadt (1992: 57) states, 'a crucial aspect of sustainability is to maintain the productivity of the resource', therefore, it is mutually beneficial for both the tourist ventures and the local population to maintain the natural environment. Long and Wall (1996: 48) stated that 'environmental impacts often occur in the forms of new facilities, infrastructure, superstructure, architectural styles, carrying capacity issues, wastes and pollution'. The only way to completely remove all forms of tourism impacts is if the natural areas remain untouched by people (Budowski, 1977).

Tourism planning and education could minimise and prevent the majority of environmental degradation that occurs in ecotourism destinations. Environmental awareness should be fostered through the ecotourism operations, among the ecotourists and the local population (Weaver, 1998). Uncontrolled development should not be allowed to occur, as it can be potentially destructive to the natural environment.

Socio-cultural appropriateness

Small-scale community tourism should be socio-culturally appropriate. In order to achieve this, the local community must be involved in tourism planning, development and decision-making. When the local community is involved in the running and ownership of the tourism ventures the well-being of the local population is more likely to be sustained, as they are less likely to be exploited from within (Chalker, 1994; Orams, 1995; Wall, 1997). The inclusion of the local population in tourism planning and decision-making is deemed very important for successful small-scale community ecotourism. In order for ecotourism to be viable, benefits for local people should be higher than costs (Chalker, 1994). Noting the difference between the tourists and the local populations can allow for the assessment of possible social impacts between tourists and the host population (Butler, 1974).

There are many positive aspects for the local populations in small-scale tourism development. Ecotourism development can empower the local community as it promotes the use of indigenous knowledge, material and labour, and provides the opportunity for the local population to generate economic benefits from tourism (Khan, 1997). Furthermore, ecotourism development can promote local ownership, perpetuate local identity and strengthen economic equity in the community (Khan, 1997). Most of the benefits for the local population accrue once the locally based tourism industry has developed. However, frequently local populations cannot afford to start tourism development without foreign assistance, which results in a loss of control and benefits. In order to minimise this, restrictions and guidelines need to be used to maintain a small-scale community based ecotourism operation. Another positive aspect is that tourism could create an appreciation of cultural relativity and international understanding of different cultures (Smith, 1989).

Utilising the community in tourism planning, decision-making and implementation is more than just maintaining good public relations. As Pigram (1992: 86) states, 'certain individuals in the communities possess specialised knowledge and awareness of attitudes because of their occupational experience and their position in a community'. The use of knowledgeable local people enables tourism planners to obtain views that provide them with insight for that specific area that they would not otherwise have been able to access. However, tourism planners often do not consult the locals for knowledge about the environment, or develop plans to fit with the socio-cultural patterns of the community (Liew, 1990). Grundsten (1994) stated that tourism could not continue to develop unplanned, as through planning it is possible to ensure that ecotourism is sustainable. Without planning there is little hope for the natural environments and the well-being of the local population.

Economic viability

Economic viability is another requirement of small-scale community tourism. According to Khan (1997), economic viability can be achieved by limiting foreign investment to loans designed to stimulate initial development, after which point the local community assumes ownership and responsibility. Additionally, a proportion of the money derived from the tourism development should go toward the maintenance, protection and enhancement of the natural resources (Lindberg *et al.*, 1996; Weaver, 1998). Local involvement in tourism means that the local population benefits; the money accrues directly to them, and leakages are limited (Boyd & Butler, 1996; Weaver, 1998).

Small islands with limited natural resources often turn to tourism, as it seems an easy means for economic profit. Unfortunately the islands often have no alternatives for producers of economic profit, and governments of these island nations latch onto tourism solely for the economic benefits that it might bring to the country and for the expected flow-on effects of employment (Bowe & Rolle, 1998).

Money spent by tourists does not necessarily remain at the holiday destination and can leak back to the market countries. These leakages occur mostly because the holiday destination imports goods and services that in turn utilise the tourists' money. Foreign owned tourism operations and tourists using their own airlines, all contribute to the money that tourists spend on their holiday which leaches out from the local economy, therefore not benefiting the local community (Khan, 1997). This problem is often exacerbated in developing countries, as these countries do not have the developed resource base that can be utilised for tourism purposes, resulting in high imports of goods and services. Milne (1990) stated that in some small developing countries leakages could be as high as 70%.

Small-scale and its importance

For ecotourism operations to be sustainable it is also important that the operations are defined as small-scale tourism. In theory this means that there are limited tourist numbers, limited infrastructure and specific tourist development or superstructure, and the tourists should adapt to the living standards of the local people (Cater, 1994; Lindberg & McKercher, 1997). Weaver (1991), indicated that tourism development should incorporate small-scale locally owned activities.

Another component of sustainable tourism is the promotion of small-scale family owned enterprises rather than imported foreign investments (de Kadt, 1992; Hjalager, 1997). As Khan (1997: 989–90) states, ideally 'ecotourism development is most likely to be at a smaller scale, locally owned with low import leakage and a higher proportion of profits remaining in the local economy', providing more benefits for the local populations. Many academics (e.g. Murphy, 1985: Sofield, 1993) include community involvement in tourism planning, decision-making and implementation as important aspects of tourism development. Without local involvement, acceptance of tourism operations within the host community is likely to be minimal.

Small-scale tourism has been said to be sustainable by a number of authors such as de Kadt (1992) and Wilkinson (1989), as it reduces the negative impacts of ecotourism on the host population and the natural environment. Small-scale development is an attempt to contain the impacts of tourism and keep ecotourism sustainable in the long term. Small islands are often ideally suited to small-scale tourism due to their size and location.

Small islands and tourism

Island environments have highly valuable habitats, and most often the islands have highly vulnerable environments, particularly when the islands are small. These islands have few species and a relatively small population, with limited natural resources apart from access to the sea (Hanneberg, 1994). Island environments interest a large number of tourists as they are exotic, interesting and unique destinations (Britton, 1987), and as a direct result there are many ecotourism operations in small islands. Tourism can benefit these small islands with contributions to the economic revenue, through employment, although the operations can be hindered by a remote location and the difficulties in developing and implementing a tourism management plan (Ringer, 1996). However, there must be strict controls placed on the development and planning of tourism operations in order to retain local control of and benefits from tourism.

Summary of Literature Findings

There are a number of aspects involved in small-scale community ecotourism. This term has been developed as a continuation of ecotourism. There are many constraints with the term ecotourism as there is little chance that a workable definition suitable for use will ever be developed. Small-scale community ecotourism involves four evaluation criteria: environmental sensitivity, socio-cultural appropriateness, economic viability and small-scale tourism. This provides a holistic approach to assessing ecotourism operations. Ecotourism in developing countries (particularly small islands) has been reviewed, as it is important to link this with both small-scale tourism and ecotourism, since most ecotourism destinations are in developing countries. Ecotourism does not always live up to the expectations, and often over-development occurs when there is little tourism planning. Environmental degradation and other negative impacts are a direct result of over-development, which leaves the local community with a less than perfect environment and additional associated problems. Due to the problems identified, it is important to test whether small-scale community ecotourism is sustainable.

Case Study: Niue

The purpose of this section is to assess whether small-scale ecotourism is in fact sustainable, through examination of the case study of Niue. Niue was chosen because it is different to surrounding Pacific Islands, which provide typical beach resort environments. It is also evident that Niue's natural resources are used as tourism attractions and there are a limited number of tourists to the island each year. Niue deals with tourists who are not the typical 'sun, sand, sea tourists', different to those attracted to other Pacific Islands. Tourism promotion in Niue is marketed to a smaller elite group of travellers. As a consequence of

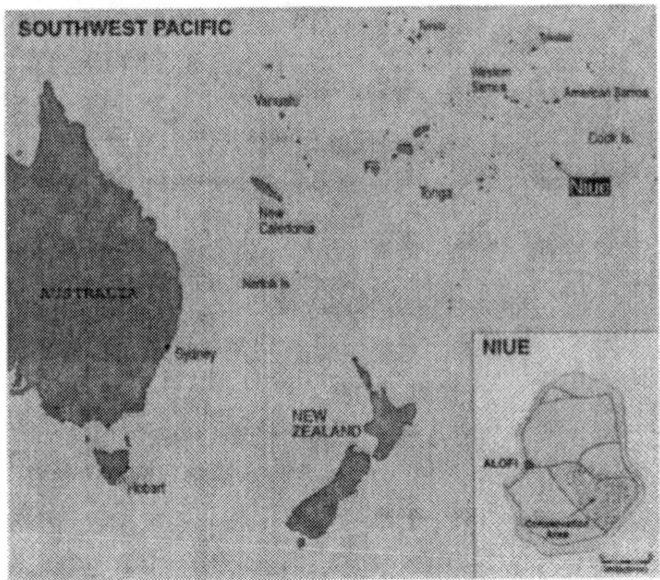

Figure 1 Location of Niue in the South Pacific
Source: Oulton, 1999

marketing strategies and accessibility, numbers of tourists travelling to Niue are relatively small; therefore it is presumed that tourism is more sustainable. The research will attempt to determine whether small-scale tourism is, in fact, sustainable in Niue.

Niue in General

Niue is a small raised coral island in the South Pacific (Lane, 1994): it is situated in a central position in Polynesia, with Tonga to the West as its closest neighbour (see Figure 1). Western Samoa lies to the North, the Cook Islands to the East, while New Zealand lies Southwest of Niue at a distance of 2400 kilometres (Yarwood, 1998). Niue has limited natural resources, with a landmass of 259 square kilometres. As Niue is an island it also has a significant marine environment. Niue's Exclusive Economic Zone (EEZ) covers approximately 390,000 square kilometres of sea (Lane, 1994). Within the EEZ there are three reef systems, the Antiope, the Harran and the Beveridge Reefs (Lane, 1994). The Niue Dive operator identified Beveridge Reef as a potential tourism attraction for diving (and fishing) (Fawcett, pers. comm., 1998; Moore, 1999).

Since the early 1970s, many Niueans have left Niue for New Zealand (with whom Niue has free association) and as a result the population has declined significantly. In 1966, the population of Niue was 5194 (Statistics Immigration Unit, 1991); however, out migration had decreased it to 2300 by 1996 (Dickinson, 1998), and in 1998 it was estimated to be 1900 (Waqa, 1998). Many of working age have migrated in search of better opportunities and paid jobs, leaving a high proportion of young and older people in Niue.

Niue's limited resources restrict options for expanding the island's economic base. Taro is Niue's major export consisting of 85% of all exports (Lane, 1994). However, the agricultural products that Niue does export do not provide sufficient income to make Niue self-sufficient. Other money earners include cash crops (such as vanilla), postage stamps and tourism (Yarwood, 1998). In 1993, exports from Niue amounted to less than one-seventh that of imports (Kiste, 1998), while in 1996 total imports reached an all-time high of five million dollars (NZ) (Yarwood, 1998). Niue receives millions of dollars annually as aid from New Zealand to supplement its economy. Tourism has been given the status and priority of solving all of Niue's financial worries; yet, at this stage there has been no indication that it can indeed provide self-sufficiency for the island, as tourism has not been a reliable money earner, although it has become increasingly popular as a possible means for providing an income. Unfortunately, there is the potential that tourism will succumb to the same fate as most of Niue's other economic projects, and fail.

Tourism in Niue

It was not until 1971, with the new airport that Niue had frequent and easy travel to and from neighbouring islands. In 1975 the Niue Hotel was built although other accommodation developments and tours for visitors did not develop until the 1980s when Niue began focusing on tourism. Unlike many other Pacific Islands, Niue has barriers and hindrances that affect the tourism industry such as isolation, lack of their own air carrier (and thus a reliance on other air carriers), and the vulnerability to natural disasters that can damage infrastructure and the natural environment. Niue's economic growth and development is restricted due to its distance from neighbouring islands, and heavy dependence on imports of goods and services (SPC, 1994).

Niue's past has proven its dependence on New Zealand aid to support its economy. Milne (1992: 569) concluded, 'While tourism will continue to be an important source of additional income and employment, Niue will remain dependent on public sector employment and international aid flows for the foreseeable future.' In particular Niue relies on remittances, aid and bureaucracy to supplement or provide income to the already depleted economic revenue. Over the past 10 years, millions of dollars in aid money have been used to develop Niue's tourism industry, either through promotion of the island as a destination or through preparation of Niue for the anticipated 'tourist boom' (Planning and Development Unit, 1998). Tourism became increasingly important for Niue as a source of income. Fortunately, most tourism ventures have been small-scale developments to reduce possible impacts to the environment and local people (Skinner, 1980).

Niue's history with tourism has not been stable. The island has not been able to attract visitors in large numbers, and thus its development has been hindered. In Niue's early stages of tourism it was hoped that 20,000 tourists annually would be attained by the year 2000. In 1994 this goal was reduced to 10,000 tourists by the year 2000. This goal, according to the Environment Unit (1995, 43), was 'dependent on the establishment of regular and reliable air links, a development which has proven difficult in recent years'. The Director of Tourism noted that the goal was lowered even further in 1997 to approximately

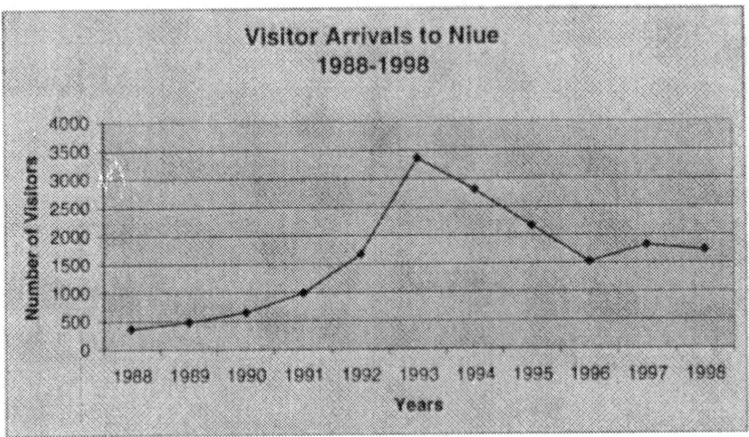

Figure 2 Total Visitor Arrivals to Niue from 1988–1998
Source: Statistics Niue, 1999

5000 tourists by the year 2000 (Rex, pers. comm., 1998). In 1993 Niue's tourism reached a peak with an all time high of 3358 visitors to the island, while in 1998 there were 1729 visitors to the island, making the assumed goal of 5000 seem distant (see Figure 2).

The lack of tourists is specifically related to the poor history Niue has had with the various air carriers that have serviced the isolated island. Its tourism industry has also been affected by factors influencing the market countries, such as New Zealand's economic downturn in 1998. Niue has had many problems with securing an air service that meets their needs. In the past there have been problems with irregular air services, the financial well-being of the air carrier and expensive airfares. Unfortunately the present air carrier charges high airfares, which makes Niue the most expensive tourist destination in the South Pacific, with a cost of $1185NZ in the low season and $1385 in the high season (Power, pers. comm., 1998). Additional to the cost of travel to Niue, the present tourism marketing problem that plagues Niue is the lack of availability of information in the source markets such as New Zealand and Australia. The low level of awareness about Niue is in part due to its small size and limited resource base.

Impacts of ecotourism in Niue

The four concepts identified earlier in the paper (environmental sensitivity, socio-cultural appropriateness, economic viability and small-scale development) have been used to determine whether Niue's tourism industry is sustainable. Its tourism industry is identified as small-scale community ecotourism due to its limited landmass, population size, infrastructure, visitor numbers and natural resources. Hess (1990) noted that small-scale tourism development is best for small islands in the long term, as it would provide more benefits to the local people than developing mass tourism. The natural resources that Niue does possess are unique and unsurpassed (see Figure 3). Inskeep provided a summary of what Niue has to offer:

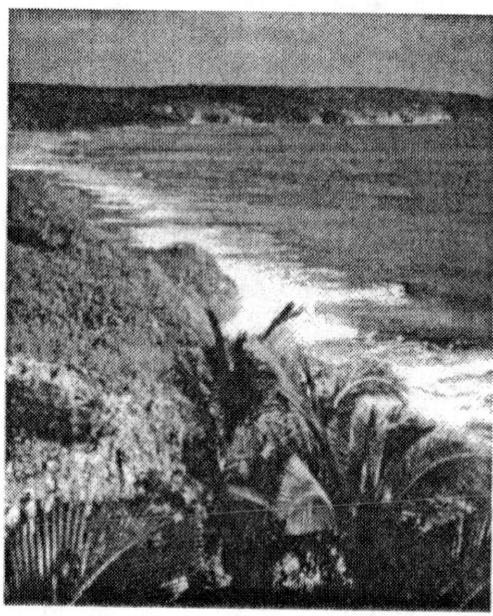

Figure 3 Niue coastline

> Niue does not have the beaches and diverse natural landscape beauty of many other Pacific Island countries, but does possess a tranquil, unspoiled and non-commercialized environment and specific natural features of high water clarity, coral formations and colourful fish which are ideal for diving combined with caves and grottos that contain impressive limestone formations, beautiful natural swimming pools and scenic views highly suitable for trekking and exploration, and interesting traditional cultural features of dance and handicrafts. (Inskeep, 1984: 6)

Niue's tourism industry was never expected to be a large one. As a result, the potential negative tourism impacts have not been addressed. In 1969 the Tourist and Publicity Department (1969: 18), stated, 'Niue ... is likely to have a relatively small inflow of travellers in the course of years [and] is unlikely to suffer the problems associated with large inflows of people.'

Environmental sensitivity

An ecotourism destination needs a resource base that is unique, fragile and natural (Pigram, 1992), to which Niue's resources conform. However, there are a number of environmental aspects in Niue that do not conform to the evaluation criteria. Firstly, the Environment and Biodiversity Advisor noted that there is no environmental law in Niue at present (Bereteh, pers. comm., 1998), as the *Niue Constitution Act 1974* has little effect regarding environmental matters (Peteru, n.d.). As there is no environmental law in Niue, there is also no tourism environmental law. However, it seems apparent that environmental law is required to protect the unique natural resources on the island through the promotion of conservation and environmental protection. The Environment Management Bill, drafted in 1995, is anticipated to be able to assist with the establishment of a solid legal framework for environmental planning and management (Environment Unit, 1995). Beyond the establishment of environmental laws however, is the crucial need to ensure that relevant laws are enforced for the tourism industry (de Haas and Cukier, in press).

Environmentally damaging practices

Secondly, there are some practices of the local population that detract from the pristine state of the natural environment. If the natural environment is damaged, either superficially or detrimentally, it detracts from the tourists' enjoyment of the resource. This could in turn lead to the Niue tourism industry losing what little tourism business it has. Local people can inadvertently cause environmental damage as a result of tourism development. In most cases, damage is caused when natural sites are altered to improve access for tourists. Tracks (generally made from concrete) have been built across the island to allow for easy access to the various tourist sites, including the coastal areas. The appearance of concrete in the natural areas is alien and unexpected; it also detracts from Niue's natural resources.

A priority concern for the present Tourism Office is developing sites in an environmentally friendly manner, in harmony with the environment. As Rex (1998) in personal communication stated, 'old sites are being made more environmentally friendly by using treated wood as it blends into the environment better than concrete'. It is hoped that over time all ecotourism sites in Niue will be aesthetically pleasing.

Another situation of environmentally damaging practices was the alteration of the caves to improve access for a cave tour. Two caves were connected through a gap known as the 'keyhole'. However, the keyhole was not large enough to accommodate some of the tourists and therefore was enlarged with a sledgehammer, thus causing damage to the ecologically sensitive cave. Both land and marine resources are important for Niue's tourism industry, and must be maintained in the best possible condition.

It can be noted that Niue has a significant problem with over-fishing by international fleets in their EEZ, while there is also over-fishing by local people for personal use. As a result of the declining fish stocks, good catches are becoming infrequent and fishing is no longer commercially viable (Fawcett, pers. comm., 1998). Some tourists travel to Niue specifically for fishing and diving, but without fish Niue again detracts from and limits its tourism attractions. Niue could lose one of its major attractions and therefore reduce the pool of tourists that are interested in travelling to Niue.

Huvalu Conservation Area

A positive environmental initiative resulting in part, from tourism, is the Huvalu Conservation Area. It was a community driven project sponsored by South Pacific Regional Environment Programme (SPREP) to promote biodiversity. Biodiversity is very important for Niue and its small land base, the local people, and as a tourism resource to be utilised by ecotourists visiting the island. The Huvalu Conservation Area contains some major tours and prominent natural attractions within its boundaries. A Forest Camp for tourists has

Figure 4 The Huvalu Forest Camp

been developed in the area though it has not been utilised for this purpose yet (seen on Figure 4). The Huvalu Conservation Area is an asset to Niue's tourism industry and is a considerable resource that can be utilised to provide benefits to the local people by the forest being used as a resource that retains biodiversity as well as assisting the local people with benefits gained through tourism in the area.

Socio-cultural appropriateness

Niue is both a traditional and modern society mixed to suit Niueans and their lifestyles. As Inskeep (1984) observed, Niue had already been through significant cultural change to the point where a small number of tourists would not negatively impact the community. However, most changes among the Niuean population cannot be directly attributed to tourism in Niue, but rather to the increased interactions with New Zealand and other countries with the opening of the airport allowing for easier travel and television. There are a number of socio-cultural changes that are expected should the tourism carrying capacity of Niue be reached. The changes are overcrowding resulting in local population dissatisfaction, increased cultural awareness, increased foreign control of tourism operations, and a loss of authenticity of tourism products.

Differences between hosts and guests

Differences between host communities and local populations are the cause of the majority of the socio-cultural impacts resulting from tourism: the greater the differences, the greater the chance of negative impacts occurring amongst the local population (Butler, 1974). Tourism plays a part in influencing host populations, as tourists are visible for all to see with their dress and behaviour being easily imitated. This 'demonstration effect' is significant to Niue particularly with reference to behaviourisms and style of dress. The demonstration effect is more common among the younger population of Niue. Changes to dress style in Niue and other Pacific Islands have been occurring since first contact with Europeans, and have changed dramatically over the years. Some of the adoptive behaviours can be positive for the local population, such as acquiring education, while others can alter the behaviour and appearance of local people in a negative way. Negative changes have been the disregard for the Niuean language or customs, particularly through the adoption of English as their preferred language.

Disillusionment

It was not until the late 1980s that tourism in Niue became the focal point for potential economic gain by the Government of Niue. While it was not expected that there would be immediate economic success, it was hoped that after 10 years of focusing on tourism promotion, tourism would be the vital ingredient to provide economic stability for Niue. However, local support has faded over recent years due to a lack of significant results from the marketing strategies and the slow growth of Niue's tourism industry. The promised economic benefits for the local community have not been realised and the social benefits, in terms of local control, are focused on a smaller group than first anticipated.

Local involvement in tourism planning and decision-making

With local participation there is also local control over aspects of tourism that influence or impact upon the environment and the culture of Niue. Simmons (1996) observed that Niueans tend to lack knowledge and awareness about tourism, yet are fairly supportive of tourism if financial benefits are realised. Often the local people are not directly involved in tourism, and not consulted in tourism matters.

There are a number of possible impacts to the local population if 'overcrowding' were to occur on Niue. In 1969 (Tourist and Publicity Department), the perceived socio-cultural impacts from tourism were mostly the disruptive effects of large numbers of people travelling around the island. Therefore, tourism must not dominate Niue, both in terms of exceeding the carrying capacity and with tourism development. Due to the island's small population base (a direct result of depopulation) it is also likely that the Niueans could see themselves marginalised in their own country (Simmons, 1996). The local people may lose their greatest attribute, their friendliness, affecting Niue's tourism industry for years to come.

However, a positive impact of tourism is the focus and interest in cultural tours and activities. Tourism can reintroduce and provide focus for the local people and their culture (Ayala, 1995). Niueans have an interesting culture and by sharing it with tourists the culture becomes stronger. Culture sharing is important to forge an understanding between Niueans and visitors.

Foreign investment in the tourism industry

Niue has easily managed to retain local ownership due to a lack of interest from foreign investors and the small visitor numbers. However, there is a high percentage of expatriate ownership of tourism ventures in Niue. Most have married Niueans and all live in Niue, but in difficult economic times they are still considered to be taking potential money away from Niueans. The lack of foreign investment is a positive aspect of Niue's tourism industry because the locals retain ownership and therefore control the tourism industry.

Economic Viability

Tourism has become a priority for the Niuean Government in an attempt to improve economic conditions and provide revenue. At present the Niuean economy is under considerable pressure to increase their exports due to an ever-increasing deficit. Much of the aid money provided to Niue by New Zealand was given with the understanding that Niue would develop its tourism industry, eventually becoming self-sufficient and thus relying less on outside sources of aid. Milne (1992: 569) stated, 'while tourism will continue to be an important source of additional income and employment, Niue will remain dependent on public sector employment and international aid flows for the foreseeable future'. An impediment to the economic viability of Niue's tourism industry is the air service as it determines the number, cost, and frequency of flights, and in essence the number of tourists to the island. Air access in Niue is the most important aspect affecting economic development, and contributing directly to the low tourist numbers (UNDP/WTO, 1997).

Tourism cannot be considered the solution to all Niue's economic problems; it contributes to the economy but has proven to be unreliable, particularly with seasonal fluctuations of visitors. Niue needs to maintain a diversity of products that earn economic profits to compensate for the difficult years it has had with tourism. Tourism is not heavily relied upon for income at present but the Minister of Tourism believed that tourism is their number one priority in terms of economic development and hopes that it will provide 80% of the Government income in the future (Pavihi, pers. comm., 1998).

Economic benefits from tourism

For tourism to have economic viability it must produce profits that filter back into the local community, with a portion spent on conserving, maintaining, and enhancing the natural environment utilised for tourism (Lindberg *et al.*, 1996; Weaver, 1998). Small-scale community ecotourism allows opportunities for the local population to be employed in tourism and to start entrepreneurial businesses. However, Niue's tourism profits are minimal and therefore only those directly involved in tourism see any benefits, and thus there are not sufficient funds to recirculate back into conserving the natural resources.

Niue does not have the resources or the funds available to develop and maintain a sustainable and successful tourism industry with the number of visitors to the island at present. The only aspect where it has exceeded capacity in its superstructure is in terms of the large number of accommodation units available, effectively swamping the market and resulting in some difficulties in making any profit. Although Niue is fortunate to maintain local control of the tourism industry, there is a need to be wary of a loss of control of the industry since this ultimately leads to the loss of local economic benefits.

Leakages

Due to Niue being a small island with restricted natural resources, it imports a large amount of goods and services from New Zealand and other countries. This effectively increases the leakage of economic profit, and the profits that Niue does earn from tourism are often spent on imports, resulting in only a small proportion of the tourists' expenditure remaining within the island (Talagi, pers. comm., 1998).

The Paradox

There is a paradox between the three concepts – environmental sensitivity, socio-cultural appropriateness and economic viability. These three concepts must exist in symbiosis for small-scale community ecotourism to be sustainable. Therefore, tourism that is not economically viable is not sustainable, as costs are not covered and there are no economic benefits for the local population or for conservation of the natural resources. The economic viability of an ecotourism operation depends on the number of tourists and the money that they spend at the destination. However, care must be taken not to exceed the number of tourists at the destination, thus surpassing the carrying capacity and resulting in negative environmental and socio-cultural impacts. Tourism can be economically viable, and environmentally and socio-culturally sustainable under certain conditions. These conditions may be when a small economy does not require large sums of money to be viable, or a tourism destination can attract 'elite' tourists who are higher spenders thus requiring fewer numbers to ensure economic viability. The paradox is dynamic and factors can influence one aspect and thus affect the sustainability of the tourism destination.

Niue

Despite meeting many of the criteria which would deem Niue 'sustainable' (such as locally owned tourism enterprises, limited tourist numbers, tourist attractions based on existing natural features and a degree of local involvement in decision-making), Niue's tourism industry is currently unsustainable as it has not achieved a balance, and therefore is not economically viable. The Planning and Development Unit (1998: 2) said it best with 'The problem can be simply stated: there are currently insufficient tourist arrivals to ensure the continued existence of a tourism industry in Niue.'

Niue has many impediments in creating an economically viable tourism industry. There are many factors both within Niue and internationally, that affect the numbers of tourists to Niue. Two factors are the isolation of the island, and not being able to support their own airline, resulting in reliance on foreign owned air-carriers. There are economic benefits gained from tourism in the form of job opportunities and earning revenue, as well as indirect economic benefits gained by the local community. There is some foreign investment in Niue's tourism industry but this does not negatively affect the economic benefits. However, the high leakage rate from the purchase of goods and services imported into Niue is of serious concern. There is also some concern with the large amount of funding allocated to tourism promotion, and the lack of results in the form of increased visitor numbers. Niue needs more visitors with more money, spread throughout the year to create a sustainable tourism industry in economic terms. However, in environmental and social terms, the limited tourist numbers has resulted in few negative impacts for the environment and the people.

In summary, Niue's tourism industry is environmentally sensitive yet could sustain more tourists. Ecotourists are generally environmentally conscious, but it can also be noted that at present there are not enough tourists in Niue to cause major negative environmental impacts. However, there are certain aspects that can be addressed to make the tourism industry even more environmentally friendly, such as the level of environmental law and promotion of environmentally friendly practices to ensure Niue's natural environment is preserved. In 1998 there was no environmental law, making it difficult to enforce environmentally friendly practices and to prevent or reduce environmentally damaging practices and behaviours, such as littering, graffiti, altering natural resources for access, and over-fishing. Creating a product in keeping with the environment has in the past been insufficient in preserving the natural character of the environment. As a result there has been damage to Niue's natural resources both in physical appearance and to its aesthetic values. Promoting the Huvalu Conservation Area is a positive aspect for Niue, although the resources are currently under-utilised for tourism purposes.

Niue's tourism industry is currently socially and culturally sustainable. There is some local control and involvement in the tourism industry, although this is more a result of the lack of foreign interest than from restrictions and planning regulations. There is some foreign investment in Niue's tourism industry, particularly from New Zealand expatriates. Socio-cultural impacts stem from the differences between the hosts and the guests that cause concern for the local population. There are few significant differences and thus impacts are minimal, though it is important that the visitors to Niue are taught and prepared to be culturally conscious of their behaviour. The target of 5000 tourists a year could be sustainable, but it is likely that this figure is very near the peak visitation rate of Niue's carrying capacity. Measures should be taken to minimise possible negative impacts that could result from an increase in tourist numbers.

Conclusion

Niue's tourism industry was determined to be unsustainable because it is not economically viable. Future tourism options for Niue are wide ranging, partly due to the fact that the tourism industry is susceptible to factors beyond its control. These factors (such as foreign air carriers servicing Niue and the Asian Economic Crisis) ultimately affect the tourism industry on the island; however, by attracting 'elite' higher spending tourists to Niue, economic benefits will begin to surface. Niue has unique natural resources and a friendly local population that makes it a 'new and different' Pacific Island destination for tourists searching for a distinct holiday. It is likely that Niue's tourism industry will remain environmentally and socio-culturally sustainable with low visitor numbers. It is also likely that while reviving the economic viability of the industry, elite tourists would not detrimentally affect environmental and socio-cultural situations. The island needs to retain the sustainability of its natural resources and the Niuean culture and social characteristics while becoming economically viable, and thus sustainable.

Correspondence

Any correspondence should be directed to Heidi de Haas, 4 Murray Road, R.D. 4, Morrinsville, New Zealand (hdh_nz@yahoo.co.nz).

References

Ayala, H. (1995) From quality product to eco-product – Will Fiji set a precedent? *Tourism Management* 16 (1), 39–47.

Bowe, C.A. and Rolle, S. (1998) A sustainable tourism development policy, guidelines and implementation strategy – the Out Islands of the Bahamas. *Eighth Australian Tourism and Hospitality Research Conference.* Canberra.

Boyd, S.W. and Butler, R.W. (1996) Managing ecotourism – an opportunity spectrum approach. *Tourism Management* 17 (8), 557–66.

Britton, S. (1987) Tourism in Pacific Island States – constraints and opportunities. In S. Britton and W.C. Clarke (eds) *Ambiguous Alternative: Tourism in Small Developing Countries* (pp. 113–39). Suva: University of the South Pacific.

Budowski, G. (1977) Tourism and conservation – conflict, coexistence or symbiosis? *Parks* 1 (4), 3–6.

Burton, F. (1998) Can ecotourism objectives be achieved? *Annals of Tourism Research* 25 (3), 755–8.

Butler, R.W. (1974) Tourism as an agent of social change. *Annals of Tourism Research* 2, 100–11.

Cater, E. (1994) Introduction. In E. Cater and G. Lowman (eds) *Ecotourism: A Sustainable Option?* (pp. 3–18). Chichester: John Wiley and Sons.

Chalker, L. (1994) Ecotourism – on the trail of destruction or sustainability? A minister's view. In E. Cater and G. Lowman (eds) *Ecotourism: A Sustainable Option?* (pp. 87–99). Chichester: John Wiley and Sons.

de Haas, H.C. and Cukier, J. (in press) Small-scale tourism and sustainability in Niue. *Pacific Tourism Review.*

de Kadt, E. (1992) Making the alternative sustainable – lessons from development for tourism. In V.L. Smith and W.R. Eadington (eds) *Tourism Alternatives: Potentials and Problems in the Development of Tourism* (pp. 47–75). Philadelphia: University of Pennsylvania Press.

Development Programme – Niue: Final Report.

Dickinson, S. (1998) Biggest little atoll in the world. *Destinations* (Winter), 83–85.

Environment Unit (1995) *Huvalu Forest Conservation Area Project: Niue Project Preparation Document.* Alofi: Government of Niue.

Grundsten, C. (1994) Heron Island: Walking the tourism–environment tightrope. *Enviro: International Magazine on the Environment* 17, 22–3.

Hanneberg, P. (1994) Ecotourism or ecoterrorism? *Enviro: International Magazine on the Environment* 17, 2–5.

Hess, A. (1990) Overview: Sustainable development and environmental management of small islands. In W. Beller, P. d'Ayala and P. Hein (eds) *Sustainable Development and Environmental Management of Small Islands* (pp. 3–14). Paris: UNESCO and the Parthenon Publishing Group.

Higinio, E. and Munt, I. (1993) Belize – ecotourism gone awry. *Report on the Americas* 26 (4), n/a.

Hjalager, A.M. (1997) Innovation patterns in sustainable tourism – an analytical typology. *Tourism Management* 18 (1), 35–41.

Inskeep, E.L. (1984) *A Tourism Development Strategy for Niue 1985–1990.* United Nations Development Programme and World Tourism Organisation.

Khan, M.M. (1997) Tourism development and dependency theory – mass tourism vs. ecotourism. *Annals of Tourism Research* 24 (4), 988–91.

King, B.E.M. (1996) *Marketing Report – Tourism and Private Sector Development Programme.* United Nations Development Programme and World Tourism Organisation.

Kiste, R.C. (1998) *Niue.* Microsoft Encarta Encyclopaedia.

Lane, J. (1994) *Niue – State of the Environment Report.* Apia: South Pacific Regional Environment Programme.

Lanfant, M.F. and Graburn, N.H.H. (1992) International tourism reconsidered – the principle of the alternative. In V.L. Smith and W.R. Eadington (eds) *Tourism Alternatives: Potentials and Problems in the Development of Tourism* (pp. 88–112). Philadelphia: University of Pennsylvania Press.

Liew, J. (1990) Sustainable development and environmental management of atolls. In W. Beller, P. d'Ayala and P. Hein (eds) *Sustainable Development and Environmental Management of Small Islands* (pp. 77–86). Paris: UNESCO and the Parthenon Publishing Group.

Lindberg, K., Enriquez J. and Sproule, K. (1996) Ecotourism questioned – case study from Belize. *Annals of Tourism Research* 23 (3), 543–62.

Lindberg, K. and McKercher, B. (1997) Ecotourism – a critical overview. *Pacific Tourism Review* 1 (1), 65–79.

Long, V. and Wall, G. (1996) Successful tourism in Nusa Lembongan, Indonesia? *Tourism Management* 17 (1), 43–50.

Mandziuk, G.W. (1995) Ecotourism: A marriage of conservation and capitalism. *Plan Canada* (March), 29–33.

Milne, S. (1990) The impact of tourism development in small Pacific Island States. *New Zealand Journal of Geography* 89, 16–21.

Milne, S. (1992) Tourism development in Niue. *Annals of Tourism Research* 19 (3), 565–9.

Moore, C. (1999) A rare find. *New Zealand Herald* (9 March).

Murphy, P.E. (1985) *Tourism: A Community Approach*. London: Routledge.

Orams, M. B. (1995) Towards a more desirable form of ecotourism. *Tourism Management* 16 (1), 3–8.

Peteru, C. (undated) *Niue Administrative, Legislative and Policy Review*. South Pacific Regional Environment Programme.

Pigram, J.J. (1992) Alternative tourism: Tourism and sustainable resource management. In V.L. Smith and W.R. Eadington (eds) *Tourism Alternatives: Potentials and Problems in the Development of Tourism* (pp. 76–87). Philadelphia: University of Pennsylvania Press.

Planning and Development Unit (1998) *Alternative Tourism Marketing Approaches – Project Document*. Alofi: Government of Niue.

Ringer, G. (1996) Sustainable ecotourism and island communities: A geographic perspective. *World Congress on Coastal and Marine Tourism*. Hawaii.

Simmons, D. (1996) *Socio-Cultural Report: Tourism and Private Sector Development Programme*. United Nations Development Programme / World Tourism Organisation.

Skinner, R.J. (1980) The impact of tourism on Niue. In F. Rajotte and R. Crocombe (eds) *Pacific Tourism: As Islanders See It* (pp. 60–4). Institute of Pacific Studies of the University of the South Pacific with South Pacific Social Sciences Association.

Smith, V.L. (1989) Introduction. In V.L. Smith (ed.) *Hosts and Guests: The Anthropology of Tourism* (pp. 1–17). Philadelphia: University of Pennsylvania Press.

Sofield, T.H.B. (1993) Indigenous tourism development. *Annals of Tourism Research* 20, 729–50.

South Pacific Commission (SPC) (1994) *Pacific Islands Populations*. Auckland: South Pacific Commission.

Statistics Immigration Unit (1991) *Report on the Niue Census of Population and Dwellings 1991*. Alofi: Government of Niue.

Statistics Niue (1999) *Tourism Statistics*.

Tourist and Publicity Department (1969) *Tourist Development in Niue Island*. Wellington: Tourist and Publicity Department.

United Nations Development Programme and World Tourism Organisation (UNDP/ WTO) (1997) *Tourism and Private Sector*.

Wall, G. (1997) Is ecotourism sustainable? *Environmental Management* 21 (4), 483–91.

Waqa, V. (1998) Tough times in Niue – are there enough people for it to survive? *Island Business* 24 (11), 23.

Weaver, D.B. (1998) *Ecotourism in the Less Developed World*. Oxon: CAB International.

Weaver, D.B. (1991) Alternative to mass tourism in Dominica. *Annals of Tourism Research* 18, 414–32.

Wheat, S. (1994) Taming tourism. *Geographical* 66 (4), 16–19.

Wilkinson, P.F. (1989) Strategies for tourism in island microstates. *Annals of Tourism Research* 16 (2), 153–177.

Yarwood, V. (1998) Life on the rock. *New Zealand Geographic* 37 (January–March), 56–86.

Personal communication

Bereteh, M. (1998) Environment and biodiversity advisor (Huvalu Conservation Area), formal interview, 19 June.

Fawcett, K. (1998) Owner and operator of Niue Dive, formal interview, 30 June.

Oulton, M. (1999) Cartographer, Geography Department, University of Waikato, 9 July.

Pavihi, A. (1998) Minister of tourism, telephone interview, 1 July.

Power, R. (1998) Air New Zealand travel consultant, telephone interview, 19 November.

Rex, L. (1998) Director of tourism, formal interview, 29 June.

Talagi, M. (1998) Director of Niue Campus, University of the South Pacific, formal interview, 24 June.

Statutes cited

Niue Tourist Authority Act, 1995.

Local Community Involvement in Tourism around National Parks: Opportunities and Constraints

Harold Goodwin
Centre for Responsible Tourism, School of Earth and Environmental Sciences, Medway University Campus, Pembroke, Chatham Maritime, Kent ME4 4TB, UK

National Parks are often major tourist attractions located in relatively remote and marginalised rural areas. The potential role of tourism in contributing to the costs of conservation and providing economic opportunities for communities living adjacent to natural heritage has long been recognised. Issues of access to tourists and capital, enclaves and bypasses and employment need to be addressed. The opportunities for local economic development through tourism at Komodo (Indonesia), Keoladeo (India), Gonarezhou (Zimbabwe) and Puerto Princesa (Palawan, Philippines) National Parks are explored, and the paper concludes with an agenda for action.

Introduction

This paper draws on material from a Department for International Development funded comparative study of tourism, conservation and sustainable development at three National Parks in India, Indonesia and Zimbabwe[1] and on consultancy work around St Paul's Subterranean National Park in Palawan. One of the objectives of the DFID study was to identify methods of raising the income and related benefits that local people gain from tourism based on biodiversity.

The idea that nature tourism could provide the incentive for conservation through the establishment of National Parks has a long history.[2] Budowski argued that it was possible to create a symbiosis between conservation and tourism.[3] Where tourism is wholly or partly based on values derived from nature and its resources it could provide an economic value for conservation of species and habitats. The IUCN's 1980 World Conservation Strategy endorsed the sustainable utilisation of species and ecosystems. The IUCN in 1982 affirmed that the 'tourist potential' of an area is an important factor in the selection of protected areas, but recognised that many areas of important conservation value have little appeal for tourists and that the pursuit of tourism revenue may result in inappropriate development.[4] Philips argued that tourism provides conservation with an economic justification, a means of building support for conservation and a source of revenue.[5] Tourism to protected areas is emerging as a development strategy. As Ziffer has argued, the development goal is to attract 'visitors to natural areas and use the revenues to fund local conservation and economic development'.[6] Tourism is one of the forms of sustainable use that potentially enables protected area managers to allow local people to derive economic benefit from the park and to encourage local support for its maintenance.

The 1992 IVth World Congress on National Parks and Protected Areas declared that tourism associated with protected areas 'must serve as a tool to advance protected areas' objectives for maintaining ecosystem integrity, biodiversity, public awareness, and enhancement of local people's quality of life.[7] McNeely reflects the changing attitudes of protected area managers, and recognition of the close links between biological and cultural diversity-links which he argues reflect long-established human activity embracing 'cultural identity, spirituality, and subsistence practices' that have contributed to the maintenance of biological diversity.[8] Cultural diversity and biological diversity are often inextricably linked, defining the management context for the protected area manager, the 'product' for the tourist and the opportunity for the local community.

Table 1 Tourist motivations for travel

National Park	*Wildlife*	*Landscape*	*Culture*
Gonarezhou NP Zimbabwe	4.8	4.5	3.7
Keoladeo NP India	4.1	3.9	4.3
Komodo NP Indonesia	4.1	4.5	4.4
St Paul's NP Palawan, Philippines[10]	4.7	4.8	4.4

Data were collected on the relative importance of landscape, wildlife and culture to visitors to four National Parks. Respondents were asked to rate the importance of a range of motivations for travel on a five-point scale.[9] Interviews took place either within, or immediately adjacent to, National Parks. The results are therefore likely to be skewed towards the importance of wildlife and landscape (see Table 1).

Large numbers of nature tourists interviewed in National Parks ranked culture as their single most important reason for travel: 45% of respondents in Keoladeo and 57% in Komodo cited culture as their primary motivation for visiting India and Indonesia respectively. In Gonarezhou the figure was only 9%, reflecting the large number of regional tourists in the sample and the under-valuation of African culture.[11] There is considerable interest among international visitors to National Parks in the national and local cultures of the destination countries. This represents an often-neglected set of opportunities for the development of locally owned complementary tourism products around National Parks.

Local culture is often an asset of the poor. Ljubljana was fly posted by a Swedish NGO in 1997 with posters declaring 'Tourism: Your every day life is someone else's adventure'. The living local culture, the fabric of the lives of local communities, constitutes a significant part of the product sought by domestic and international tourists. National Parks attract tourists and are able to 'sell' to them a limited range of wildlife and landscape experiences; there are additional products that can be sold by local people enabling them to diversify their livelihoods and to raise their household incomes.

Over the last 15 years there have been a series of initiatives to implement projects which enable local economic development whilst maintaining or furthering conservation objectives. Zebu and Bush produced clear survey evidence that park authorities had realised that local populations could no longer be ignored in the establishment, planning and management of National Parks and other protected landscapes. The same survey reported that tourism formed part of the park management strategy of 75% of respondents.[12] Wells and Brandon surveyed Integrated Conservation Development Projects (ICDPs) many of which had promoted nature tourism in order to provide funds for protected area management and to generate income gains for local communities. They reported that the results had been disappointing, with all visitor spending in the parks going directly to the central treasury or to concession holding private corporate interests. Although, at some popular sites, revenues may exceed local protected area operating budgets, it is unusual for any of the additional revenues to be returned to park management 'and extremely rare for a revenue share to go to local people'. Wells and Brandon reported that local employment opportunities linked to tourism were 'insufficient to attract much popular local support for the parks'. In any event 'only a small minority of protected areas attract significant numbers of visitors'.[13] However, it is clear that National Parks visitor numbers are increasing at a significant rate (see Table 2).

Table 2 Indicative visitor figures for four National Parks – rounded figures

National Park	*1991–1995 Visitor average annual growth rate (%)*	*Total number of visitors 1995*	*International visitors as % of total visitors*
Gonarezhou NP Zimbabwe	10	6,400	40
Keoladeo NP India	7	125,000	30
Komodo NP Indonesia	15	30,000	90
St Paul's NP Palawan, Philippines	45	17,300	26

National Parks attract large numbers of relatively wealthy domestic and international tourists to relatively remote rural areas. Many National Parks attract significant numbers of customers to the 'product'; the customer travels to the place of production to consume their holiday in and around the National Park. These relatively wealthy consumers, attracted by nature-based tourism, constitute a potential market for tourism products based on natural resources and local culture.

For the purpose of the management of tourism in and around National Parks, nature tourism and ecotourism need to be distinguished. Nature tourism is concerned with the enjoyment of nature, ecotourism additionally requires a contribution to conservation. Ecotourism is a management aspiration:

> low impact nature tourism which contributes to the maintenance of species and habitats either directly through a contribution to conservation and/or indirectly by providing revenue to the local community sufficient for local people to value, and therefore protect, their wildlife heritage area as a source of income.[14]

If tourism to National Parks can be managed into ecotourism it can enable local people to gain economically from the protected area with which they live. Protected areas cannot co-exist in the long term with communities that are hostile to them. Local people are important stakeholders with whom protected area managers must co-operate. More of the benefits of conservation need to be delivered to local people by enabling them to benefit from the protection of the park – their use of which is now regulated. If local people secure a sustainable income (a tangible economic benefit) from tourism to these protected areas, they will be less likely to exploit them in other less sustainable ways – obvious examples include fuel collection, charcoal burning, over-fishing, poaching or coral blasting. If local people gain from the sustainable use of, for example, a coral reef or wild animals through tourism they will protect their asset and may invest further resources into it.

Aspirations of Local Communities

It is unsurprising that people in relatively impoverished local communities aspire to become involved in tourism. Tourists are wealthy consumers with money to spend; it would be surprising if large numbers of people in marginalised rural communities were not interested in finding a means of securing some of that disposable income and securing a contribution to their household income. People in local communities do recognise that tourism can have negative effects and these are reported in the case study reports.[15]

In Palawan, nature tourism at St Paul's Subterranean River National Park attracted fewer than 40,000 visitors in 1997 of which 21% were international. They contributed some £3.5 million (₱153 million) to the local economy but most of it was spent in the urban economy where the accommodation is available. Filipinos spent an average of ₱1,431 per day more than the international visitors who spent ₱1,346 per day, although foreign tourists did stay longer (8.1 days as compared with the average Filipino stay of 4.6 days). Not surprisingly, independent tourists spent on average 1.6 times as much as a backpacker and 1.1 times as much as a group traveller. It is often argued that backpackers spend more money in the local economy, but in Palawan backpackers stay an average of 9.1 days and spend ₱7,360, independent travellers stay 7.4 days and spend an average of ₱8,529, on average 16% more than backpackers. Clearly attracting more independent travellers and extending their length of stay would increase local revenues. In the three years between 1992 and 1995 there was an increase in the number of people employed in tourism of 219%, from 402 (3.9%) to 1284, some 9.6% of the employed population. In Sabang, the gateway community to St Paul's Park, 28% of households were involved in tourism establishments (lodges, restaurants, cafes or guiding) while 19% were involved in the running of tourist boats. Most of the benefits of tourism accrue to the urban area, and the rural lodges at Sabang are finding it increasingly difficult to provide the kind of accommodation (with private facilities) now demanded by backpackers since the park is easily accessible as a day trip from Puerto Princesa City. Local communities seek to attract tourist dollars by providing additional excursion opportunities (visits to caves and guided walks often to view points and including a wildlife viewing opportunity or canoeing), handicraft sales and home stays, camping and picnic sites. One of the major difficulties confronting these local communities is of encouraging the day excursionists to stop along the road to visit local communities and spend money there.[16]

Mico, a local entertainer in Dominica, has a calypso which defines the problem clearly: 'They pass on a bus, they don't make a stop, they pass on a bus, they don't stop and shop.'[17] At Keoladeo the large number of international tourists who visit the Forest Lodge for lunch bypass the local economy completely as do cruise ship passengers stopping at Komodo. Coaches, boats and hotels, lodges and resorts can all create enclaves containing tourists who are then inaccessible to the informal sector and the local economy. One response to this is the hawking, which is the only way in which many traders can access the market as the tourist moves between vehicle and site or hotel.

Table 3 Attitudes to tourism in local communities adjacent to National Parks in Indonesia and Zimbabwe

	Indonesia[20]		*Zimbabwe*[21]	
	Labuan Bajo (%)	*Sape (%)*		*South-east Lowveld (%)*
Would you be happy to see more tourists here?	94	91	Would you like to have more contact with tourists?	82
Would you be happy if your children worked in the tourism industry?	81	96	Tourism has created more jobs for local people	49
Tourism benefits the whole community?	46	57	Tourism would benefit our community	71
Tourism only benefits rich people?	35	59	Tourism benefits only a few already wealthy people	64
Only outsiders benefit from tourism here?	35	14		
My family has more money because of tourism	20	25	Tourism would benefit me and my family	74

Komodo National Park in Indonesia generated over US$1.25 million for the local economy in the mid-1990s and over 600 jobs were at least partially supported by tourism.[18] There are economic costs associated with tourism. Local people perceive inflation to be due in part to tourism. There are also considerable changes in land ownership taking place, with non-local speculators purchasing waterfront land in Labuan Bajo. Although not a prime focus of this research, there are some social costs identified by local people. These appear to be more prevalent in Labuan Bajo, which receives more tourist contact.[19]

In the communities around Gonarezhou and Komodo there is considerable enthusiasm for tourism, although there are marked differences between villages in the Zimbabwe data. Tourism jobs are valued; 71% of respondents in the Zimbabwe villages agreed that tourism would benefit their community. In Sape and Labuan Bajo, in Indonesia, where there is more experience of tourism, respondents were markedly less confident that tourism could benefit the whole community. In Sape (59%) and the villages around Gonarezhou (64%) there was stronger feeling than in Labuan Bajo (35%) that tourism benefits only the wealthy; this reflects problems over access to the industry. In Indonesia one-third of respondents in Labuan Bajo felt that 'only outsiders benefit from tourism'. In the villages around Gonarezhou three-quarters of respondents expect their household to benefit, reflecting high expectations in an area only just

Table 4 Ways that respondents thought that local people could earn money from tourism

How could local people earn money?	*Frequency*	*(%)*
By increasing employment opportunities	2	1.4
Sell firewood	3	2.1
Other	4	2.8
Levy for community development on tourists	5	3.5
Wildlife hunting/ranching	5	3.5
Set up enterprises	8	5.6
Construction/building cultural village	12	8.4
Entertainment	15	10.5
Produce & sell agricultural products	18	12.6
Guides	24	16.8
Produce & sell handicrafts	47	32.9

beginning to develop tourism, although there were significant variations in responses by village. By contrast, in Labuan Bajo a relatively developed destination, only 20% of respondents expected their households to benefit directly (see Table 3).

In the south-east lowveld of Zimbabwe 83% of respondents thought that local people could earn money from tourism and gave a range of unprompted answers about how this could be achieved (see Table 4).

Issues

National Parks and the communities that live in and adjacent to them share a common difficulty in relation to domestic and international tourism. International tourists arrive from the tourists' originating countries and domestic tourists from metropolitan centres. This process is driven by demand and by the international and domestic tourism industry. Whilst local tour operators and hotels may have some, often imperfect, knowledge about the patterns of visitation which can be expected in the medium term, National Park managers and local communities have none. They are both on the receiving end of a process they do not control and over which they are able to exert very little influence. Whilst the tourists may be welcome, it is rare for park managers and local communities to be entirely happy with the arrangements for their visits or with the contribution they make to the local economy or to the park.

Access to tourists: location

Location is a critical issue; proximity to park entrances and to flows of tourists creates opportunities. In Komodo NP 99% of revenue to the local economy accrues to neighbouring town communities, and not to those communities living within the park who are most disadvantaged by restrictions over resource use within the park and who lack the capital and opportunity to develop tourism facilities because of park restrictions.[22]

The Keoladeo case study demonstrates how local families, well located to the tourist flows to a National Park, can opportunistically develop accommodation businesses. Almost all of the private hotels used by visitors to Keoladeo National Park are run by entrepreneurs often on the (former) site of the owner's home. Many involve family labour and brothers and sons often move on to start their own hotel on adjacent plots. Two *Jat* Bharatpur families own six of the hotels, all within 500 metres of each other and adjacent to the entrance to the National Park.[23] The pattern of land ownership around the north end of the park where most of the hotels are situated accounts for this. Since Independence much of this land has been owned by a handful of *Jat* families – which now control the private hotel sector. Only one hotel has close associations with the rural communities around Keoladeo National Park. A family of Brahmins runs it, formerly from Jatoli village (on the north-east side of the park).[24]

Access to capital

At Keoladeo at least two entrepreneurs have entered the hotel business after several years accumulating experience and capital from guiding, working in state hotels, with the Forest Department or even with foreign research projects. Small, cheap 'backpacker' hotels require relatively little capital to set up – and are run almost entirely with family labour. One such family owns three small hotels. The number of very small hotel enterprises in Bharatpur appears to be declining in favour of larger establishments although family labour and networks play an important part at almost all levels of operation. Hotels with more than two or three rooms often employ non-family labour, but they are still essentially family businesses.

Jat entrepreneurs (75% in the sample) run the majority of private hotels, typically in their mid-30s, but as the industry develops, the barriers to entering the market for hotel proprietors with little capital are increasing. The budget end of the foreign tourist market appears to be saturated and most new entrants are competing at the mid-price level while existing hotels attempt to specialise for particular types of client. The degree of linkage to the local urban economy is high, but connections with the rural economy are generally low and although hotel ownership is also 'local' it is concentrated into the hands of a few entrepreneurs with connections to the traditional elite.

Employment

At Komodo employment in tourism-related enterprises is mainly secured by the young (under 30), and mainly to males, although the full role of women has not been fully explored and requires more research. The levels of education and capital possessed by local people restrict their involvement in the industry. Existing skills and capacities have been utilised to enter the industry at basic levels, but there is considerable external ownership of businesses, and opportunities for retraining appear to be sparse.[25]

Around Keoladeo National Park hotel labour is largely drawn from the urban sector, with more expensive hotels having a higher propensity to employ non-local professionals. Wages within the hotel sector are often below the national minimum, but include many payments in kind; provision of seasonal accommodation, clothing and food are the norm. Wages are higher in the public sector, and provide more regular incomes than in the private sector where there is a high degree of family labour. However, despite the strong seasonality in tourist arrivals, labour demand is less seasonal than might be expected. Hotels rarely close for the off-season. In terms of employment, the *Jat* community dominates the sector, but local *Jatavs* also have relatively high representation. *Jatavs* traditionally occupy low occupational positions, but within the hotel sector they have been able to secure employment in fairly large numbers and at most levels. In contrast, *Gujjars* and *Thakurs* (traditionally cattle herders and farmers) are less well represented. The only tangible links to the rural economy in this sector is through the sale of milk and the employment of a few waiters and domestics from the *Jatav* communities. Despite the location of the hotel sector at the edge of the National Park, and its proximity to rural suppliers of produce and labour, Bharatpur city maintains a stronger influence. Consequently the hotel sector, although dependent on nature tourism, retains an essentially urban character.[26]

Enclaves and bypasses

All too often, particularly in rural areas, local people are denied any significant opportunity to participate in the tourism market. Tourists are not accessible to the local community when they are within their hotels, coaches (at Keoladeo), boats (cruise ships at Komodo), safari vehicles (in and around Gonarezhou) or inside sites and attractions such as museums. These are all enclave forms of tourism, where those wishing to sell to tourists are often reduced to hawking at the enclave entry and exit points. Cruise ship passengers and tourists on 'all inclusive' packages are particularly difficult for local entrepreneurs to access (and these sectors are growing rapidly). Tourism needs to be managed in ways that enable local people to have better access to tourists.

Although the average cost per trip of different types of visitor presented in Table 5 is not entirely comparable,[27] they do give an indication of the relative contributions of different types of visitor and the magnitude of tourist spending on trips to Komodo NP, which completely bypasses the local economy. Package tours provide a visit to the park in the minimum amount of time, but with a certain (fairly basic) level of comfort. Only 17.5% of revenue from this source accrues to the local economy. Cruise trips, whilst advertised principally for their inclusion of Komodo NP on the itinerary, do fulfil other recreational functions (multiple destinations, luxury service, etc.). As such it is a little unfair to imply that the total expenditure on cruise tours is contingent upon the inclusion of KNP on the itinerary. Nevertheless, it remains true that cruise passengers visiting KNP spend over US$6.5 million for the privilege, of which almost nothing (0.01%) accrues to the local economy.

Table 5 Distribution of tourist spending by type of tourist

Tourist type	*Mean cost of trip (US$)*	*Total expenditure (US$)*	*Total local expenditure[28] (US$)*	*Mean local expenditure per visitor (US$)*	*Proportion of total cost of trip spent locally (%)*
Cruise	600	6,763,200	388	0.03	0.01
Package	300	1,032,000	180,450	52.46	17.49
Independent	97	1,071,727	1,071,727	97.43	100.00
Total	345	8,866,927	1,252,565	48.72	14.13

At the other extreme, independent tourists, once they have arrived in the region, spend all their money locally although, as already highlighted, a substantial proportion leaks out again. It would appear, then, that the amount of tourism spending based on Komodo NP that bypasses the local economy is substantially greater than that which accrues to it. In addition, there appears to be an inverse relationship between average spend on a visit to KNP and average contribution to the local economy. Independent visitors, demanding a lesser level of comfort and service, provide a greater contribution to the local economy than the more affluent travellers seeking higher, Western levels of comfort and service. Approximately 85% of tourist expenditure on a visit to KNP bypasses the local economy due to the dominant involvement of non-local carriers and package tour operators in the market.[29]

Leakages

Lindberg and Enriquez[30] (1994) identified four factors that will affect the contribution of tourism to local economies: the marketability of the attraction; the type of tourist; the infrastructure/facilities, and the extent of local involvement and linkages. Leakage of revenue from the local economy is related to the magnitude of importation of goods from outside the region, and the level of non-local ownership of tourism-related enterprises.

Leakages occur because of the paucity of linkages between tourism and the existing local economy. Tourism is a tertiary industry, which at Komodo is developing in an area where the dominant industry has been primary, i.e. fishing and farming, without the development of intermediate secondary industries. Tourism relies on secondary, manufacturing industries for the supply of processed and packaged retail goods, and for much of its infrastructure (furniture, etc.). The absence of such industries locally, and the lack of linkages where they do exist, accounts for much of the leakage that is witnessed.

In the local economy surrounding Komodo NP, at least 50% of revenue leaks out of the local economy as a result of imports and non-local involvement in the local tourism industry (Table 6).[31] A high proportion of public transport services is government-owned or run by external operators. Similarly, a number of the higher-cost charter operations are externally run and operate out of Lombok or Bima. The high proportion of leakage from retail outlets is due to the tourist demand for manufactured goods (bottled drinks, snacks, cigarettes, postcards, etc.) that are not produced locally. The proportion of leakage from restaurants is lower, given that much of the goods sold by restaurants is fresh produce

Table 6 Estimates of leakage of tourism revenue from the local economy

Sector	*Estimated leakage (%)*	*Revenue remaining (US$)*
Hotels	Unknown	150,000
Restaurants	20	160,000
Charter boats	58	233,000
Shops/Goods	60	87,000
Transport	93	9,000
Total		639,000

obtained locally. It is difficult to estimate a figure for leakage from hotels. A number of hotels are non-locally owned but some of these owners are locally resident. The proportion of revenue that is removed from the local economy is unknown.

Although tourism earning opportunities within Komodo National Park are relatively limited, it is important to note that leakage from revenue generating activities in Kampung Komodo are negligible, since they are based upon the provision of labour and primary produce. Whilst the ownership of the shuttle boats appears to be held by Sape residents, much of the revenue is still retained by the village, and all remains within the wider local economy embracing the rural population bordering the park.

Raising the financial contribution of tourism demands two things: increasing the contact which tourists have with the local economy, and increasing opportunities for tourists to spend. Currently, the cruise ship sector of the tourist market based upon Komodo NP is essentially an enclave development. Visitors are completely isolated from the surrounding local community in a self-sufficient, exclusive environment that denies local people the opportunity to benefit. The same is virtually true of most package tourists using charter boats from Sape. Of particular importance is the lack of opportunities for people living within the park to benefit from tourism. Training and development of small-scale projects, and a greater integration with the tourism developments within the park, would greatly improve the benefits that inhabitants of the park receive from tourism.

Policy Implications

One of the key issues at the turn of the century is how tourism can become more pro-poor and make a larger contribution to the livelihoods of people living in, or adjacent to, national parks. The Department for International Development initiated debate *on Sustainable Tourism and Poverty Elimination* in October 1998[32] and subsequently commissioned research on *Tourism and Poverty Elimination: Untapped Potential.*[33] Pro-poor tourism is defined as tourism that generates net benefits for the poor, economic, social, environmental and cultural benefits and costs are all included.[34]

Traditional tourism development generally focused on macro gains to national economies,

> but there are a number of challenges to be met if the potential for sustainable local development and poverty elimination, through the localisation of benefits, is to be realised. These challenges include issues of ownership, economic leakage (from the local economy and through imports), local employment, benefit distribution, social and environmental impacts and dependency. These problems can only be effectively addressed at the destination level with the active participation of the local communities.[35]

Tourism needs to be organised in ways that enable local people to have better access to tourists. There is a strong case for intervention at a local level in tourist destination areas to:

- enable local community access to the tourism market and avoid enclaves;
- maximise the linkages into the local economy and minimise leakages;

- build on and complement existing livelihood strategies through employment and small enterprise development;
- evaluate tourism projects for their contribution to local economic development not just for their national revenue generation and the increase in international arrivals;
- ensure the maintenance of natural and cultural assets;
- control negative social impacts;
- control the rate of growth of tourism.[36]

Local involvement in the tourism industry depends largely on access to the market. Frequently, local benefits are maximised in the informal sector where the scale of capital investment is low. Interest groups outside the rural community (tour groups, hoteliers and government agencies) exercise more power within the formal sector because of their command over financial resources.[37] The ability of the local population to gain access depends in part upon the expectations of tourists themselves and local suppliers have little control over the way in which the experience is marketed. At the Indian and Indonesian study sites, those populations who reside nearest to the protected areas and who have therefore borne most of the costs of exclusion appear to participate least in the tourism industry. Tourism in the south-east lowveld of Zimbabwe is not yet sufficiently established to measure the benefits for rural populations, although expectations are high.[38]

The potential for rural populations to participate in the nature tourism industry and secure livelihood benefits is dependent on a range of factors, in particular the transferability of existing skills, the opportunity to acquire and develop new skills, patterns of land ownership and the ability of external interests to dominate the industry locally. Research from Keoladeo, Komodo and Gonarezhou National Parks suggests that although tourism presents additional income and employment opportunities, rural populations remain largely marginalised from development associated with protected areas. Despite the rural location of National Parks, the industry retains a distinctly urban bias.

At each of the parks different initiatives have been suggested, each intended to increase the livelihood opportunities for local communities living in and around the National Parks. In the examples that follow only some of the ideas which emerged from the case studies are reported. They are only intended to show the wide range of opportunities and 'solutions': for a full understanding of the different situations in and around each of the parks it is important to look at the original reports.

Komodo National Park

At a workshop held as part of the Tourism, Conservation and Sustainable Development project in Labuan Bajo in April 1996 a series of local solutions were identified by local people and members of the tourism industry in East Nusa Tengarra.

Leakages from the local economy are significant. Local people have had little exposure to foreign tourists and their needs, and without the necessary skills to transfer from traditional livelihoods, and with no capital to invest they experience great difficulty in entering the industry. If change is to occur, training needs

- Labuan Bajo should be the centre for tourist transport to the island. The already established co-operative should play more of a role in organising charter transport. Better quality boats, with improved safety facilities, are necessary for tourists.
- Residents of K. Komodo and K. Rinca should be involved in a service co-operative, and permitted to provide drinks and souvenirs to visitors in some capacity.
- Training needs to be provided for local communities, particularly ecological knowledge and language skills for residents of K. Komodo, K. Rinca, and Labuan Bajo, so that they may become involved as quality tourist guides.
- Training should be provided in the making of tourist souvenirs, for residents of K. Komodo and K. Rinca.
- There should be further investigation into zoning in marine areas for tourism, fishing and mariculture. There are areas of conflict and of complementarity.
- The Labuan Bajo Guiding Association should start a licensing scheme to improve guiding standards and prevent unlicensed hawking.
- There should be improvements in the educational facilities for children in K. Komodo and K. Rinca.
- The Kader Konservasi should be involved in planning and management of tourism activities in the park.
- There should be increased tourist events in Labuan Bajo. Boat races, kite flying, and festivals should be organised.

Figure 1 Recommendations from Labuan Bajo workshop on ways of increasing the involvement of local communities in tourism and securing increased benefits.[39]

must be addressed, and local enterprises given support to establish themselves. The simplest way to achieve this may be through the establishment of co-operatives similar to that which operates the tourist infrastructure within the park.[40]

Keoladeo National Park

In September 1996, a series of workshops was held in Bharatpur in order to discuss the development of tourism. Participants included representatives from all sections of the local tourist industry, park staff and sarpanches from communities adjacent to the park. Three schemes for using tourism to re-orient the benefits of the park back to rural communities were discussed.

Raising the entrance fee of the park for foreign tourists, and diverting some of the revenue to local development schemes

At Keoladeo National Park, the entrance fee is currently far below that which the majority of foreign tourists are willing to spend. Part of the extra income raised by increasing the entrance fee of the park could be directed towards local development such as roads, schools, biogas and water sources for the surrounding villages. A fund could be advertised within the park visitor centre whereby tourists could make contributions to local development initiatives. This suggestion has been a frequent topic of discussion between park managers and community leaders. However, the idea is discussed with less enthusiasm among villagers themselves, principally because of the lack of appropriate institutions that could administer it. The success of such a scheme would depend upon the transparency and representation of the committee responsible for distributing the revenue. Park employees, while generally supportive of the idea, suggest that the sharing pattern should be made clear at the start of such a project – particularly with regard to the powers and responsibilities of the park management, tourists and local government.

Opening another gate at the site of the old Aghapur entrance to the park

An additional entrance to the park exists close to Aghapur, which was closed in 1981 when the park was created. It has been suggested that this gate be opened so that visitor pressure on the main road might be reduced and so that people living in Aghapur might be able to participate in the tourism industry. Currently, the road on the west side of the park running through Mallah village is too small to accommodate tourist traffic, and the opening of the Aghapur side gate might well encourage local non-tourist traffic to enter the park. Again, this suggestion has been met with enthusiasm from local leaders, but there is little support for it within the communities themselves. This is largely because of the pattern of land and capital ownership in the local rural areas. Creating another tourism 'centre' is not regarded as the answer to the problems facing many of the rural poor.

Encouraging a local handicraft industry

Unlike many parts of Rajasthan, traditional handicraft skills are not exploited in the Bharatpur district. Surveys with foreign tourists revealed that many wanted to purchase local crafts but could not find them. Some already exist, and are mostly made by women, for example baskets and fans made from local grasses. Other crafts such as knitting soft toys and weaving 'endri' (for carrying water pots) could be adapted to suit tourist tastes. Some training in handicrafts would be necessary and various methods of marketing explored. However, the potential impact on women is unknown. The lives of women around the National Park have changed significantly since the wetland was gazetted as a National Park. In the absence of grazing, the labour requirements for fodder collection are high and this task falls largely on women and children. However, rural unemployment among women as well as men is of increasing concern. One of the principal obstacles for income generation of this kind is the lack of a suitable institution in the area.

Guiding is often regarded as a way into the travel business and nature guides have the opportunity to make international connections. Of those that were recruited in 1976, two have subsequently become travel agents (at least one now lives in England) and two others have become local hotel proprietors. Many have become tour escorts, associated with particular companies and travelling across India. The changing approach of the park to the training and issuing of guide licences demonstrates what can be achieved by local park managers and the consequences of setting unnecessarily high standards for the qualification of guides. Many visitors to Keoladeo are more than adequately guided around the park by the cycle rickshaw drivers, almost exclusively lower caste.

There are approximately 20 licensed nature guides working inside the National Park. Several groups have been trained and licensed since 1976, with increasing resistance from existing guides. Incomes amongst the nature guides vary considerably and are largely dependent upon the extent of pre-booked business they are able to secure. On a routine basis, nature guides offer their services to tourists at the main gate to the National Park. For this group, incomes are highly seasonal – with two to three months of regular work. However, those who have connections with the travel trade are able to pre-arrange their services with tour companies, while others secure additional work as tour escorts throughout India. Those who derive *all* of their income from *ad hoc* guiding from the main gate typically earn Rs40,000/- per year. The few who supplement their income through tour escort work earn more than Rs100,000/- per year.[41] Of the guides that maintain a regular presence at the main gate, the average income per guide for 1995/96 was over Rs 60,000/-.

Originally guides were recruited by way of advertisements in local newspapers and candidates had to be graduates. Guides were largely drawn from the *Jat* community that owns a large part of the medium tariff hotels close to the park entrance. In recent years, there has been a shift towards the recruitment of guides from the rural areas around the park. This has been accompanied by changes in the selection technique whereby recruitment is no longer advertised in local newspapers and fewer qualifications are required. One-third of the most recent batch of qualified guides is from the rural area surrounding the park. The more established guides have taken the Forest Department to court over its licensing procedure, with charges of nepotism, undermining existing incomes, and lowering the standard of guiding in the park. The park has responded by stating its aim for increasing its support base among the rural poor.[42]

During the course of the research around Keoladeo NP it became increasingly apparent that despite the significant potential for increasing tourist spending at Bharatpur, there were few mechanisms that could orientate revenue and employment benefits towards rural communities. Although leakage of tourism revenue from the regional economy is low, there is a strong urban bias to the accumulation of profit due to existing patterns of land ownership and the transferability of urban skills. Access to tourist spending is highest among the rural population where existing skills and capital are utilised, i.e. those that are easily transferable and complementary to existing livelihood patterns. Few such opportunities exist within the tourism industry, and those that do are of sufficiently low status to exclude large sections of the population (for example rickshaw pulling). By far the most common suggestions for local rural development made during the field research in 1995/6 concerned access to the resources of the wetland itself suggesting that the potential for park-people conflict remains high.[43]

South-east lowveld, Zimbabwe

In the southeast lowveld of Zimbabwe there are high expectations in local communities of the opportunities which tourism could bring to a relatively isolated and impoverished area. Surveys of tourists in Gonarezhou and the conservancies and of local communities demonstrated that there are significant areas of overlap between supply and demand in handicraft sales, village meals, village tours, wildlife tracking, music and dance performances, story telling and bush survival training. There are local people wanting to provide the services and tourists wanting to purchase them. As numbers of tourists increase in the lowveld there is the potential to develop a number or local enterprises, owned by people from the local communities and being able to diversify their sources of income through tourism.

People expressed an interest in providing certain suggested services to the tourism industry if they had the opportunity to do so. The most popular services were producing and selling handicrafts (74.7% expressed an interest), cooking a meal in their homes for tourists (64.6%), tours round their village (61.2% were interested in providing this service to tourists) and music and dance performances (56.2%). The figures on the number of tourists interested in the various activities are drawn from the lowveld tourist questionnaire conducted in the same period. The figures are presented where a comparable question was asked of the tourists, those marked * are services which the Conservancies, Conservation Trust and/or Zimsun at Mahenye and Chilo have expressed interest in purchasing (see Table 7).

Table 7 The services respondents would be interested in providing for tourists

Service	*(%)*	*Frequency of a 'Yes' response*	*Level of interest expressed by tourists or local enterprises (%)*
Selling handicrafts in your village	74.7	133	10.3
Cooking a meal in your home	64.6	115	10.3
Tours around your village	61.2	109	14.0
Music & dancing performances	56.2	100	10.3
Teaching wildlife tracking	11.8	21	48.6
Providing vegetables to lodges	11.8	21	*
Boat trips on the river	9.0	16	18.7
Bird watching tours	6.7	12	
Storytelling & theatre	5.1	9	10.3
Providing chickens/eggs to lodges	5.1	9	*
Bush survival training	4.5	8	38.3
Selling beverages in village	1.1	2	
Providing textiles to lodges	0.6	1	*
Canoe safaris	0.6	1	
Botany tours	0.6	1	

The continuation of communal land ownership in Zimbabwe and the CAMPFIRE programme enabled the Mahenye community down on the Mozambique border to secure a land rent and planning gain. Zimbabwe Sun Ltd (Zimsun) has leased land from the local community for two lodge developments, bringing tourists to a remote part of Zimbabwe that was previously virtually unvisited. The lease commits Zimsun to pay a significant yearly minimum lease fee and a percentage of gross trading revenue, rising to 12% in the final four years of the 10-year lease. Zimsun also undertook 'wherever reasonably possible' to employ local labour. In the construction phase 120 permanent and 40 casual labourers were employed on the project, amounting to some 7300 months of labour at an average of US$110 per month, amounting to some US$800,000. In March 1997 the Mahenye and Chilo Lodges were employing 63% of their labour from the local community; and whilst only seven women were employed in the lodge, six of them came from the local community. The Chipinge Rural District Council and local community are both pressing for more local employment and for the training necessary for members of the local community to fill more skilled posts. This lease agreement points to the value of formal development and lease agreements in laying the basis for local employment and associated training.[44]

The changes of land use in the lowveld as overgrazed cattle ranches switched to wildlife and consumptive and non-consumptive tourism caused the conservancy entrepreneurs involved to think very carefully about how linkages into the local community could be maximised. There was an urgent political and economic imperative to identify ways in which economic linkages could be forged. Table 8 shows the initiatives that have been discussed and the progress towards implementation that had been made by March 1996.

Table 8 Tourism related complementary enterprise development in the Lowveld

	Zimsun Mahenye/ Chilo Lodges	*Malilangwe Conservation Trust*	*Bubiana Conservancy*	*Chiredzi River Conservancy*	*Save Valley Conservancy*
Supply of goods					
Curio manufacture	●	●	●		●●●
Furniture manufacture			●		●●
Manufacture and supply of building materials	●				●●●
Uniform manufacture		●●●	●		●
Food and vegetable production			●		●
Supply of services					
Game meat retailing and distribution			●●		●●
Provision of transport					●
Retailing and distribution of fuel wood					●
Complementary tourism enterprises					
Cultural tourism	●		●		●
Tourist accommodation	●				
Traditional show village	●●				●●
Community based wildlife projects			●	●	●
Joint ventures					
Accommodation joint ventures		●●			
Incorporation of resettlement of communal lands into conservancies			●	●	●
Wildlife ownership on conservancy land earning dividends				●	●

● Idea has been discussed ●● Implementation has been commenced ●●● In operation

Palawan

At St Paul's Subterranean River National Park there are large numbers of tourists who pass by local communities and the park management would welcome a reduction in visitor pressure experienced by the park. Both the park and local communities share an interest in developing additional tourist attractions in the rural areas between Puerto Princesa City and the park. The priorities for development identified in consultations with the local communities and the tour operators based in Puerto Princesa City are:

- Craft work. This requires training and the opening up of access to a market through the development of craft markets and labelling. A tribal market (a tabuan) is proposed. The branding would increase sales by assuring the consumer that the labelled product is locally produced; handcrafted; uses renewable resources sustainably; meets a minimum quality standard and is authentic. The park could also assist by producing computer-printed labels (in Tagalog and English) with a brief description giving the product name, the use and details of the material used to make it.
- The park is withdrawing from providing picnic and campsites, this provides opportunities for local communities and entrepreneurs.
- Wildlife viewing opportunities, trails, walkways and viewing platforms/hides are a priority for visitor satisfaction. However, without skilled development – including walkways, hides, planting and some limited 'natural' feeding – this will be difficult to accomplish.
- A local river kayaking enterprise is possible between Tagabinet and the sea.
- An approved trail with appropriate campsites should be developed between the road on the San Raphael side and the park. This is necessary both to minimise ecological impact and to protect the privacy of the Batak who live in this area and who feel harassed by tourists.

A Batak visitor centre would create an economic opportunity for this marginalised community, act as a buffer zone between the Batak and tourist and enable them to exercise some control over the tourists who currently walk through their territory, often in a very intrusive way. The Batak Visitor Centre emerged as a mechanism through which the Batak might exercise some control over the tourism that they currently experience and enable them to harness it to their purposes. For the Batak one of the key issues is to gain control over the access of tourists to their home territory, in order to earn something from tourism and to gain some control over its impact on their communities. This can be achieved by creating a Visitor Centre through which entrance to the area is controlled, and if it works closely with SPSNP that controls the point of exit, then the whole tourist visit can be controlled. With the support of the Park Rangers and the Community Rangers the rules negotiated with the Batak can be policed. The Batak do not currently receive a fair share from the tourism to their area.

A Visitor Centre is to be preferred over a Cultural Village because it avoids the idea of tourists coming in to a show or mock village to 'see the natives' and to photograph them. The Visitor Centre places the emphasis on the Batak interpreting and showing their culture – on their terms – to the visitors. It is their culture and they should control its presentation to the visitors. One of the key purposes of the Visitor Centre is to empower the Batak as teachers, guides, hosts – to give them the major say over the terms upon which visitors enter their home territory. The visitors should be placed in the *subservient* position as *learners*. The centre would act as a *cultural buffer zone*.

The Batak Visitor Centre could contain:

- A small museum of the history, ethnography and cultural history of the Batak (this would be for visitors and for the Batak themselves).
- A display about the ecology of the area and the ways in which the Batak live from the land (including gathering, hunting and farming – and medicinal plants). This display should also address the issue of sustainability.
- A School of Living Traditions – with a dual teaching function: the development of Batak culture and craft skills *and* a place where the Batak could teach craft or life skills to tourists – if they choose to do so.
- A craft exhibition, a market and a café.
- A starting point for the trek across to the park or for short trails to introduce the visitor to the ways in which the Batak use the forest – including *sagbay*. Batak guides would accompany all walking groups.
- Seasonal demonstrations of agricultural and hunting practices – including *kaingin* and honey gathering.
- A venue for closed and open cultural performances – including music, dance and story telling.[45]

Guidance notes and action lists

Whilst some common themes can be abstracted from the agendas for action which emerged from the four case studies, it is important to recognise that particular local solutions need to be identified which address the concerns of local communities and for which there is evidence of tourist demand. Tourism is a business and initiatives can only be successful if visitors are willing to pay for the goods or services offered. The solutions have to be made to work and poor people's livelihoods are at stake.

However, the level of income and employment opportunities arising from tourism at protected areas depends largely on the form of tourism development (enclave or dispersed), and the articulation of particular social structures in the host population. Histories of land ownership, political representation and engagement by the state have a special relevance. Research in at least two of the study sites suggests that while protected area managers, tourism professionals and researchers prefer to make a clear distinction between the tourism and conservation objectives of National Parks, the views of local inhabitants often combine them. Programmes for increasing the degree of local control over tourism development can only proceed from techniques and approaches that seek to address local concerns. Where tourism is identified as an appropriate area for growth, the following principles may be useful in guiding development for the benefit of the poor and relatively poor in local communities.

Focus assistance to non-capital intensive enterprises

Local involvement in the tourism industry depends largely on access to the market. In many cases local benefits are maximised in the informal sector. Local skills and services are often maximised where the scale of capital investment is low. This aspect is sometimes neglected in tourism planning, and access to tourists by the informal sector is restricted. Training in market research, understanding consumer tastes and product promotion may increase sales for small traders.

Maximise tourism based on local skills and technology

Transferability of skills and hence local involvement is largest where existing capital and know-how can be utilised. Tourism developers should be encouraged, wherever possible, to use and promote existing local modes of transport, accommodation and art and handicrafts, food production and preparations – remembering that a significant motivation for travel is the natural and cultural diversity that can be experienced.

Discourage enclave practices

Resist the tendency of some tour operators to bypass local business opportunities by regulating traffic (for example through the judicious location of parking spaces and entry restrictions). Ensure local access to the tourism market though the development of markets and opportunities for visitors to interact with the local economy and local people. Prioritise local outsourcing and encourage tourists to purchase local goods and services directly from producers.

Encourage flexible partnerships between public and private sectors

Despite the wishes of protected areas to increase rural support, efforts are sometimes frustrated by emergent monopoly practices within the local private sector. For example, local Nature Guide training and selection should be based upon a clear agreement of recruitment practices with participation from existing guides, protected area managers, and rural development associations.

Create and strengthen appropriate institutions

Local concerns regarding tourism development and attempts to retain some of the revenues from tourism are often hampered by the lack of local representation at an institutional level. Nature tourism, conservation and income generation often fall between the jurisdictions of several institutions. A clear destination focus is important. Local government and donor agencies should explore means of establishing an appropriate forum for the articulation of local concerns with representation from, and managed engagement of, all stakeholders (park management, tour companies, hotel developers and small businesses).

Developing revenue sharing policies

Some park directors are considering the introduction of local development levies on entrance fees. Collaborative policies may be pursued in order to raise the total revenue for both local people and parks.

Some generalisations can be made, but circumstances *do* alter cases. Questions can be useful in provoking different groups to take action and the Department for International Development also produced *Changing the Nature of Tourism*[46] which drew media and travel industry representatives and NGOs into the process of developing agendas for action (See Figure 2).

- Can airlines use their in-flight magazines and videos to encourage tourists to make a greater contribution to the local economy through their choice of activities and the purchasing of products and services?
- What can airlines and tour operators do to encourage tourists to be culturally sensitive?
- Can tour operators provide more information about destinations and local activities and encourage tourists to diversify their experience?
- What can tour operators and hoteliers do to enable local people to engage in the industry by providing goods and services?
- What can the industry do to encourage tourists to pay a fair price for local attractions?
- How can hotels be developed more sensitively to avoid enclave practices?
- Can hoteliers host local craft producers to demonstrate their skills and sell their products?
- Can tour operators work with local communities to develop markets where tourists can purchase local art and crafts?
- Can the hoteliers work with local entrepreneurs to develop a wholesale market where they can source food and other consumables?

Figure 2 Opportunities for action?[47]

Correspondence

Any correspondence should be directed to Dr Harold Goodwin, Centre for Responsbile Tourism, School of Earth and Environmental Sciences, Medway University Campus, Pembroke, Chatham Maritime, Kent ME4 4TB (z0007842@zoo.co.uk).

Notes

1. Copies of the three case study reports and of the Comparative Report can be obtained from http://www.ftsl.demon.co.uk. There is a summary volume by Goodwin, H.J., Kent, I.J., Parker, K.T. and Walpole, M.J. (1998) *Tourism, Conservation and Sustainable Development*. International Institute for Environment and Development.
2. Myers, N. (1972) National parks in savannah Africa. *Science* 178, 1255–63.
3. Budowski, G. (1976) Tourism and environmental conservation: Conflict, coexistence or symbiosis? *Environmental Conservation* 3 (1), 27–31.
4. IUCN (1986) *Managing Protected Areas in the Tropics*. Gland: IUCN.
5. Philips, A. (1985) *Tourism, Recreation and Conservation in National Parks and Equivalent Reserves*. Derbyshire: Peak Park Joint Planning Board.
6. Ziffer, K.A. (1989) *Ecotourism: The Uneasy Alliance*. Washington, DC: Conservation International.
7. IUCN (1993) *Parks for Life: Report of the IVth World Congress on National Parks and Protected Areas*. Gland: IUCN.
8. McNeely, J.A. (1993) Diverse nature, diverse cultures. *People and the Planet* 2 (3), 11–13. Cf. Kemp, E. (ed.) (1993) *The Law of the Mother: Protecting Indigenous People in Protected Areas*. San Francisco: Sierra Club Books.
9. Likert scale from 1 'unimportant' to 5 'very important'.
10. The St Paul's survey included both international and domestic visitors – the other figures are for international tourists specifically.
11. Goodwin, H., Kent, I., Parker, K. and Walpole, M. (1998) *Tourism, Conservation and Sustainable Development: Case Studies from Asia and Africa*. Wildlife and Development Series No 11. London: IIED.

12. Zebu, E.H. and Bush, M.L. (1990) Park-people relationships: An international review. *Landscape and Urban Planning* 19, 117–31.
13. Wells, M. and Brandon, K. (1992) *People and Parks – Linking Protected Area Management with Local Communities*. Washington, DC: World Bank.
14. Goodwin. H. (1996) In pursuit of ecotourism. *Biodiversity and Conservation* 5, 277–91.
15. See in particular the Indonesia and Zimbabwe case studies.
16. Goodwin, H. (1998) Recommendations to the protected area management board of the St Paul's Subterranean River National Park, Palawan Tropical Forestry Protection Programme, Palawan, Philippines (unpublished).
17. Voluntary Service Overseas (1998) *Worldwide Campaign Leaflet*. London: VSO.
18. Goodwin, H., Kent, I., Parker, K. and Walpole, M. (1998) Tourism, conservation and sustainable development (vol. 3). Komodo National Park, Indonesia (unpublished). Department for International Development, London. On WWW at http//www.ftsl.demon.co.uk.
19. Goodwin, H., Kent, I., Parker, K. and Walpole, M. (1998) Tourism, conservation and sustainable development (vol. 3). Komodo National Park, Indonesia (unpublished). Department for International Development, London. On WWW at http//www.ftsl.demon.co.uk.
20. Goodwin, H., Kent, I., Parker, K. and Walpole, M. (1998) Tourism, conservation and sustainable development (vol. 3). Komodo National Park, Indonesia (unpublished). Department for International Development, London. On WWW at http//www.ftsl.demon.co.uk.
21. Goodwin, H., Kent, I., Parker, K. and Walpole, M. (1998) Tourism, conservation and sustainable development (vol. 4). The South-East Lowveld, Zimbabwe (unpublished). Department for International Development, London. On WWW at http//www.ftsl.demon.co.uk.
22. Goodwin, H., Kent, I., Parker, K. and Walpole, M. (1998) Tourism, conservation and sustainable development (vol. 3). Komodo National Park, Indonesia (unpublished). Department for International Development, London. On WWW at http//www.ftsl.demon.co.uk.
23. Goodwin, H., Kent, I., Parker, K. and Walpole, M. (1998) Tourism, conservation and sustainable development (vol. 2). Keoladeo National Park, India. (unpublished). Department for International Development, London. On WWW at http//www.ftsl.demon.co.uk.
24. Goodwin, H., Kent, I., Parker, K. and Walpole, M. (1998) Tourism, conservation and sustainable development (vol. 2). Keoladeo National Park, India. (unpublished). Department for International Development, London. On WWW at http//www.ftsl.demon.co.uk.
25. Goodwin, H., Kent, I., Parker, K. and Walpole, M. (1998) Tourism, conservation and sustainable development (vol. 3). Komodo National Park, Indonesia (unpublished). Department for International Development, London. On WWW at http//www.ftsl.demon.co.uk.
26. Goodwin, H., Kent, I., Parker, K. and Walpole, M. (1998) Tourism, conservation and sustainable development (vol. 2). Keoladeo National Park, India. (unpublished). Department for International Development, London. On WWW at http//www.ftsl.demon.co.uk.
27. Given that the point of departure of different trips is not universal.
28. Before consideration of leakages.
29. Goodwin, H., Kent, I., Parker, K. and Walpole, M. (1998) Tourism, conservation and sustainable development (vol. 3). Komodo National Park, Indonesia (unpublished). Department for International Development, London. On WWW at http//www.ftsl.demon.co.uk.
30. Lindberg K and Enriquez J (1994) *An analysis of ecotourism's economic contribution to conservation and development*. In Belize, WWF & Ministry of Tourism and Environment.
31. This does not take into account leakages associated with initial infrastructural and development costs, or overheads.

32. Goodwin, H. (1998) Sustainable tourism and poverty elimination. Discussion paper. Department for International Development and Department of Environment, Transport and the Regions.
33. Deloitte & Touche, the International Institute for Environment and Development and the Overseas Development Institute, London, April 1999.
34. Ibid.
35. Goodwin, H. (1998) Sustainable tourism and poverty elimination. Discussion paper. Department for International Development and Department of Environment, Transport and the Regions.
36. Sustainable Tourism and Poverty Elimination
37. Koch, E. (1997) Ecotourism and rural reconstruction in South Africa: Reality or rhetoric. In K.B. Ghimire and M.P. Pimbert *Social Change & Conservation*. London: Earthscan.
38. Goodwin, H., Kent, I., Parker, K. and Walpole, M. (1998) Tourism, conservation and sustainable development (vol. 1). Comparative Report (unpublished). Department for International Development, London. On WWW at http//www.ftsl.demon.co.uk.
39. Goodwin, H., Kent, I., Parker, K. and Walpole, M. (1998) Tourism, conservation and sustainable development (vol. 3). Komodo National Park, Indonesia (unpublished). Department for International Development, London. On WWW at http//www.ftsl.demon.co.uk.
40. Ibid.
41. Five guides who now have their own businesses as hotel proprietors of permanent positions with tour companies earn more than Rs200,000/-. They no longer wait for business at the main gate.
42. Goodwin, H., Kent, I., Parker, K. and Walpole, M. (1998) Tourism, conservation and sustainable development (vol. 2). Keoladeo National Park, India. (unpublished). Department for International Development, London. On WWW at http//www.ftsl.demon.co.uk.
43. Goodwin, H., Kent, I., Parker, K. and Walpole, M. (1998) Tourism, conservation and sustainable development (vol. 2). Keoladeo National Park, India. (unpublished). Department for International Development, London. On WWW at http//www.ftsl.demon.co.uk.
44. Goodwin, H., Kent, I., Parker, K. and Walpole, M. (1998) Tourism, conservation and sustainable development (vol. 4). The South-East Lowveld, Zimbabwe (unpublished). Department for International Development, London. On WWW at http//www.ftsl.demon.co.uk.
45. Goodwin, H. (1998) Recommendations to the Protected Area Management Board of the St Paul's Subterranean River National Park, Palawan Tropical Forestry Protection Programme, Palawan, Philippines (unpublished).
46. Goodwin, H. and River Path Associates (1999) *Changing the Nature of Tourism*. Environment Policy Department, Department for International Development.
47. Goodwin, H., Kent, I. and Walpole, M. (1998) Guidance notes (unpublished). Department for International Development.

References

Budowski, G. (1976) Tourism and environmental conservation: Conflict, coexistence, or symbiosis? *Environmental Conservation* 3 (1), 27–31.

Deloitte and Touche (1999) *Tourism and Poverty Elimination: Untapped Potential*. London: International Institute for Environment and Development and the Overseas Development Institute, April 1994.

Goodwin, H. (1998a) *Sustainable Tourism and Poverty Elimination* (discussion paper, October 1996). London: Department for International Development and Department of Environment, Transport and the Regions.

Goodwin, H. (1998b) Recommendations to the Protected Area Management Board of the St Paul's Subterranean River National Park (unpublished). Palawan Tropical Forestry Protection Programme, Palawan, Philippines, June 1998.

Goodwin, H. (1996) In pursuit of ecotourism. *Biodiversity and Conservation* 5, 277–91.
Goodwin, H. and River Path Associates (1999) *Changing the Nature of Tourism Environment Policy Department.* London: Department for International Development.
Goodwin, H.J., Kent, I.J., Parker, K.T. and Walpole, M.J. (1998) *Tourism, Conservation and Sustainable Development.* International Institute for Environment and Development
Goodwin, H.J., Kent, I.J. and Walpole, M.J. (1998) Guidance notes (unpublished). Department for International Development, London.
— Volume I: Comparative report (unpublished) UK Government's Department for International Development, London.
— Volume II: Keoladeo National Park, India (unpublished) UK Government's Department for International Development, London.
— Volume III: Komodo National Park, Indonesia (unpublished) UK Government's Department for International Development, London.
— Volume IV: The South-East Lowveld, Zimbabwe (unpublished) UK Government's Department for International Development, London.
— *Case Studies from Asia and Africa.* Wildlife Development Series No. 11.
IUCN (1986) *Managing Protected Areas in the Tropics.* Gland: IUCN.
IUCN (1993) *Parks for Life – Report of the IVth World Congress on National Parks and Protected Areas.* Gland: IUCN.
Kemp, E. (1993) *The Law of the Mother: Protecting Indigenous People in Protected Areas.* San Francisco: Sierra Club Books.
Koch, E. (1997) Ecotourism and rural reconstruction in South Africa: Reality or rhetoric? In K.B. Ghimire and M.P. Pimbert (eds) *Social Change and Conservation* (pp. 214–38). London: Earthscan.
Lindberg, K. and Enriquez, J. (1994) An analysis of ecotourism's economic contribution to conservation and develoment. In *Belize.* Belmopan: WWF & Ministry of Tourism and Environment.
McNeely, J.A. (1993) Diverse nature, diverse cultures. *People and the Planet* 2 (3), 11–13.
Myers, N. (1972) National parks in savannah Africa. *Science* 178, 1255–63.
Philips, A. (1985) *Tourism, Recreation and Conservation in National Parks and Equivalent Reserves.* Derbyshire: Peak Park Joint Planning Board.
Wells, M. and Brandon, K. (1992) *People and Parks – Linking Protected Area Management with Local Communities.* Washington DC: World Bank.
Voluntary Services Overseas (1998) *Worldwide Campaign Leaflet.* London: Voluntary Services Overseas.
Zebu, E.H. and Bush, M.L. (1990) Park–people relationships: An international review. *Landscape and Urban Planning* 19, 117–31.
Ziffer, K.A. (1989) *Ecotourism: The Uneasy Alliance.* Washington DC: Conservation International.

Large-scale Ecotourism – A Contradiction in Itself?

Michael Lück
Department of Recreation and Leisure Studies, Brock University, St Catharines, Ontario, Canada

In a large number of attempts to define ecotourism researchers often suggest that one vital aspect of ecotourism is the scale of the operations. Ecotourism, so the argument goes, should be small-scale tourism. This view is often illustrated with a number of negative impacts of mass tourism on the environment and on the host communites. However, this paper introduces the reader to two major players in mass tourism, Europe's largest package tour operator TUI and Germany's second-largest charter carrier LTU. Both are certainly not ecotour operations; however, both implemented a variety of policies and actions, which attempt to keep the environmental and social impacts in the destinations as low as possible. The examples show that positive action can be taken without compromising company operations and customer comfort.

Introduction

A wide variety of researchers and authors attempted to describe and define the term ecotourism. One of the most prominent and most quoted definitions, maybe because it was the first conscious use of the term, came from Hector Ceballos-Lascurain (1987:13), who stated that

> we may define ecological tourism or ecotourism as that tourism that involves travelling to relatively undisturbed or uncontaminated natural areas with the specific object of studying, admiring and enjoying the scenery and its wild plants and animals, as well as any existing cultural aspects (both past and present) found in these areas'.

Later on, a variety of researchers stated that ecotourism should be small-scale tourism (Gilbert, 1997; Jones, 1992; Khan, 1997; Lindberg & McKercher, 1997; Lück, 1998; Orams, 1995; Thomlinson & Getz, 1996; Warren & Taylor, 1994; Wheeller, 1994). It is argued that with ecotourism growth it starts to become a mass-venture and the old problems of mass tourism re-occur.

The goal of this paper is to introduce the reader to two large companies, which deal with enormous numbers of tourists. Without doubt both are big players in mass tourism. The first example is TUI's Robinson Club Baobab in Kenya. Club holidays are certainly not associated with ecotourism and the reader might be surprised when reading some facts about this club. The second example is LTU International Airways, Germany's second-largest charter carrier with a fleet of 35 modern aircraft. Air travel is the section within the tourism industry with the worst environmental image (Gwinner, 2001). The two projects 'C.A.R.I.B.I.C.' and 'Ökobeutel' ('eco-bag') of LTU will be introduced.

Robinson Club and LTU do not give themselves the label of an 'ecotourism operator/airline'. However, they are proud about their share in environmentally conscious (mass-)tourism and the awards they received for their commitment.

The Case of the Robinson Club Baobab in Kenya

The brand Robinson Club is a subsidiary of TUI (Touristik Union International). TUI is Europe's largest tour operator with about 12.9 million pax in 1998/1999 (Fremdenverkehrswirtschaft, 2000). In 1990 TUI employed a highly skilled full-time environment-strategy commissioner (Dr Wolf Michael Iwand), who is responsible for a more environmentally friendly development of the company's products. He is head of the 'environment strategy commission' and in direct contact with the board of directors (Kirstges, 1995).

TUI, including the branch Robinson Club, set a variety of criteria for their holiday destinations, hotels and carrier (Table 1). They set up an environmental database, which is used for planning and information in catalogues.

While these criteria are applied to all TUI products, this chapter focuses on the case of the Robinson Club Baobab.

The Robinson Club Baobab lies in a tropical coastal forest at the Diani Beach, about 35 kilometres south of Mombasa, Kenya. The club comprises 80 double rooms in two-storey houses and 70 double rooms in bungalows. Only 2.5% of the

Table 1 TUI´s environmental criteria for destinations, hotels and carrier

TUI Destination criteria	*TUI Hotel criteria*	*TUI Carrier criteria*
Bathing water and beach quality	Wastewater treatment	Energy consumption
Water supply and water-saving measures	Solid waste disposal, recycling and prevention	Pollutant and noise emissions
Wastewater disposal and utilisation	Water supply and water-saving measures	Land use and paving over
Solid waste disposal, recycling and prevention	Energy supply and energy-saving measures	Vehicle/craft, equipment and line maintenance techniques
Energy supply and energy-saving measures	Environmentally oriented hotel management (focus on food, cleaning and hygiene)	Catering and waste recycling and disposal
Traffic, air, noise and climate	Quality of bathing waters and beaches in the vicinity of the hotel	Environmental information for passengers
Landscape and built environment	Noise protection in and around the hotel	Environmental guidelines and reporting
Nature conservation, species preservation and animal welfare	Hotel gardens	Environmental research and development
Environmental information and offers	Building materials and architecture	Environmental cooperation, integrated transport concepts
Environmental policy and activities	Environmental information and offers of the hotel	Specific data: Vehicle/craft type, motor/power unit, age
	Location and immediate surroundings of the hotel	

Source: TUI (undated)

total area of 250,000 m^2 is built on, and the whole area has been established as a nature preservation park with endemic plants, which are already extinct in other parts of Kenya's coast (Lerner & Hagspiel, 1999).

The architecture

When renovating and redecorating the club, TUI placed emphasis on the use of local materials. This resulted in a typical African architecture with straw-roofed bungalows in an African style, made of coral blocks and mangrove timber. The bungalows have been carefully integrated in the park (Lerner & Hagspiel, 1999).

Rubbish issues

The main goal for TUI is to avoid rubbish rather than to just dispose of it. Robinson Club Baobab does not use any disposable cutlery and crockery. Softdrink cans and beer cans are unknown in the club, too. When supplying the club with food, emphasis is put on low package products. For example, jam, butter and marmalade are not served in small individual packages, but bought in bulk and served in bowls.

When it comes to food, Robinson Club Baobab relies heavily on local supplies. This guarantees freshness and supports the local community. In addition, food is freshly made and the buffet is always served through a cooking station, where every meal is freshly prepared. In the case of leftovers, the club's staff is allowed to take unused food home. Non-usable leftovers are composted in their own device and passed on to those local farmers the club buys their products from. Additional humus is used as fertiliser in the club's gardens (Lerner & Hagspiel, 1999).

Water issues

The club has a need for about 7000 m^3 fresh water every day. This is an enormous amount of water, especially in a country with seven rainless months. The club's wastewater is not pumped into wild soak-aways or even into the sea (as is common practice). The club has built their own fully biological sewage system. This system consists of three 30 m by 10 m large ponds, which are used for all wastewater produced by the club (see Figure 1).

Water runs from pond to pond, evaporates and gets cleaned by a special plant (Nil Cabbage) and fish (Tilapiafish). Arriving in the third pond, the water is clear enough to be used to water the gardens. The soil acts as an additional filter and the clean water finally flows back into the ground water system (Lerner & Hagspiel, 1999).

Social issues

Club Baobab is fully aware of the situation of being a guest in a foreign country. The above-mentioned points not only affect the visitors, but also the local community in a positive way. In addition, the club offers a trainee programme for young local people. In all departments of the club, young local people are trained (Lerner & Hagspiel, 1999). (See Figure 2.)

Figure 1 Biological sewage system at Robinson Club Baobab
Source: Courtesy of TUI Hannover

Figure 2 Members of the Trainee Programme at Robinson Club Baobab
Source: Courtesy of TUI Hannover

The holistic approach

As Europe's largest tour operator, TUI tries to follow a holistic approach regarding the environment. All departments are involved in the process and trained. Continuous monitoring attempts to establish and keep to high standards. SWOT analyses are repeatedly undertaken and weaknesses identified.

For quality control, reports of TUI's tour guides and clients' correspondence are evaluated. In addition, when TUI staff travel on holiday, they get an 'environmental' questionnaire as means of quality control of the product management, local guides and hotel management. Consultation is offered to local hotel owners. Expertise on composting and sewage management, noise pollution and alternative energies, and sources for governmental subsidies are only a few examples of the help offered (TUI, 1993)

The Case of LTU International Airways

With more than 7 million passengers per year and a fleet of 35 modern aircraft (7 Airbus A330-300, 1 Airbus A320-232, 6 Boeing 767-300ER, 15 Boeing 757-200, 6 Boeing 737-700), LTU is Germany's second-largest charter carrier (LTU, 1999a). Already in 1992, LTU added the principle of environmental protection to its company philosophy. Continuous work on reducing the amount of kerosene and thus the amount of exhausts through modernising the fleet is a high priority task. All LTU planes are matching the strong noise regulations of the International Civil Aviation Organisation (ICAO Chapter III, Annexe-16-certification). Moreover, LTU obliges their pilots to kerosene and noise reducing start and landing procedures (Immelmann, 1996).

LTU also supports environmentally friendly travel between passengers' homes and the airport. LTU passengers are eligible for a reduced Rail&Fly ticket on the whole German railway net. Passengers flying out of Düsseldorf or Cologne/Bonn (about 50% of LTU's passengers) have the advantage of free use of public transport within these areas. In 1996, more than 250,000 travellers used this environmentally friendly and stress-free service. Finally, LTU connects the two major airports of Düsseldorf and Frankfurt with a daily coach shuttle service, called LTU SKY SHUTTLE (Immelmann, 1996).

LTU also continuously reduces the amounts of rubbish produced during the flights. The majority of goods used on board are now bulk goods. Here alone, LTU was able to reduce about 80% of the produced rubbish. As for the rest of the rubbish, LTU already separates it on board and transfers it for proper recycling at the final destination. The results speak a clear language: Although the number of passengers increased from about 4 million in 1990 to more than 6.9 million in 1996, the amount of rubbish in that period could be reduced from 1093 tons to 824 tons. Taking the increase of passengers into consideration, this is a reduction of almost 50% (Immelmann, 1996). It seems to be a matter of course that LTU also supports environmental research and protection projects in different parts of the world.

The above activities show the variety of LTU's commitment to the environment. However, the focus of this chapter is on two major projects, the C.A.R.I.B.I.C. project and the 'Ökobeutel' ('eco-bag'). Those two projects are unique within the industry.

The C.A.R.I.B.I.C. project

C.A.R.I.B.I.C. stands for **C**ivil **A**ircraft for **R**emote Sensing and **I**n-Situ-Measurement of Troposphere and Lower Stratosphere **B**ased on the **I**nstrument **C**ontainer and is a project for scientific research on the atmosphere. The 'green-

Table 2 Participating partners in the C.A.R.I.B.I.C. project

Partner	*Subject*
Max Planck Institute for Chemistry (MPI), Mainz, Germany	CO-Concentration, Whole-Air-Sampler
Institute for Meteorology and Climate Research (MK), University of Karlsruhe, Germany	Ozone Concentration
Institute for Tropospheric (IfT), Leipzig, Germany	Aerosol Concentration
GFAS Gesellschaft für angewandte Systemtechnik, Immenstaad, Germany	Coordination of the project/Development of the container system
LTU International Airways, Düsseldorf, Germany	Modifications on the aircraft/Avionics & Technical Engineering/Coordination with Boeing/Certification and test flights
Also joined in the second phase of the project	
Royal Meteorologic Institute, De Bilt, Netherlands	University of East Anglia, Norwich, England
Institute for Nuclear Physics, Lund, Sweden	Max-Planck-Institut für Aeronomie Katlenburg-Lindau, Germany

Sources: Immelmann (1996); LTU (1999b); Hoffmann (2000)

house effect', 'climate change' and the 'depletion of the shielding of the ozone layer' became keywords for constantly growing damage of the atmosphere due to emissions from human activities on the earth. C.A.R.I.B.I.C. is unique and under the leadership of Prof. Dr Paul Crutzen (awarded with the Nobel Prize for his research on the ozone layer). Several participating institutes and companies (Table 2) also contribute to this project. The aim of the project is to gain a better understanding of changes in the atmosphere and achieve better predictions about the consequences of global climate changes (Immelmann, 1996; LTU, 1999b).

LTU's Boeing aircraft B767-300ER 'Uniform November' was modified with a probe system and a cockpit control for the container. The container is equipped with measuring and monitoring tools to measure aerosols, ozone and carbon monoxide. Furthermore it contains 12 bottles of 20l content for automatic flooding during flight through the 'whole air sampler', which is fixed at the bottom of the fuselage. This 'whole air sampler' can collect air samples for later analysis in laboratories back in the institutes. The advantage of this system is that samples can be collected during regular passenger flights (Immelmann, 1996; LTU, 1999a).

Since the inaugural flight from Malé (Maldives) to Munich (Germany) on the 5th of May 1997, the modified B767-300ER is employed on a variety of routes throughout LTU's network, such as flights from Düsseldorf to Mombasa (Kenya), Miami, Daytona Beach and Fort Myers (Florida/USA), San José (Costa Rica), Puerto Plata and Punta Cana (Dominican Republic) and from Munich to Malé (Maldives), Colombo (Sri Lanka), Denpasar (Bali/Indonesia) and Mombasa (Kenya) (LTU, 1999b).

The C.A.R.I.B.I.C. project aims to get a better understanding about the physical and chemical processes in the tropopause and the stratosphere. First results show some surprising facts, as shown by the following three examples.

Figure 3 The C.A.R.I.B.I.C. Container is loaded on LTU´s B767 'Uniform November'
Source: Courtesy of LTU Düsseldorf

(1) In November 1997, for example, high concentrations of carbon monoxide (CO) were registered above the Indian Ocean and the Arabian Sea. This high concentration was a result of the extensive forest fires in Southeast Asia in the second half of 1997. Due to the El-Nino phenomena this concentration was clearly higher than in the previous years (Hoffmann, 2000).
(2) In 1998, an unexpected high concentration of carbon monoxide and aerosols was identified only a few 100 metres above the tropopause. This is clear evidence of the fact that 'polluted air' in the troposphere moves up to the stratosphere. There is only little knowledge about frequency and size of exchange processes between troposphere and stratosphere and this project aims to gain further data about those processes (Hoffmann, 2000).
(3) In August 1997, high concentration of methane was found above the Indian Ocean. Meteorological investigations proofed that the air masses with a high content of methane above Southeast Asia moved from the surface up to a height of 10,000 meters. There is evidence that this methane was emitted from the extended rice fields in North India and China. These results show that processes on the ground have a clearly higher influence on higher atmospheric layers than the emissions of today's air traffic (Hoffmann, 2000).

LTU and the associated institutes continue research with the C.A.R.I.B.I.C. project and more results are expected subsequently (Figure 4).

The Ökobeutel ('eco-bag')

The Maldives is a state comprising 1200 islands (202 inhabited) and 19 atolls (Preuss Touristikinformation, 1995). The Republic is heavily reliant on tourism and is a paradise for watersport lovers. Owing to the geographic state of the

Figure 4 The C.A.R.I.B.I.C. Container in the Body of the B767
Source: Courtesy of LTU Düsseldorf

country, waste disposal is a severe problem. The small islands do not offer the opportunity of waste dumps and most of the waste is dumped into the open sea. LTU alone is generating almost 20% of the total inbound tourism to the Maldives (Hoffmann, 2000). Due to these high numbers of visitors, LTU took over the ecologic responsibility and started a new programme in 1993. Flight attendants hand out 'eco-bags' to every passenger on LTU-flights to the Maldives. They ask the tourists to collect all inorganic waste during their stay and bring the bag back to the airport at the end of their holidays. At the check-in LTU staff take care of the bags, and after sorting the bags they are loaded in special containers and flown out of the country back to Germany (Figure 5). In Germany the waste is finally transferred to recycling stations for recycling or proper disposal (LTU, 1999b). Over the first six years of the programme LTU distributed more than 300,000 eco-bags and about 80% of all passengers participated in the programme. The result is an amount of more than 400 tons of rubbish, which has been flown back to Germany instead of being dumped into the ecological sensitive ecosystem of the coral reefs. Subsequently, LTU was awarded with the 'Green Palm Tree' of the renowned tourism journal *GEO Saison* in 1996. In 1995, LTU received the governmental conservation award by the President of the Maldives (Hoffmann, 2000; Immelmann, 1996).

Related to the eco-bag project is the 'Clean up the Reefs' scheme. Once a year, divers from the world's largest diving organisation PADI in co-operation with LTU clean the coral reefs around the hotel-islands of the Maldives. The collected rubbish is brought to Germany by LTU for adequate disposal or recycling. PADI awarded LTU with the conservation award AWARE in both years 1995 and 1996 (Immelmann, 1996; LTU, 1999b).

Figure 5 Happy tourists checking in their 'Ökobeutel' after their holidays in the Maldives
Source: Courtesy of LTU Düsseldorf

Conclusion

It is often argued that ecotourism is working with small-scale operations only. This chapter introduced two major players in 'megamass tourism' (Wheeller, 1994: 652). Neither of the companies use the label 'ecotourism' for more effective marketing. However, it is fair enough that they are proud of their commitment and the received awards. It was clearly shown that it is possible for large-scale ventures, such as a large tour operator or a charter airline, to operate according to a code of conduct. Compliance to (self-set) regulations is strictly enforced and contributes to a better environment not only at the destination. Taking responsibility means investing in the future and in the host communities. It also comprises taking action and active support of vital research for a better understanding of the impacts tourism has on the host communities and the environment in general.

Acknowledgements

The author would like to thank Mechthild Latussek, Karl Lerner, Thomas Hagspiel, Karl J. Pojer and Dr Wolf Michael Iwand of Touristik Union International (TUI) and Robinson Club in Hannover for the supply of detailed information and photos about TUI's environmental activities and strategies. He also wants to acknowledge Christoph Schröder and Jutta Hoffmann of LTU International Airways for their assistance, information, and photos about LTU's C.A.R.I.B.I.C. project as well as the environmental activities in the Maldives.

Correspondence

Any correspondence should be directed to Michael Lück, Department of Recreation and Leisure Studies, Brock University, St Catharines, Ontario, Canada L2S 3A1 (mlueck@brocku.co/ michael.lueck@brocku.ca).

References

Ceballos-Lascurain, H. (1987) The future of ecotourism. *Mexico Journal* (January), 13–14.

Gilbert, J. (1997) *Ecotourism Means Business*. Wellington: GP Publications.

Hoffmann, J. (2000) *Umweltschutz rund um die Welt*. Düsseldorf: LTU Group Holding.

Immelmann, T. (1996) *LTU Stichwort: Umwelt – Eine Bilanz 1996*. Düsseldorf: LTU Lufttransportunternehmen.

Jones, A. (1992) Is there a real 'alternative' tourism? Introduction. *Tourism Management* 13 (1), 102–3.

Khan, M.M. (1997) Tourism development and dependency theory: Mass tourism vs. ecotourism. *Annals of Tourism Research* 24 (4), 988–91.

Kirstges, T. (1995) *Sanfter Tourismus – Chancen und Probleme der Realisierung eines ökologieorientierten und sozialverträglichen Tourismus durch deutsche Reiseveranstalter*. München/Wien: R. Oldenbourg Verlag.

Lerner, K. and Hagspiel, T. (1999) Der Umweltschutzgedanke unter den Bedingungen eines Entwicklungslandes. Personal communication, 9 June.

Lindberg, K. and McKercher, B. (1997) Ecotourism: A critical overview. *Pacific Tourism Review* 1, 65–79.

LTU (undated) *C.A.R.I.B.I.C.: A Project for Scientific Research on the Atmosphere*. Düsseldorf: LTU International Airways.

LTU (1999a) Die Airline. On WWW at http://www.ltu.de. Accessed 20.8.99.

LTU (1999b) Umwelt: Was tun wir? On WWW at http://www.ltu.de. Accessed 20.8.99.

Lück, M. (1998) Sustainable tourism: Do modern trends in tourism make a sustainable management more easy to achieve? *Tourismus Jahrbuch* 2 (2), 141–57.

Orams, M.B. (1995) Towards a more desirable form of ecotourism. *Tourism Management* 16 (1), 3–8.

Preuss Touristikinformation (eds) (1995) *Länder-Info '95*. Bonn: Preuss Touristikinformation.

Thomlinson, E. and Getz, D. (1996) The question of scale in ecotourism: Case study of two small ecotour operators in the Mundo Maya region of Central America. *Journal of Sustainable Tourism* 4 (4), 183–200.

Touristik Union International (TUI) (1993) In Sachen Umwelt ... TUI auf dem Prüfstand. Praxistest: TUI-Urlaubshotels und Umweltverträglichkeit. Presentation and public debate. March. Touristik Union International, Berlin.

Touristik Union International (TUI) (undated) *General Information for Customers on TUI's Environmental Policy in the TUI Travel Catalogues*. Hannover: Department of Environment, Touristik Union International.

Warren, J.A.N. and Taylor, C.N. (1994) *Developing Eco-tourism in New Zealand*. Christchurch/Wellington: New Zealand Institute for Social Research and Development.

Wheeller, B. (1994) Egotourism, sustainable tourism and the environment – a symbiotic, symbolic or shambolic relationship? In A.V. Seaton (ed.) *Tourism: The State of the Art* (pp. 647–54). Chichester: John Wiley & Sons.

Looking into the Future of Ecotourism and Sustainable Tourism

Michael Lück
Department of Recreation and Leisure Studies, Brock University, St Catharines, Ontario, Canada

The World Commission on Environment and Development (WCED) launched the report *Our Common Future* in 1987 and set a milestone in terms of the world's development (World Commission on Environment and Development, 1987). Sustainable Development became a key issue in all parts of our daily lives, and tourism, the world's largest industry, adopted the idea and is striving for a Sustainable Tourism Development (STD). Over the short and long term STD should:

- meet the needs and wants of the local host community in terms of improved living standards and quality of life;
- satisfy the demands of tourists and the tourism industry, and continue to attract them in order to meet the first aim; and,
- safeguard the environmental resource base for tourism, encompassing natural, built and cultural components, in order to achieve both of the preceding aims. (Hunter, 1995: 155–6)

Clearly, the objectives of STD are similar to those identified in the wide variety of definitions of ecotourism. A look into the different definitions shows all too clearly that we are far away from any all-encompassing definition. However, there are a few aspects that seem to be apparent and re-occurring in the STD aims, such as a sense for the host community, conservation of natural, built and cultural heritage and resources, and the generation of revenue. Similar to ecotourism, everyone seems to agree that there is a need for STD, but what it actually entails remains somewhat vague (Wheeller, 1994). The complexity of the tourism industry makes it almost impossible to find a suitable definition (and code of conduct) for all parts within the wide spectrum of tourism. The market is extremely heterogeneous and can be influenced, but certainly not totally controlled (Wheeller, 1991).

Experts still have different views about the 'real' sustainable tourism. While Poon (1993), for example, sees a trend away from mass tourism (although 'mass tourism will not disappear'), Wheeller (1994) predicts the trend to even more mass tourism:

> I am, however, amazed by their assertion, that [. . .] the concept of mass tourism [. . .] has no relevance for growth in the next decade. To me it has every relevance as we move towards, not away from, megamass tourism. (Wheeller, 1994: 652)

No matter which form of tourism we will see predominantly in the future, all sorts of tourism are dependent on resources, especially natural and cultural. The challenge is to manage the use of those resources in a sustainable way. Ever increasing numbers of tourists all over the world are setting resources under a growing pressure. One school of thought suggests that sustainable does not necessarily mean small-scale tourism. In fact, 'large-scale, spatially concentrated tourism may, as it is argued, act as a 'safety-valve' syphoning off potential demand for scarce resources elsewhere and it may keep mass tourism firmly in its place' (Wheeller, 1991: 93–4). Eco and similar forms of tourism are seen as the most destructive forms of tourism. Ecotourists endeavour to constantly discover new, untouched areas. Negative impacts often are not avoided, but rather spatially spread. The classic word of 'mass follows class' applies perfectly and ecotourism destinations soon have to cope with large amounts of 'normal' tourists. Destinations, such as Costa Rica, Zanzibar and Belize are examples of this development. Formerly difficult to travel to and examples of best practice ecotourism, now all are served by major charter airlines, which paved the way for mass tourism in these ecologically and culturally sensitive destinations.

There are lots of obstacles to overcome with the attempt to implement ecotourism and/or STD codes. The example of the small island of Niue in the South Pacific, introduced by Heidi de Haas, shows that constraints include the dependency on the schedules of major airlines. This very well illustrates one of the conflicts of sustainable tourism: small destinations would appreciate more frequencies by major airlines in order to receive sufficient numbers of visitors for viable operation, while once they got the numbers as mentioned above, it can result in adverse effects due to too many tourists. Political instability means a major financial risk for investors. Changing policies and laws make it very difficult for small companies and communities to develop a healthy operation, as shown in Thea Shoeman's article about tourism in the Qwa-Qwa National Park in South Africa.

The major task will possibly be to define common rules and codes of conduct. This is necessary in order to establish a transparent system for the consumer. With the advent of the term ecotourism, many tour operators and hoteliers adapted the term without changing anything within their actual behaviour and operational procedures, as illustrated in Ron Mader's contribution 'eco sells' and they use the term for effective marketing. The need not only for a common code of conduct but also for independent audits and certification arose. There have been many local and national attempts to find common grounds and labels, for example, the 'Top Team Natur(e)' and the 'Gruene Koffer' (Green Suitcase) in Germany (Krause, 1998), and the *Best Practice Ecotourism* programme of the Commonwealth Department of Tourism in Australia (Commonwealth Department of Tourism, 1995). However, a global system was absent for a long period of time. After the Earth Summit in Rio de Janeiro in 1992, Agenda 21 became an issue in tourism operations throughout the world. Subsequently in 1994, the idea of 'Green Globe 21' (GG21) was developed as a global system for individuals, companies and communities. Green Globe 21 means:

- quality alliances for global coverage and local implementation;
- state of the art environment management and support systems;
- clear standards based on ISO and Agenda 21;
- independent certification;

worldwide, web-driven promotion of brand holders for consumers. (Green Globe, 2000)

The advantages are obvious: participating companies and communities are independently assessed and certified and consumers have the opportunity to check Green Globe's website free of charge and can rely on the quality of certified companies in their destination. The costs for participating companies are relatively small. Depending on the size of the company, costs range from $US350 to $US5000, while communities are charged with $US50,000 in the first phase. Consecutive costs depend on the size of the community and the intensity of service and consultancy required. Assessment and implementation of the standards are time consuming and it can take up to a few years until a participating company is officially certified. However, the effort alone is also awarded by the right of using the GG21 logo. Once certification has been completed, the GG21 logo with a tick may be used for advertising purposes (Green Globe, 2000). (Figure 1.)

Figure 1 **Green Globe logos**

The future in ecotourism and sustainable tourism certainly lies in a symbiosis of different forms of tourism. Mass tourism has its place in this development and it would be naive to think that the ever growing tourism on this planet could be without mass tourism. Therefore, it is the challenge for planners and managers to make a difference. Exemplary projects worthy to copy are those of TUI and LTU (as shown before in my paper Large-scale ecotourism – A contradiction in itself?), who take responsibility for their actions. Education and interpretation is crucial for a better understanding and a more conscious behaviour of the tourists. Green Globe 21 also is a valuable approach and deserves attention all over the world. 'Eco-Pirates' will not be able to use the logo and the consumer benefits from an independent transparent system. Problems, for example for SeaCanoe (as described by Noah Shepherd), can be overcome. Local poaching operators would not be certified and once Green Globe 21 is well established, ideally would be avoided by tourists.

Correspondence

Any correspondence should be directed to Michael Lück, Department of Recreation and Leisure Studies, Brock University, St Catharines, Ontario, Canada L2S 3A1 (mlueck@brocku.ca/michael.lueck@brocku.ca).

References

Commonwealth Department of Tourism (1995) *Best Practice Ecotourism: A Guide to Energey and Waste Minimisation*. Canberra: Commonwealth of Australia.

Green Globe (2000) Green Globe 21. On WWW at http://www.greenglobe21.com. Accessed 04.10.2000.

Hunter, C.J. (1995) On the need to re-conceptualise sustainable tourism development. *Journal of Sustainable Tourism* 3 (3), 155–65.

Krause, R. (1998) Dem einheitlichen Ökosiegel auf der Spur. *Fremdenverkehrswirtschaft International* 32 (26), 93–4.

Poon, A. (1993) *Tourism, Technology and Competitive Strategies*. Wallingford: CAB International.

Wheeller, B. (1991) Tourism's troubled times: Responsible tourism is not the answer. *Tourism Management* (June), 91–6.

Wheeller, B. (1994) Egotourism, sustainable tourism and the environment – a symbiotic, symbolic or shambolic relationship. In A.V. Seaton (ed.) *Tourism: The State of the Art* (pp. 647–54). Chichester: John Wiley & Sons.

World Commission on Environment and Development (1987) *Our Common Future*. Oxford: Oxford University Press.

Printed in the United States
19800LVS00003BC/7-12

9 781873 150405